Changing Ti

A LIFE IN JOURNAL

Changing Times

A Life in Journalism

Frank Kilfeather

BLACKWATER PRESS

Editors
Aidan Culhane
Rosemary Dawson

Design & Layout
Paula Byrne

Cover Design
Slick Fish Design

ISBN
0 86121 726 8

© – 1997 Frank Kilfeather

Produced in Ireland by
Blackwater Press
c/o Folens Publishers
8 Broomhill Business Park,
Tallaght, Dublin 24.

In memory of my father, T.P. Kilfeather, who instilled
in me a great love of journalism.

Acknowledgements

The author and publisher wish to thank *The Irish Times* for photographs used in this book.

Contents

Introduction ix

Beginnings 1

Progress 11

Hard Times at The Herald 19

Good Times at The Irish Times 31

Tense Years in The North 47

The Lighter Side of the North 56

The Dáil 61

Dáil Antics and Personalities 67

Jimmy Tully 79

Who'd Be a Politician? 84

Brian Lenihan 92

The Dublin Bombings 98

The Herrema Kidnapping 103

Dark Days 108

The Lighter Side 113

Journalists and Gardaí 125

Threats, Bribery and Intimidation 132

The Beef Tribunal 138

The Irish Press Closure 146

Charlie Haughey 152

And Finally 162

Introduction

Friends often say to me: 'You're lucky; you have a very exciting job...' They then invariably add, enviously: 'You must meet a lot of very interesting people?'

I usually reply: 'It's a living,' and think no further about it. I stress that journalism can be just as boring and as frustrating as any other job – trying to produce hundreds of words against a tight deadline for a daily newspaper that is going to be wrapping fish and chips the next day.

However, now that I am in what I might describe as my anecdotage, when every sentence begins with 'I remember...', I am coming to realise that my friends are right. It is an interesting and fascinating job; the last 39 years have indeed been quite eventful and exciting. I have now stopped to reflect and have become more philosophical in my outlook. In the early years I was always too involved in the story on hand to see exactly how lucky I was. In fact the more I think of it, to work as a journalist is a privilege. It may be a topsy turvy existence, full of unpredictability and tension, but it has wonderful compensations.

Being a journalist means sitting in the front row of the theatre of life, seeing the drama of history unfolding before your eyes. Ensconced in that theatre every day, I had the added bonus of recording it for others, making it interesting and informative for the public. Since 1958, I have worked on provincial, evening and daily newspapers. I have seen many changes in Irish journalism and Irish society – mostly for the better. I was present at the civil rights marches in Northern Ireland in the late 60s; the subsequent riots and social unrest; Jack Lynch sacking Charles J Haughey and Neil Blaney; the Arms Trial; the Dublin and Monaghan bombings, which left 33 dead; the Herrema kidnapping; the burning of the British Embassy in Dublin after the Bloody Sunday murders in Derry. I spent many years covering political events in the Dáil and the old Stormont. I have seen much political turmoil; a lot of street violence and demonstrations; dramatic court cases, covered the visits of US Presidents Nixon and Reagan; and, most recently, the Beef Tribunal, the longest tribunal in the history of the state. And lots more.

Yes, it has been enjoyable. I have accumulated enough good stories to dine out on for the rest of my life. I started chronicling the stories in this book as they arose. This was mostly for my own interest and enjoyment, as a kind of diary, notes attached to faded press cuttings. I have now put them into book form. This is not a pompous, academic, in-depth look at Irish journalism in the past four decades. No, it is basically a humorous look at what it has been like 'on the road', providing a news service, earning a living. It is also about the colleagues who worked with me; the fun we had, the disappointments, the frustrations, etc.

As Oscar Wilde might have said: 'Journalism is too important to be taken seriously.'

Beginnings

I knew instinctively, from the time I was 15 years old, that I was going to be journalist. I was, even at that early stage, a sharp observer of life. I had a natural curiosity and a genuine interest in what was going on around me. My biggest advantage was that my father was a journalist. He was always bubbling with energy, talking authoritatively on various topical subjects, as he puffed his way through about 50 cigarettes a day – a habit which eventually killed him. The phone was always ringing and there were plenty of what appeared to be important conversations taking place. There was always a buzz about the house when Dad was there. There was a palpable urgency about his life. I watched, fascinated. Dad was larger than life and was playing what appeared to be a big part in everything that was going on. He obviously revelled in it. Young as I was, I could see the satisfaction he was getting out of his work. Dad – or T.P. Kilfeather, to give him his full title – was a journalist of the old school. He had done everything from reporting, sub-editing to specialisation. He was a political correspondent in the *Irish Press*. He later joined the *Sunday Independent*, where he was the chief feature writer and television critic, using the *nom de plume* Peter Clery. From watching him in action, I developed a love for the business. I wasn't quite sure what it was all about, but I could see it was enjoyable. When T.P., like many a curious father before him, popped the question 'What would you like to be when you leave school?', I had no hesitation in proudly replying 'a reporter.' I thought he would be delighted, but he wasn't. Some parents don't like their children to go into the same profession. Parents always want their kids to do better. Maybe that was the reason he looked disappointed. Maybe he wanted me to be a barrister and get £2,000 a day at some beef tribunal.

The subject was dropped for a few months ... when the question was put again, and when I gave the same answer, he accepted that I was serious. In fact, from that day on he began to train me for journalism. Even though I was only 15 and still going to school, he sent me twice a week to a man in Mount Merrion who taught me shorthand at 2/6 an hour. He gave me his second typewriter, a battered old Remington, and taught me how to type with two fingers. He spoke to me about the profession and patiently explained how to cover news stories. 'Okay, Frank, your news editor sends you out to cover a big car crash, what's the first thing you do?' He would explain the difference between the District Court and the Circuit Court, or the High Court and the Supreme Court. He gave me a lot of useful hints.

He stressed the importance of psychology in the business. For instance, he warned me not to rush at people with heavy, embarrassing questions: that is guaranteed to get a door closed in your face or the phone put down abruptly. To be a journalist, it's important to be diplomatic. He emphasised the importance of building up contacts and getting to know the right people, the people who had access to news. I can still hear him telling me: 'If you are working in a provincial town, get to know where the Garda Superintendent or the President of the Chamber of Commerce is from. If he is native of Kerry or Galway, make sure you know if they won in Croke Park last Sunday. Always be able to talk to them on a personal level.' He spent two years quietly coaching me. He talked about descriptive writing, 'always paint a picture in words for the reader'. Be courteous, build up trust. Never push or bully.

He was also very strong on old, traditional values. Always wear a collar and tie. Appearance is very important. When I did start work, he was very annoyed a few times when I got my face scarred or damaged playing rugby. He almost asked me to give up the game. 'You can't go around interviewing people looking like THAT,' he used say. It was all a very helpful, homespun philosophy, and even now, so many years later, I can look back on it with gratitude and appreciate his words of wisdom. He also did the 'practical' end of the business with me. He brought me to election rallies where I saw de Valera addressing the populace from the back of a lorry; I was shown the Dáil in action. I visited the courts and was smuggled into press conferences. I also accompanied him on interviews. It was all very exciting and enjoyable for a teenager. I knew I was the envy of all my school pals who all seemed to be leading a very mundane existence. Yes, it was a pleasant childhood.

So I was proficient in shorthand and typing and had my father's briefings behind me. All I needed was to finish school and get a job on some newspaper. This happened two years later, but still sooner than I thought. I had just completed fifth year in Blackrock College when, nearing the end of the summer holidays, Dad came home one evening and said there was a vacancy for a junior reporter, or 'cub' reporter as it was quaintly called in those days, in the *Drogheda Argus*. Would I like to start? Would I what – so I killed two birds with the one stone. I got out of school, which I hated intensely, and I was on my way to becoming a big-time writer with the *Drogheda Argus*. If my friends were envious before, they were speechless when they heard I had left school and had an important job. I was 17. My princely salary was two pounds ten shillings a week. Not much, but it was a start. I knew if I could get my foot in the door I could make a go of it. It later transpired I was being underpaid and the National Union of Journalists' rate was three pounds ten pence.

I vividly remember the early months there. The paper was practically on its last gasp. It had very little money and the circulation was small, and getting smaller by the week. Whether you got paid or not depended on the number of advertisements cajoled out of the business community that week. If you made a phone call it had to be logged into a big ledger for accounting purposes (and these were only local calls).

The office was spartan, to say the least. The few bits of furniture were old and falling apart. It was heated by a two-bar electric fire, which had to be reduced to one bar in times of real stringency. During the very cold periods, the editor worked with his overcoat and scarf on. It was all quite Dickensian. We were the poorest newspaper in the land. It had to be to hire me.

It was a happy office, though. People were always calling in for a chat or dropping in little news items, very parochial, but nevertheless entertaining. Some were inclined to overstay their welcome and it was difficult to get them out. We did do the odd bit of work and we wanted to do it without lengthy interruption. Still, everyone was encouraged to call. Our door was always open. After all, that's how we got the news. A lot of it was gossipy rubbish, of course, but every now and again someone did bring in some newsworthy item which filled another few blank spaces in the paper. When we were really stuck for news – on a bad week – we would have to increase the size of the pictures and the headlines. Our little paper therefore often had huge headlines and large pictures, but wasn't exactly brim-full of news. We got very little advertising – the life-blood of any viable newspaper. We were poor, very poor and on the point of collapse.

The main reason for this predicament was the opposition – the *Drogheda Independent*, a very wealthy, progressive newspaper, with a large staff, plenty of well-paid correspondents, more advertising and better machinery. It was impossible to compete with them. Still, we did our best and managed to produce the odd exclusive.

My first assignment was to go to the Drogheda Grammar School and interview two students who were the sons of an ambassador or some important foreign dignitary. Apparently, it was a great feather in the cap of the school to have these students enrolled and the proud headmaster had tipped off the local press. The story would be interesting for the readers and of course would lend a bit of prestige to the school. This should have been the simplest of stories to write.

Having just left school myself and being only 17 years old, the last place I wanted to be sent to on my first assignment was to a school. I got an attack of nerves. I remember standing on the steps of the fine old building and saying to myself: 'I can't do it, I can't do it.' I knocked ever so gently on the door, making sure that nobody could hear. Naturally, the door did not open. So I went back to my editor and said there was no reply. Oh, my innocence.

My lame excuse cut no ice and I was sent back immediately, even more terrified. This time I picked up courage and knocked hard on the door. I was ushered in and introduced to the headmaster as 'Mister Kilfeather.' Nobody had ever called me 'Mister' before. I didn't feel old enough to be called Mister.

The two students were ushered into the room. They were about the same age as myself. I then set about my first interview. Their names were unpronounceable and most definitely unspellable. I groaned. I asked them three times to spell it, but was so nervous I couldn't get it written down correctly. There was simply no link between their voices, my brain and the pen in my shaking hand. Eventually, I pretended I had it right and asked a few innocuous, stupid questions, expressed my thanks and left. On the way back to the office I knew I had nothing to write. After all, I hadn't even got the names spelt correctly. I didn't understand much of what they were saying. They spoke in broken English and I was too nervous and over-polite to persist in asking the same question. The headmaster had stood over me while the interview was going on – thinking he was going to see a real pro in action. His presence didn't make things any easier. He must have been quite shocked at the bumbling fool in front of him. Maybe if he had left the room it might have worked out better. I then tried to bluff my editor. I told him there was no real story there and it wasn't worth using. He insisted that he wanted it. I had no option but to admit that I couldn't do it and explained my difficulties. Thankfully, he was very understanding and sent a senior reporter out to conduct the interview. The senior reporter came back with a great 'colour story'. This was the first time I had heard the expression and it means a lightweight, off-beat, easy-to-read story. He thought it was so good that he sent it to the Dublin papers and made a few quid out of it.

Well, it wasn't what you would describe as an auspicious start to a career in journalism. My chances of becoming a big-time reporter didn't look very promising. If things were to continue like this I would be lucky to hold on to my low paid, bottom-of-the-pile job. My confidence was zero and I was beginning to think I had made a mistake. But there was worse to come – much worse. I cringe, even now, looking back on some of my earlier assignments. Things looked so bleak. Another silly foul-up still rankles. It upsets me thinking about it, but it did, in retrospect, have its amusing aspect.

The Drogheda Chamber of Commerce invited the *Argus* to a lunch at which Enid Lakeman, the famous authority on the Proportional Representation voting system, was guest speaker. While Miss Lakeman may have been famous, I certainly had never heard of her, nor had I ever come across a voting system called PR. I mean, I was only a youngster and wasn't even eligible to vote. All the Drogheda captains of industry were at the dinner. I wore my best suit – my only suit – and hoped that I looked like an experienced reporter. Even though I was only a child, all the 'captains' swarmed around me, shook my hand and spoke about weighty world affairs. I bluffed and bluffed for all I was worth.

I did so well I could have been given an Equity card. They wanted to talk to me because I was 'the reporter' and probably thought I might put their name in the paper. I couldn't believe I was so popular.

I sat at the bottom of the table for the meal. There I could get a good view of what was going on and less people could see me. When the lunch ended Miss Lakeman started her speech. It went on and on and on. The longer it lasted the more complicated it became. I kept writing, but I didn't know what I was writing. It's one thing to have shorthand but it's a different ballgame altogether trying to read it back. Eventually, she sat down with a loud burst of applause ringing around her.

I knew in my heart and soul that I hadn't understood one word of what she had said. There was no question of me being able to put one paragraph together or to produce any type of intelligent report for my paper. I was dying of embarrassment, but I kept smiling and pretended I understood it all and continued to bluff profusely. I then left and went back to the office, like a turkey shuffling up to Christmas. I told the editor that the story wasn't worth carrying, that it was too technical and that the readers wouldn't be interested in such balderdash. He replied: 'Okay, Frank, if that is your opinion, we won't use it.' My relief knew no bounds. I believed I had survived the ordeal. I had been shot, but the bullet hadn't hit any vital organ, so to speak. Or so I thought. When the *Drogheda Independent* came out that week, they had a front page story on Miss Lakeman. They had sent John Patton, one of their most experienced reporters, to the dinner. He had naturally understood every word spoken by the woman. John just happened to be one of the best shorthand writers in Ireland (and later went on to be a court stenographer). He wrote a brilliant synopsis of the lecture and it was accompanied by a two column picture. I didn't know John Patton at the time and was not aware that he was at the dinner. It is so easy to get caught out in this game. When I was confronted with the Patton story, all I could do was plead guilty and admit that I was not up to covering such complicated stories. I needed a bit more time. Worse was to come. This story wasn't going to die a natural death. It was going to hang around to haunt me. The Drogheda Chamber of Commerce, outraged that no report of their big event had appeared in the *Argus*, incensed that they had paid for a lunch for a reporter and got no publicity in return, wrote to the editor complaining bitterly. They went even further. They demanded that the paper reimburse them the price of the meal (2/6). The editor of course ignored it, but they wrote again. We eventually sent them the money. The boss was good enough not to dock it from my small salary.

The moral of this story is that there is no such thing as a free lunch. I was finding journalism to be a very tough profession indeed. After a few months I was still wondering if I would ever get anywhere in the business. Depression was setting in. I was losing any little bit of confidence I might have had. It certainly wasn't as easy as I thought it would be. In fact, it wasn't easy at all. The sheer variety and complexity of the job, being expected to know something about everything, had me quite despondent. The hardest part, as I have illustrated, was dealing with the public. I was very young and had always been shy and reserved. This was a big drawback. I was extremely fortunate that I had as my editor one of nature's greatest gentlemen – John McDonnell. He had infinite patience and treated me with the utmost courtesy. I know only too well that no other editor would have tolerated my shaky beginning. John was a very calm and relaxed person who took everything in his stride. Thanks to his encouragement I managed to persevere.

Nowadays, the colleges of journalism spew out graduates and these youngsters come into the business full of knowledge and confidence. In my day you operated on a wing and a prayer – flying by the seat of your pants, you might say. My father's little talks had never prepared me for the reality of journalism.

After four months of floundering around, I got my first scoop. The story still pleases me when I think of it, even though I only stumbled on it by accident and a senior reporter wrote it. I had called to a member of the bridge club to get the results of some big tournament. After getting the results, we began to chat. It was the autumn of 1958 and Pope Pius XII was dying in Rome. He had been dying for weeks and the Irish papers were full of the story and Radio Éireann was giving regular bulletins on his latest condition. Special masses were being said for him throughout the country. Churches were full with people praying for his recovery. 'It's so sad about the Pope,' said the woman after giving me the list of results. I nodded and she went on to talk about what a great man he was. I listened patiently. I could see that she had more than a passing interest in the Pope's illness. She then recounted the story of her brother, who was a priest, who met the Pope a year earlier in Rome. Her brother was a member of a crowd in St Peter's Square waving to the Pope. As the pontiff walked by he shook the young priest's hand.

Then he exchanged his skull cap for the one being worn by the priest. The young priest naturally treasured this souvenir of his visit to St Peter's. Some months later a very sick friend asked to borrow it. The priest lent it to him because he knew Pope Pius meant so much to the man.

Not long afterwards the sick man made a full recovery and was in no doubt that it was the Pope's cap that had done the trick. 'It undoubtedly was a miracle,' said the lady, who added that her brother still had the cap in his possession. I was a bit sceptical, but said nothing to dispel her happiness. We then chatted about a few more things and I headed back to the office. After going a short distance I realised that this was a great story and highly topical. I ran back to the office and told the editor. Naturally, they weren't going to let a novice like me write this one. A senior reporter was dispatched straight down to the woman's house for a major interview. He did a great job on it and then flogged it to every national and international newspaper. Everybody was talking about it. He must have made a fortune out of it. It was really a good story at the time. I didn't get any monetary reward out of it, but I was as proud as punch. Yes, I was beginning to develop a real news sense. Maybe I could make it as a reporter.

The senior reporter was none other than Michael 'Mickser' Hand, who later went on to become editor of the *Sunday Independent* and one of the country's best known and loved journalists. He died in July 1997. He was only 60 years old.

There was an amusing sequel to the story. I met the 'bridge' woman a year later and she jokingly shook her fist at me and shouted: 'It's all your fault. You have no idea of what you did.' Apparently, the Pope's cap was now in tatters. She said that when the story appeared the family was inundated with many heart-rending pleas to borrow the cap. The unselfish priest lent it to a lot of people and it naturally became badly worn and damaged.

Still, the family maintains that it was worth it and that many more people who had it in their presence were cured. 'We can't lend it out any more because it's in bits,' she added. 'We have it stuck together with sellotape, but it's now too fragile to lend.'

Being the 'cub' reporter on the paper, I did all the menial, unglamorous jobs, picking up stuff just to fill space. I used to check the death notices in the daily newspapers to see if any local person had died. If they had, it was my duty to go to the house, interview the next of kin, and write an obituary. It was not pleasant talking to relations after a loved one had died. It didn't matter that the dead person wasn't well known. Everyone who died got their name in the paper. At least they were known on the street where they lived. Even if half the people on the street bought the *Argus* it represented a little increase in circulation or so the thinking went. The obituary always described the deceased as being 'a respected member of the community, held in high esteem by neighbours, who was a popular member of the Legion of Mary and who bore her illness with great fortitude.' You would also add in the deceased's age, how many children she had, where she was educated and what hobbies she had. I became very efficient at writing obituaries and stringing the clichés together.

I built up my list of 'contacts.' I used to call to the secretaries of the local clubs to get the latest results of their competitions; call to the chairman of the local drama society to see what they were doing; call to the local barber, who was a great contact and who knew all the gossip of the town. There was also a man who worked in a shoeshop who always seemed to know what was going on, but who would always say when I was leaving: 'Remember, if anyone asks, you didn't get it from me.' I used to wink knowingly and reply: 'Who are you? I've already forgotten.'

One of my contacts tipped me off about a 'very sad story' which he stressed was very important and should be written. It was all very furtive and conspiratorial. 'Fine, but what's the story. I'm not going on a wild goose chase,' I said, looking for more information. All he would give me was the address of a house in a council estate and told me to call there and see for myself. He was not going to enlighten me further. 'Just go there and you'll find out,' he growled. This was all very mysterious, but I decided to trot along anyway, fearful that I might be missing something and I didn't want the dreaded *Drogheda Independent* publishing the story first. I arrived at the little red-bricked, terraced houses and knocked on the door. No reply. I knocked again a few times. I was just about to leave, thinking there was nobody in (and also that I had been hoodwinked), when the door slowly opened. I looked in and there was nobody there. Then I heard a slight voice say 'Hello, what do you want?'

I looked down on the ground and there was this tiny little woman in a kind of wheelbarrow contraption. She had no legs and pulled herself along a rail line in the hall from the kitchen to the door. She was a helpless invalid. I had not been expecting this and was a bit taken aback. I introduced myself and said I understood that there was some story which should be written, but that I did not know what it was.

She invited me into the dark kitchen, where she told me her sad little story. 'I have been handicapped all my life and live here alone,' she said. 'Some people call in to see me once a week to ensure that I'm all right. My food is brought in every day.'

So what was the story? 'The only company I have are my two cats. They are great friends,' she rambled on.

I was beginning to wonder what the hell was going on, when she added: 'I now have no friends; I'm alone in the world. My cats have been killed.'

I asked if they had been knocked down by a car or a lorry?

'No, they were poisoned by the man next door,' she snapped, bursting into tears.

It transpired that the man next door had a big loft of fine racing pigeons and apparently the cats and the pigeons were not compatible, so she claimed he poisoned 'my two lovely little friends.'

It was all heart-rending stuff and the word had gone around the area. The neighbours were incensed and feelings were very high. I came back to the office with the story. I thought it was a great human interest story, but I was told to just write a paragraph about it. I thought I would get plenty of space for this human interest 'scoop.' But my wily editor said you have to be careful of stories like that. 'Why?' I asked innocently. He explained that there was no proof that the neighbour had poisoned the cats and the man could sue the paper for ruining his good name, or something to that effect. I then wrote a little story to say that Miss

X was distraught at the loss of her cats who appeared to have been poisoned by someone unknown. No mention of the neighbour or of the pigeons.

During the summer, news was always very slack. This is called the 'silly season' because the usual sources of copy have dried up, with the courts closed, no local authority meetings, no chamber of commerce or other type of meetings taking place and many contacts on holidays. You are really put to the pin of your collar trying to dream up some stories to fill all those intimidating blank spaces in the paper. Many years later, a news editor told me there is no such thing as a silly season, pointing out that both World Wars started in the summer. 'A good reporter should always be able to find a good story, whatever.'

One of the pathetic ways we had of filling space in the summer was to interview returned emigrants, back for their summer holidays. They did not even have to be prominent people who had emigrated and 'made their fortune.' No, they could be unemployed builder's labourers who had managed to rustle together a few quid to make their first return to the town of their birth since they left ten years previously. Suddenly, they are answering their door to a reporter, notebook in hand, interviewing them about their life abroad and putting penetrating questions to them like 'How do you think the town has changed since you left?'

I have seen such unfortunates nearly expire from embarrassment on such occasions as they searched for words. 'Why me? What do you want to interview me for?' they gasp. 'What have I done?' I cheerfully explain that the *Argus* always liked to welcome back emigrants and ask them a few questions. I don't let them know that we are scraping the barrel and are fresh out of ideas on how to fill a bit of space. I don't tell them that if they had returned a few months earlier we wouldn't be the slightest bit interested in them because there would be plenty of events to cover.

Sometimes, through good fortune, I managed to get interesting stories from them, but usually it was all quite embarrassing and tedious.

Another one of my insignificant tasks was to cover weddings. These were always a great source of interest. I used to drop in to the local hotel every day to see if there was a wedding reception. If there was I used to look for the best man or bridesmaid and ask for all the details about the happy couple. This was easy until you reached the part where you had to describe the bride's dress. This was always tricky, but I became quite accomplished after the first hundred receptions.

Another tricky question was: 'Where are you going on your honeymoon?' Most did not like answering that, and the usual answer was 'travelling.' When I would say 'Travelling where?' they might vaguely say 'around Ireland'. In those days there wasn't much money around and you didn't have couples flying off to the Canaries or to Rome after the reception.

In many cases they just went home or spent a weekend in some small hotel in rural Ireland. Anyway, I was the man who recorded the happy event for posterity. They later came back from their honeymoon and cut out the little report out of the *Argus* and placed it in the photo album.

One day I arrived at the hotel, having heard that there was to be a wedding reception, but I was immediately rebuffed. The manager, who was always pleased to get the name of his hotel mentioned in dispatches and naturally delighted with the free advertisement, said I wasn't to go near the room where the wedding party was. I was puzzled by this, but I left, philosophically concluding that if they didn't want publicity that was their business. Most couples on their wedding day will knock you down to get their names and maybe a picture, if they are lucky, into the paper.

Later that day, I mentioned this excessive secrecy to a friend, who confided that the couple were farmers in their 80s and did not want the news to be splashed across the local press.

Progress

After spending two interesting and enjoyable years in Drogheda, I got restless and decided I could get more experience and be given more responsibility on a different paper. I moved down the coast and joined the *Wicklow People* in 1960. I was based in the branch office in picturesque Wicklow town, beside the sea, and within striking distance of Dublin. I wasn't described as a 'cub' reporter any longer. No, I was known as Paddy Noonan's 'assistant'. Paddy, a frail, white haired gentleman in his mid sixties, had been working in Wicklow for 40 years.

He had been in poor health before I arrived and I was, more or less, expected to be his 'legs' and to look after the more energetic assignments. Always formally dressed in a dark suit and tie, he used to travel around the county in an old blue Volkswagen with his big sheepdog Lassie sitting in the front seat beside him. He was deeply respected in the area. He loved County Wicklow – the Garden of Ireland – and he wrote an informative and interesting book on Glendalough. Our branch 'office' was Paddy's sitting room. It was all very quaint, but it did not affect our efficiency. It must have been upsetting for Paddy's ever-patient wife, Alice, having so many people traipsing to her door every day with advertisements and news items. She bore it stoically though and seemed to like chatting to the people. In a way she was an unpaid secretary, taking messages, keeping us informed.

She was a vital cog in our operation. The system worked very well. Paddy was a talented reporter of the old school; his copy was always perfectly accurate, fair and impartial. He was a brilliant shorthand notetaker but he would never use a proper notebook. Instead he wrote on the backs of envelopes or old county council stationery; in fact any documents which he had no further use for. He certainly knew how to economise. His ingenuity knew no bounds. He once got a load of out-of-date election registers and they kept him going for months, writing on the back of them. I was always introduced to people as his 'assistant'. He used to address me in his old world fashion as 'Mister.' It was always Mister, do this or Mister do that.

The amount of actual 'assistance' I provided was debatable. He had very high standards and my sketchy reports fell very far short of his ideas of good, solid journalism. When he wrote a report nothing was left out. His reports were long and comprehensive. When you read a Paddy Noonan report you got the lot; you were fully informed; there were no questions left unanswered. Mine just gave the basics. That's all I was capable of giving. At that time you were expected to have a fast shorthand note and be able to take down everything practically verbatim. I had shorthand but nowhere near the speed he could reach. He would tut-tut, scratch his head and wonder where they had found this young lad. The first few months were therefore rather traumatic for both of us.

I was immediately thrown in at the deep end and given some heavy work to do. I remember covering a very complicated embezzlement case in the Circuit Court which went on for about three days. I was in a total daze. Reporters are advised to check everything twice; I checked everything about ten times. To make matters worse in this particular case the defendant's name was Maguire, the prosecuting counsel's name was McGuire, and the counsel for the defence, believe it or not, was MacGuire. However, I managed to stumble through. I also plodded through long county council meetings and numerous and varied local human interest stories. Paddy was always there to read the copy and make the corrections. He could be very strict and at times it was worse than being at school.

The months went by. I was quite happy and was building up a good relationship with my old colleague, whom I looked on as a second father.

I was beginning to feel that I was going to make it as a reporter. I now had two fruitful years behind me. Everything was right with the world. Unfortunately, like as so often happens in this life, the good times quickly come to an end. Paddy suffered a massive heart attack and died instantly while out visiting a friend one Saturday afternoon. He dropped dead while getting into his Volkswagen. Lassie stood guard over him and was very reluctant to let anyone come near. We were only together a short time, but I had come to like and respect him and will always be grateful for the appreciation he instilled in me for honest and fair journalism. It is 37 years since he died, but, being a bit of a sentimentalist, I like to look back and think of the happy times we had together.

Nick Lawlor, an experienced reporter from Wexford, arrived to replace him. I was only 19 and far too young to take over Paddy's job, nor did I want it. I am probably the least ambitious person you will find anywhere. I have never in nearly four decades in the newspaper business applied for even the most lowly management job, even though I became much more highly qualified than those who did seek promotion. I have always been content to be a reporter and to be out among the people, seeing life as it is, working at the coal face. I'm proud of this, as was John 'Backbencher' Healy. When John died, his death notice simply said: 'John Healy, reporter.' It was a nice touch, but very much in keeping with the man.

Ironically, Nick, like Paddy, also died of a massive heart attack. He was only 50 years of age. He was a major loss to the paper and to the hundreds of people who got to love and respect him in his adopted county. A first class reporter, he was highly conscientious and built up a strong reputation for integrity and fairness during his 25 years in the area. Even though he had nobody looking over his shoulder, checking his work, he diligently covered every bunfight. Quite a few of the jobs weren't worth covering, but Nick felt that even the smallest organisation should get a mention in the paper. He was right of course and this aspect was deeply appreciated by the readers. He was a very modest man, one of the most unassuming individuals I have ever met. He never let his own views or prejudices enter his reports, unlike a lot of younger reporters today. He never had any ambitions to work on a national newspaper. If he had moved to Dublin, he would have made excellent executive material, as he had tremendous stamina and was a great organiser.

* * *

Wicklow town was the capital of the county and all the main administration was located there – the county council, courts (District, Circuit and High Courts), etc. It was a busy station, but it was ideal for gaining invaluable experience. At times it was that bit too busy, while on other occasions it was slack. During the quiet summer times you could lie on the beach or stroll down to the harbour. Our hours were, to say the least, flexible. We might have all afternoon off, but then have to go to a meeting at night, which might not end until 11 p.m. It became really hectic when the High Court clashed with the monthly meeting of the county council. Both provided an enormous amount of copy and when they came together we really had to work hard. We were a good little team though and we always produced the goods.

It was pleasant working in a branch 'office,' with no bosses present to harass us. They trusted us and we worked well on our own initiative. The head office was in Wexford and the copy was posted down each evening in a big brown envelope. On Wednesday – the day before publication – there was a greater urgency, so the envelope went by train. Looking back on it now, I suppose it was the next best thing to carrier pigeon when you relate it to the speed of communications today. The reporters on the *Wicklow People* today send their copy by computer or fax. When I think of all the Wednesday evenings I got soaked walking to the station outside the town to make sure the news got through. It was like a stagecoach.

One of the most tedious and annoying jobs, which had absolutely nothing to do with journalism, was having to call around to company offices and shops to collect advertisements. At the end of the month we had to call again for payment. Such was the lifestyle of a reporter in those days. You could never get away from the job. Every time you walked down the main street someone would stop you and ask you to put an advertisement in the paper for them. Even sitting in the cinema, people came up to me with small advertisements, placing the grubby bit of paper and the money into my hand. You literally lived the job in those days.

All I could do was smile, accept the advert and get a receipt for them the next day. And we were supposed to be reporters! The National Union of Journalists would not allow it to happen today. Now the *Wicklow People* has an office with a staff who deal with all that sort of thing. The reporters stick to producing news. They don't know how lucky they are.

Yet, working on a provincial newspaper can be very enjoyable and personally rewarding. You are situated firmly at the hub of the community and you know everything that's going on (or if you don't, you should). You know most of the people in the area and you are familiar with all the issues affecting them. In fact, you are probably affected by them yourself. You take a much greater personal interest in news items than you would on a daily newspaper. Generally, you have so many local contacts it is easy to get a story done quickly. You know the telephone numbers of the top people in the town off by heart. You know them personally and they will talk to you. In Dublin, because it is so big, you have to find out who are the spokespersons for the various organisations. After getting that far, you then have to persuade them to talk. You have to build up a trust. In the provinces that trust is there, developed over a long period. Of course, this can work to your detriment too. These same people can get to know you too well and start pressurising you for publicity. You can meet some very ambitious people who will try to use you and the paper as a ladder to move on to greater things. The politicians are masters at this. Big advertisers will also use their clout for a little bit of blackmail. Like, for instance, the big auctioneer doesn't have to push too hard to get his daughter's wedding photograph into the paper. Auction advertisements are the backbone, the lifeblood, of most provincial newspapers and auctioneers are therefore held in great esteem, bordering on reverence. Big names and monied people will also try to persuade an editor to leave court cases out of the paper. A lot of responsibility lies on the editor's shoulders and he has to be strong to resist the constant approaches. But, overall, most people were fair and understanding and there weren't too many problems.

I enjoyed my years in the small, vibrant provincial press. There was a great feeling of belonging, seeing things develop, watching ideas become reality, taking a genuine interest in the community's progress, of being totally immersed. You knew that the local people would buy the paper and later discuss the issues with you. There is no rapport between you and the public in a big city like Dublin. There is a chasm between the journalist and the people. Thirty-five years ago, impoverished reporters didn't own cars and relied on public transport, hitch-hiking or the more favoured 'bumming' of lifts. If you were going to cover one of the outlying courts, you cadged a lift from the local garda superintendent. As well as being provided with transport, this had other advantages. The superintendent could fill you in on what cases were going to be interesting and worth using. He would also give you the background to the case, in confidence of course. This made the courts a lot easier to cover. Once you were in with the superintendent you were all right. On the way back from the courts he would discuss the day's business and express satisfaction or disappointment at the outcome of the various cases. He would talk about the various local criminals and how they were proceeding against them.

For a young chap like me, it was all very educational, quite riveting at times, and I fully realised the trust being put in me. I quickly realised the importance of confidentiality and how essential it is not to reveal a source. You can grow up very quickly learning the journalistic profession.

You also bummed lifts from the secretaries of the various organisations in order to attend their meetings or functions. It worked to both sides' advantage. It suited them because it guaranteed your presence and provided them with a few columns of welcome publicity.

However, there were some people who weren't anxious to give the 'press' a lift and they had to be persuaded and cajoled. This was highly embarrassing. It was humiliating not having transport of your own and having to cadge a lift from someone every few days. It was something I always felt bad about, but it was the usual practice of reporters in the 50s and early 60s, as none could afford to buy a car of their own. My salary was three pounds a week in 1960.

That is all completely changed today. In fact this is one of the reasons I'm writing this book – to give a historical perspective on my profession. A reporter in the provinces today is well paid and enjoys a comfortable lifestyle. That is why young provincial reporters don't rush to Dublin any more. Even a junior reporter will now have a car of his own, a 'banger' maybe, but still a set of wheels under him to get him from A to B, probably picking up expenses from the office at the same time. I never got any expenses. Yet, I was expected to get to jobs and back and produce a full report of the proceedings. Reporters in the provinces today not only have cars of their own, but probably have mobile phones in them. What is more, when they get back from a job they key their report into a computer. In the 50s and 60s we used to write it in longhand. If you were covering a court or a council meeting you wrote it in longhand as it progressed and finished it off on a broken-down typewriter back in the office. You had a bit of carbon paper stuffed into the back to have a copy for yourself (in case there were any complaints). In addition, we were expected to write reams of copy, practically verbatim, of the most insignificant events, just to fill space. Nowadays, the rule is to 'keep it short and snappy,' which the youngsters do very efficiently. The writing is quite good and the standard is excellent. The clichés have been banished. Things have certainly changed for the better.

While I envy the new generation, I still like to look back nostalgically on the old days and the old ways. Certainly, it was all very Dickensian, but there was something dignified, gentlemanly and pleasant about it. There was of course that quality of leisurely gentility which is missing today. There was a lot of hardship and extremely long working hours, but there was a lot of fun and satisfaction too.

Before my time – in my father's days in journalism – they used to cycle to jobs. Now, that was really tough. It is something I never did and I was extremely grateful to those who drove me around the towns and villages of the county. Reporters used to repay their drivers by giving them as many 'plugs' as possible, never forgetting to mention their names in dispatches. It was a case of you scratch my back and I'll scratch yours. It's many a garda, teacher or local authority worker who got promoted as a result of his or her public relations with the press and many a GAA official moved up the ranks because he acted as a driver for a young press man.

When I worked in Wicklow, I lived in 'digs.' My landlady was an elderly God-fearing Protestant woman. A lovely person. Her one big rule was that I had to be back early for tea on Sunday evenings. She did not want to be late for evening service. When I would get back from covering some GAA match she would already be dressed up in her smart, purple Sunday suit and matching hat with a big feather sticking out of it. It was invariably a cold meal of cooked ham on a Sunday.

One day I was reading up in my bedroom when I heard Mrs Kerr shouting: 'Frank, come down quick, come down quick ... look at this.' I didn't know what the commotion was all about. She was standing by the window, practically jumping up and down. 'Look, look, look ...' she said, excitedly.

I looked out and didn't see anything earthshattering. 'No, look over there,' she screamed, 'it's a black man.' She had never seen a black person before and she was astounded. It was amusing. I told her Dublin was full of black people. 'Is it really?' she asked. 'Yes,' I replied knowledgeably, 'they're all in Trinity and the College of Surgeons.' I was, after all, a man of the world.

As it transpired, I later got to know this black man and became friends with him. His name was Samson Mwanza and he was from some recently liberated African country and was over studying local government in Ireland. He was studying with Wicklow County Council for a few weeks. He was in digs nearby so the two of us used to go out in the evenings and have a few pints. You can imagine the astonishment in Wicklow pubs back in 1960 to see an African drinking a pint of Guinness.

He knew I was only starting off in the world of journalism and offered to get me a job in his country. He knew some people in a large newspaper and he was sure there would be a job for me with great opportunities for promotion because it was a developing country. I politely thanked him, but I said I was happy where I was. I have often wondered how I would have got on if I had gone. He promised to write, but I never heard from him again. He is now probably some senior administrator in his country. He was a nice guy, excellent company. He certainly gave poor Mrs Kerr a fright nearly 40 years ago.

My young predecessor warned me when I joined the *Wicklow People* not to leave out any stories, no matter how sensitive they were, or regardless of what pressure was put on me. Before taking up my post, I had arranged to meet him to find out what it was like working in the beautiful, then very small town of Wicklow. He explained that it was a nice town, with very friendly people, and that the *People* was a good paper to work on, but stressed that all major decisions must be left to the head office in Wexford.

'Just shovel everything down to them and let them decide what they want to put in or leave out,' my friend advised. 'And when you are covering court cases make bloody sure you give the full list of those 'found-on' the premises by the Gardai in pub raids,' he added ominously. This surprised me. Even in 1960, most provincial papers had dropped the practice of using the names of the 'found-on,' satisfied just to report how many were there and how much they were fined. Of course the offending public house and its proprietor were always prominently featured.

I made this point to my young predecessor, but he was adamant: 'Doesn't matter a damn, just use the names ... and make sure you remember what I say,' he warned.

Well, sure enough, it came to pass – as Luke or John might have said – when I came face to face with this very issue. Boy, was I in a quandary. I was about six months in the town when the day of reckoning came. The Inter-Pubs darts final, sponsored by a well-known brewery, was taking place in a big pub down in The Murrough, on the sea front. The competition had aroused intense interest in the town and each pub had been battling for months to try to get to the final. Because it was such big news, I went along in my official capacity to write a few paragraphs about the happy occasion. When you are a reporter on a small paper you cover all sorts of off-beat stories. This one appeared innocent enough, but it was to have serious repercussions.

To say that the drink was flowing would be an understatement. Everyone was inebriated, transmogrified, sozzled.... They say that time flies when you are enjoying yourself: well, that's certainly true. Before I knew it, it was very late, and my photographer, who was a bit older and wiser than me (and more sober), was mumbling that we had better get out as it was well past closing time. It would be risky to stay on. I wasn't too keen to leave, as I was having a ball (mixing business with pleasure is one of the perks of being a journalist), but he persuaded me it was for the best. The two of us staggered out into the balmy summer night and gulped in the pure sea air, clearing our heads.

We were about three minutes out the door when – lo and behold – two hefty young gardaí swept past us and raided the pub. I groaned with a mixture of relief and fear. Relief because I wasn't caught and fear because I knew what was going to follow.

The following week all those 'found-ons' were up in the District Court. Yes, you've guessed it. There was I, crestfallen, sitting at the press bench, following the proceedings, diligently taking down the names of my colleagues with whom I had enjoyed such a great night. It was an unenviable task to have to jot down all those names and addresses, some of them my best friends and neighbours, even my fellow lodgers, and publish them in the paper that Friday.

My name, of course, was mud for months afterwards – rightly so. I was the biggest bastard in the town. My friends could not understand my predicament. They couldn't accept that I had no option. They thought all I had to do was turn a blind eye to the matter. Maybe I could have done that, but if Big Brother down in Wexford found out about it I would have been sacked on the spot.

I was then put into the category of the infamous garda who some years earlier had drunk and sung all night with a group of locals in a pub, but at closing time rushed home, put on his uniform and raided the pub. He was never forgiven for that. I was never forgiven for reporting the 'found-ons.' My big regret was that I hadn't been caught in the raid.

That would have turned the tables completely, as I could then have put my own name on the list of 'found-ons' and shown how conscientious I was. After all, it wasn't such a big disgrace to be 'found-on' and the fine was usually small. In fact, some fellows looked on being caught as a kind of status symbol. Unfortunately, others are worried about their wives or employers seeing it.

So to this day, I have never had the pleasure of been summonsed for being found on the premises of a public house after closing time, although I have come close to it on a few occasions. In those days the gardaí in Wicklow had very little to do. There was hardly any crime worth talking about. It left them plenty of time for tracking the publicans and their unfortunate customers. I remember a particularly dedicated garda coming to town who became the scourge of the publicans. He hated drink, wore a big pioneer pin, was highly ambitious and anxious for promotion, who spent every night checking on pubs. One publican, fed up with the excessive attention being paid to his hostelry, suggested to the young lad that he should 'take a look' at the golf club and leave the town pubs alone.

Fair enough, the garda went to the golf club the next night, and, surprise, surprise, lo and behold, there large as life, in front if his surprised eyes, was all the town's gentry, including captains of industry and local personalities, all knocking back their balls of malt. The outcome? Well, nothing really, but the Garda never went back to the club again.

After five years in Wicklow it was time to leave and move to Dublin. In those days it was always the ambition of young reporters to get on to one of the daily newspapers. Similarly in England the target was to get into Fleet Street. I had always wanted to work in the 'big time' so I headed off to Independent Newspapers Ltd to try my luck.

Hard Times at The Herald

Joining a national daily newspaper from the provinces can be quite a culture shock. Everything is much faster and harder. You are working to very tight deadlines and instead of one newspaper a week, you are facing three editions a day. Still, I was delighted in 1965 to have become a member of the staff of Independent Newspapers Ltd, the biggest group of newspapers in the country. Having had a good apprenticeship in the provinces, I quickly adapted to the major changes and soon I was taking the deadlines in my stride. There was a fine staff there and quite a few were around my age so we socialised a lot together.

The big difference between a provincial newspaper and a daily is that on the small paper you know all your contacts personally, while in Dublin every story is a problem because you have to find out who to ring to give you the information. In the provinces you have a small telephone list of important, influential people, the pillars of society, and it is just a matter of making a call and they will know everything that is going on. Similarly, when you go into a council meeting or the courthouse you know all the officials and they oblige you with all the facts. It's easy.

In Dublin they are not quite as helpful. They can be suspicious of the press and you have to spend a long time building up trust with people in vital areas. There is a saying in journalism that you are only as good as your contacts. That is very true. In the provinces you can be walking down the street and someone will walk up to you and give you a story because they know you. In Dublin, you have to make an awful lot of telephone calls before you get the information you require. Down the country you are a big fish in a small pool, someone respected and looked up to, while in Dublin you are nobody.

Back in those days in the *Independent*, we thought we were superb journalists, doing a great job, providing a fine news service – interesting, informed and entertaining service. However, in retrospect journalism in Dublin back in the 60s was generally very low-key with little flair or originality. It has developed considerably over the years. Investigative journalism was practically non-existent. Most big stories of the time tended to be hyped-up, exaggerated accounts of fires, car crashes and the odd murder or fracas. This was backed up by saturation coverage of the Dáil, the Seanad, the courts and local authorities, often printed verbatim. It was a very simple, innocent kind of reporting. Everything was taken on face value and not a lot of hard questions were asked of the establishment.

Statements by leaders of Church and State were carried in full. These were used in their entirety for fear of offending anyone. The newspapers did not want to be accused of being unfair. That was the biggest charge you could make against a paper and none of them wanted to be found guilty on that count. They all proudly boasted of being fair and impartial. They bent over backwards to ensure that every sector was given space to put its case across. This meant everybody was happy and there was no conflict. The papers could say they were providing a service, giving the news as it happened; the public was getting its money's worth and the politicians, Church and business were getting their message across. The Government was aloof and ministers were inaccessible, except to political correspondents or journalists with whom they had a good relationship. If you were privileged to be honoured with an interview with a real live Government minister it was usually after weeks of negotiations, often in writing. Important people like ministers might then stipulate – and quite often did – that you submit your copy to them before it was used. When this was done they had little hesitation in deleting the passages they did not like. Sometimes when the copy arrived back it bore very little resemblance to what had originally been written, but it was duly used because the paper had managed to secure an exclusive interview with an important man – it was always a male minister then.

It was basically a journalism of its time: it reflected the easy-going society and quieter way of life. There wasn't a lot of money around and there weren't many major controversial issues occupying the Government or the public mind. We were a new, developing nation and the main priority was to build factories and provide work. There were no big business scandals, divisive debates on contraception, divorce and abortion. We chronicled the words accurately as they were solemnly boomed out on the floor of the Dáil chamber; we reported the course of justice from the courts; county councillors got great mileage out of their long-winded speeches – and were quick to complain if they did not get into the paper or if their words of wisdom were cut to any degree.

[The Church reigned supreme and if the Archbishop of Dublin, Dr John Charles McQuaid, made a speech at a Confirmation ceremony not a comma was changed. His Lenten Pastoral Letter was like a Papal Encyclical. The name McQuaid back in the 60s was not just looked on with reverence and respect by newspaper executives, but with the deepest fear, and they were not going to jeopardise their jobs by offending the man in Drumcondra.] It was all quite paranoid really. Yet, I heard people say that Dr McQuaid was in fact a shy man and that the stories of him being a stern, authoritarian figure and difficult character were untrue. If he was shy he had a strange way of disguising it. The recently published de Valera papers show that the American bishops succeeded in pressurising Pope Pius XII not to make him a cardinal and Bishop Dalton got the plum job instead.

How things have changed. Now the politicians and Church leaders are regularly the subject of critical comment. Speeches of our leaders, however major or insignificant, are carefully scrutinised, interpreted, welcomed or sharply criticised. There is now a greater openness on both sides and a healthy respect for each other, keeping one another at arm's distance. This is good for democracy and for our society generally.

Today, the fire, the car crash or fracas does not get huge headlines. Often they are confined to a paragraph on an inside page. They will still of course get prominence in the evening papers, but overall the dailies don't give them the big treatment they used to when they were the main bread and butter stories.

* * *

The problem with working in Independent Newspapers in the 60s was that general reporters worked for all three papers in the group. This was very frenetic and difficult to get used to – three different papers, three different styles, three different sets of editorial executives. I enjoyed working on the *Independent* and the *Sunday Independent*, but hated being rostered for the *Herald*. Two years after I arrived a major decision was taken at the top to 'liven up' the *Herald*, jazz it up and dramatise stories. A wildly enthusiastic news editor was put in charge of the operation and he terrorised the staff from early morning until 4 p.m. in the afternoon. He has since gone to the great newsroom in the sky but he left his mark on many a young and old reporter. This was all quite traumatic for the staff and it pressurised us into hyping-up and exaggerating even the most trivial of stories. If you were not prepared to carry out orders without question you were categorised as driftwood.

This lasted for a few years and it was neither beneficial to the reporters nor to its readers. During the period there were numerous union meetings to protest about the direction the *Herald* was taking and the stories we were expected to write. We accepted that there was need to brighten and improve it, but we were going to the extreme and there was as lot of ill feeling as a result. The atmosphere was, to say the least, very sour.

At the best of times anyway, working on an evening newspaper is exciting. There is never a dull moment – you are constantly balancing on a tightrope – and you develop a sixth sense which would put any talented magician to shame.

There is a real buzz, a feeling of things happening quickly – too frenetically at times. The deadlines are extremely tight and the pressure is intense. You are always working against the clock, which makes it difficult to check out stories properly, and there is constant tension. It is exhilarating and infuriating. It is a lot more competitive than working on a daily paper. In fact, there is no comparison. You deal with a lot of what are called 'human interest' or 'colour' stories as distinct from issues, which are generally dealt with by the more serious dailies, where they have more time and space for 'in depth' and analytical reporting. Evening papers can only scratch the surface and give a quick, easy read. Due to the incredible pressures involved they are mainly for young reporters, strong in wind and limb, madly enthusiastic, and able to cover the hundred metres in Olympic-qualifying time. It is an ideal training ground for young reporters. But I can vouch for the fact that you don't stay young very long – at least not if you have any sensitivity.

When the big decision was made to liven-up the *Herald*, the main rule was to 'flame-up' every story. Make it jump out at the readers, hit them over the head with it, force them to read it, embellish it with as much drama as you could possibly manage. Every fire, car crash or fracas was built up into earth-shattering proportions; all it then required was for the sub-editor to put on an even more sensational screaming banner headline. Walter Mitty would have risen to executive level in the *Herald* in those days. In fact, I can honestly say there were some stories we produced which even Walter Mitty would not have believed.

For instance, a fire always became an inferno. A small fire could be made much more significant if you wrote 'the brigade averted a major disaster,' pointing out that if it had spread down the road it would have reached a petrol filling station or an orphanage. You always had to think ahead. Use your imagination, be creative, write with style and vigour. Never be satisfied with the bland, the ordinary; you were an evening paper reporter and you had to produce slick, snappy copy. It was show business, not journalism, as far as I could see.

A road accident had to be treated the same way. If it didn't speak loudly enough for itself, you introduced the 'What Might Have Been' scenario. This meant putting blatantly leading questions to eye-witnesses, suggesting that if there had been 10 children walking to school at the time the car mounted the footpath and struck the wall it would have been disastrous. They, of course, reply 'yes'. By prompting eye-witnesses it was possible to get some good quotes to inflate rather ordinary stories. This was particularly the practice on a 'slow day' – when things were quiet and there was a big blank space on the front page to be filled. There was nothing more likely to give even a young man a heart attack than a slow day in the *Evening Herald*.

To get an evening newspaper out on to the streets in the time available is a miracle of dedication in a sea of chaos and unbelievable aggravation, where the warfare of insults and frayed tempers has to be seen to be believed. It is a hard life with a lot of burn-out.

However, it is all taken as part and parcel of the job and everyone 'gets on with it' as best as they can. All the chaotic cut and thrust is accepted as part of the job of producing an evening paper. *Evening Herald* reporting in those days was kamikaze stuff indeed and quite a lot of very good reporters left Middle

Abbey Street totally disillusioned around that time, mostly to RTE. I left after a few years of it. It was a crazy existence. It wasn't good for the reporters or for the readers, whom I believed weren't getting good service. You lost a lot of very good contacts because your stories were often flamed up and totally exaggerated. The next time you rang your contact he just didn't want to know you. I also noticed during my time on the *Herald* that a lot of people who promised to 'ring back' never did. Who could blame them? If it was me, I wouldn't ring back either. Nobody wants their words twisted to mean something else to fit in with a news editor's imagination.

When I think back on some of the stories I had to do at that time I break out in a cold sweat. All stories, big or small, were chased with dedication, based on the fear that if you did not come up with the goods you would be accused of 'not trying'. And that is the biggest humiliation any reporter can face. Some of the middle-aged or older reporters of the time who had no stomach for exaggerated human interest stories became surplus to requirements. It was made known they weren't wanted on the *Herald* and they should be rostered on the *Independent*.

One story which still leaves a bad taste in my mouth involved a young nurse who died in an accident in Australia. I was asked to go out to a northside housing estate and interview the parents. The news editor, foreseeing the problems, said: 'The parents won't want to talk to you, but tell them if they give us an interview the *Herald* will fly the body home.' Then he complimented me by saying that I was the ideal man for this job, as I was always diplomatic and he was sure that I would come up with the goods. He then warned that there was a big hole on the front page that had to be filled.

I arrived at the house: knocked, waited, but no reply. After the third attempt, a voice at the end of the hall shouted out 'Who's there?' I replied *'The Evening Herald'* and got the answer I expected. 'Go away,' said the woman's voice. I then had to put my sixth sense into full play. 'Hold on, hold on a minute, I might be able to help,' I replied, making it clear that I was there to help, not just for a story. After a bit of gentle persuasion I eventually got in. I wasn't called the diplomat for nothing.

The woman was the mother of the dead girl and she was naturally terribly upset. She was most emphatic that she did not want any report in the newspapers. I explained the *Herald* was prepared to fly the body home if she would give us a few details of her daughter's short life – such as where she went to school, what she was working at in Australia, was she single or married, how many brothers and sisters had she, etc.

Pretty harmless stuff, really, and nothing to disturb her unduly in her time of grief. No grisly intrusion of privacy. She was very interested in having the body repatriated and I think she said something about the neighbours trying to help in that regard. She started to answer some of the questions without realising it. I was relieved. Then she stopped and repeated she did not want anything in the papers. 'Look, I just don't want anything in the papers; please go away, this is all very hurtful ....' At this stage I was batting for her and wanted to ensure that she did get the remains of her daughter back. However, the woman was adamant; nothing was going to appear in the papers, full stop.

Then it dawned on her. 'Does this mean that the *Herald* won't bring the body back?' she asked. This was the situation I had been dreading. I wished a hole would open and swallow me. I said I did not know and gave her the name of the news editor and his telephone number. I then left, expressing my sympathy about her sad loss.

When I got back to the office the news editor rushed up to me and asked if I had got the story. When I said no, there was a loud, angry: 'WHAT ... did you not tell her we would bring back the body?' I said I had, but the woman just did not want to talk. I told him that she had been interested in the offer but she just did not want to want to discuss the accident; it was too hurtful. She was deeply distressed. She was a quiet, retiring sort of woman who was heavily shocked and did not want any publicity. The news editor was apoplectic, hurled a shower of abuse at me and accused me of not trying, of not handling the situation properly.

I asked him if he was going to make the arrangements to repatriate the remains. At this stage I was taking a personal interest in the matter, having got to like the mother and having sympathy for her plight. He said 'Forget about it' and went off. I never did forget about it. It was 30 years ago and I still think about it. I don't know what the final outcome was. I don't know if the woman rang. I doubt it. I don't know if the neighbours were able to rally around and collect enough money to help out. Thirty years ago Australia was a long distance away and the money involved would have been substantial, too much for this old lady and her poor neighbours to raise.

Another story which still haunts me concerns a young Dublin girl who was stabbed to death by a psychopath in New York. We got the story from the wire service and once again I drew the short straw and was asked to go out and interview the mother. I cringed, but had no option but to grab my coat and hat. You don't make excuses when the boss is issuing orders. I didn't realise at the time that this was a story which was even worse than it looked at first sight.

I called a taxi and was at the doorstep within 20 minutes. A small, smiling old woman opened the door to me. She was very pleasant and seemed to be in good form. I introduced myself and began asking her a few questions about her daughter. She was chatting away about the daughter. I thought she was very easy-going for a mother who had just lost her child in a gruesome killing. After a few minutes, she asked me what I was doing there. Then it dawned on me. She didn't know her daughter was dead. Jesus Christ, what a situation to be in. I didn't know what to say. You are supposed to be able to think on your feet in this business, but I was numb. She got suspicious and asked 'Is there something wrong?' I told her as discreetly as I could that her daughter was dead, leaving out a lot of the gory details contained in the Reuters report. I think the poor girl was stabbed about 20 times in the frenzied murder. She began to tremble and broke into tears. She invited me into the kitchen where she made a cup of tea for the two of us. She just wanted someone to talk to. She thought I had a lot of information, but I only had a paragraph from Reuters (an Irish woman murdered in New York is very small news over there). She spoke a lot about her daughter and I got plenty of information. When I was leaving, I asked her if she had a photo of her daughter. She went over and took a framed picture off the wall and gave it to me, saying I could have it if I promised to get it back to her. I ensured that she got the picture back, but it was one story I would not like to have to do again.

The housing shortage 'crisis' in Dublin in the mid-sixties provided many headlines. There were numerous demonstrations and protests. There was a huge waiting list for houses. Angry families living in dreadful conditions took to the streets to make their case for proper housing. The Lord Mayor of Dublin, Tom Stafford, nearly had his car overturned by protestors outside City Hall. 'It was one of the most frightening experiences of my life,' he told me afterwards, visibly shaken. There were also a number of clashes with gardaí. It was a hectic time, with Dublin Corporation under severe pressure. It provided great copy for the newspapers.

At the centre of the crisis was Dennis Dennehy, who had been waiting for a house for a long time and was one of the leaders of the protest campaign. The *Herald* used to interview him regularly. One morning I was sitting in the office when it was decided that he should be interviewed again. Two reporters refused to go out on the story. They explained that Dennehy had not liked what they wrote previously. They had written up his communist allegiance in a way he felt was offensive. He angrily accused the *Herald* of being more interested in knocking communism than solving the housing problem. I was then selected to go out to have a chat with him to see if there were any developments in this long-running story. It was a case of being in the wrong place at the wrong time. Full of trepidation, I arrived at the flat in Mountjoy Square where he was squatting with his wife and children. I knocked on the door and his wife shouted out: 'Who's there? If it's the *Herald* go away.'

I had expected trouble, but nothing as prompt and as direct as this.

'Press,' I replied deliberately vaguely.

As I expected, she thought I was from the *Evening Press*. She let me in but Dennis wasn't there. He was down at the Labour Exchange. She then began a tirade against the *Herald*. I stood there feeling very uncomfortable indeed, in a deep sweat, waiting for an opportunity to get out. She ranted on: 'There is only one crowd worse than the *Herald* and that's the fucking Legion of Mary.'

'What did they do on you?' I asked, taken aback, wondering what such a highly reputable, harmless movement like the Legion of Mary could have done to get her so incensed.

'They keep calling in here to see how I'm getting on. They keep saying they'll pray for me. It's not fucking prayers I want; I'm looking for a fucking house,' she explained, spitting out each word with venom.

Eventually, I managed to extricate myself and got my taxi to go to the Labour Exchange. Dennehy was coming out the front door when I arrived. Perfect timing. The first and only break I was to get that day. Again, I introduced myself as 'press', now well aware of the Dennehys' views of the *Herald*. He asked for a lift into the centre of town. On the way down he spoke about the housing situation and warned that it would soon spill over and reach the stage where people would revolt. He said people would be forced to take the law into their own hands and force the establishment to give them the basics of life. It was very strong stuff. Elaborating on his theme, he said that he was not in favour of violence, but this was becoming a real possibility. He was very sincere and had very strong socialist principles. I liked him.

I left him off and went back to the office. I got a great kick out of telling the news editor and editor that the *Herald* was worse than the fucking Legion of Mary. I gave them a blow for blow account of what Mrs Dennehy thought of the paper. I explained that because of the Dennehys' strong views about the *Herald* I had no option but to get the interview under what was basically false pretences and it was now up to them to decide whether they would use it or not. They were not too happy about this. As we were talking, the phone rang. Who was on the line? Yes, Dennis Dennehy, no less. He had rumbled on to what had happened. Apparently, he had been in touch with the *Evening Press* to make an amendment to his story and they naturally informed him that none of their reporters had spoken to him. He realised straight away that he had been duped and that it was the *Herald* who had interviewed him. He warned that if we used one line from the interview he would sue. The *Evening Press* came out that night with the story he had given me on its front page. This was the galling end of the scoop that never was.

I had been put in an impossible position by our earlier reporting of Dennehy. In retrospect, I should have gone straight back to the office after Mrs Dennehy had made her views known. It was obvious I wasn't going to get a story. But in this business, especially if you are working on an evening paper, you don't put up the white flag that easily and you press on and hope for a change in the climate.

Dennis Dennehy was a man of great courage and integrity who was fighting for himself and the other homeless of Dublin. He deserved a more balanced and sympathetic press coverage than he got. He died in June 1984. He was only 45. He had been arrested for squatting in the flat in Mountjoy and was sent to prison where he went on a hunger strike for 10 days.

Another *Herald* story which I wrote which was subsequently totally exaggerated concerned a small robbery in a Dublin hotel. It was hardly worth a paragraph, but it ended up splashed across the front page.

It was about 2 p.m. when the news editor jumped from his chair flushed with excitement and rushed down the newsroom. He had just received a tip-off that there had been a robbery in a hotel on the southside of the city. We had no decent lead story that day and he wanted this to fit the bill. There was no time to wait for a photographer because it was so late (2 p.m. is an awkward time for the evening papers as it is close to their final deadline). I was to get out there as fast as I could and the photographer would follow.

I arrived at the hotel breathless. I looked for the manager or someone in charge. I was told that there had been a minor incident but that it was now all over; there was no problem. After being told by my news editor that this was a big story I thought I was being fobbed off, that the manager was trying to play down the matter. I asked him for the details. He had no hesitation in telling me. It transpired that some unfortunate, mentally defective man who had got out of a psychiatric hospital had walked up behind a woman paying her bill at the reception desk, pretended he had a gun in his pocket and demanded her cheque book.

She was terrified and gave it to him. He then rushed away, but in doing so ran straight through a plate glass door, seriously cutting himself. He was taken to hospital, bleeding profusely. Undeterred, I went to the hospital to get some details about the poor chap. A detective garda told me more or less what the manager had outlined. He patiently pointed out that there was no story in it and that this was just an unfortunate poor devil who was not aware of what he was doing. Just a sad case. I accepted that there was no real story there, certainly not a lead. I got to a phone and dictated a few short paragraphs for what I thought would be an innocuous story. As I was doing this, the news editor, who already had decided what the story was going to be, came on to the line.

He started chastising me and telling me this was a much bigger story than the one I was putting over. I explained the background to it, but he was not satisfied. He latched on to the fact that the hotel door had been smashed and that the gardaí were in the hospital. When the story appeared it was splashed across five columns of the front page. I hardly recognised it, even though my by-line was put on it. He had totally rewritten it and had the gardaí 'standing by the bedside' of a hardened gunman who had held up the hotel, terrifying the people in the foyer, seriously injuring himself as he tried to evade chasing gardaí and detectives who were now keeping a close watch on him and hoping to get him to make a statement. There was no reference to the fact that the gunman was an unfortunate youth who did not know what he was doing. To make a lead story out of an attempted larceny of a cheque book was pathetic.

In cases like this a reporter loses all credibility. He cannot go back to the manager of that hotel again, because the honest statement he (the manager) had made was not used. The gardaí also knew the story was blown totally out of proportion. Both the manager and the gardaí involved would be very slow in future to talk to the press. That is the unfortunate long-term repercussions of such journalism. It might push up circulation for one issue, but the long-term credibility of the paper and its reporters is brought into question. Working on an evening newspaper can lose you a lot of good contacts very quickly. You have no defence when members of the public accuse you of being irresponsible.

There was a lot of reporting in the *Evening Herald* in the 60s which bordered on the irresponsible. Admittedly, a lot has changed since then, but those years left a lot to be desired. Things have changed for the better over the years and the *Herald* has now found a successful formula. As a result it is a much better and more reliable paper than it was 30 years ago. Sometimes I even went beyond what was sensible, half through determination to get the story and partly through fear of the news editor, who was a hard task master. Older and wiser now, I wonder why I was so silly.

There is one excellent example of such stupidity. When I look back on it, I don't know whether to be amused or angry. I was told to go out to a big fire which was engulfing a factory on Shelbourne Road. A passer-by had phoned the news desk and said it was quite serious. I bolted out of the newsroom and got there within 15 minutes. I did not see any flames shooting into the sky, as I had been led to expect. There was a wisp of smoke coming out of the back of the premises, but that was about all. I confidently walked up to the security man on the gate and asked him about the fire. He told me it was nothing really, only a minor blaze which they had quickly extinguished. Well, I knew that that wasn't going to go down too well back in the office, where they were expecting a conflagration and had designated quite a bit of space for it on the front page.

I asked could I go in and see the damage? At least then I could describe the charred remains. 'Sorry,' said the man on the gate, 'no one is allowed in.' No amount of persuasion could convince this conscientious sentry to let me through those gates. The immortal words 'It's more than my job is worth' were repeated ad nauseum. It was an expression I used to hear quite a lot working on the *Herald*. Through a mixture of enthusiasm and anxiety I went around the back of the premises to find out if I could get a view of the fire. No luck. There was a ten foot wall between me and the factory. After a few of moments deep thought, I said 'To hell with it, I'll get in somehow.' Being young and fit, I scaled up the wall and dropped down on the other side, spraining my ankle in the process.

After a few minutes of muffled curses, I hobbled around the yard, making sure I kept myself hidden behind large timber crates. I got to the part where the smoke was coming from. Sure enough, the man on the gate was right; it was quite a harmless fire. I saw there was very little damage caused and the factory was operating normally.

My next big problem was how the hell was I going to get out. My ankle was quite painful and there was no possibility of being able to climb back the way I had come. The only other exit was through the front gate.

I sheepishly hopped to the gate, where I got the reception I expected from the perplexed security man who thought he had seen the last of me.

'How the hell did you get in here?', he shouted, or words a little stronger. He roared at me to 'get the bloody hell out of here and don't come back.' I could have assured him that I had no intention of going back, but instead I went looking for the nearest telephone to report back to base.

I got to the nearest telephone kiosk and told the news editor there was no story. It was only a minor fire and hardly worth a paragraph, I explained. News editors hate when you don't turn up with the goods. 'Ah, you're not trying,' he growled. Well, you can imagine how I reacted to that. Here I was with a badly injured ankle and all I was getting was abuse. The conversation that ensued cannot be repeated here.

Some days later, still annoyed at my experience, I told an older colleague of my unfortunate experience. He thought it was hilarious and hadn't much sympathy for me. He recalled how he had been sent to another 'fire that wasn't a fire' story. He, like me, thought he was going out to cover something big. When he arrived, it transpired that it was only a harmless incident where a carpet went on fire in a house. My colleague knew that you always had to produce something even if it was only to prove you were there and he turned a non-story into a front page picture story.

After realising that there was in fact no fire story to write, he started to look for an angle. He then came up with an ingenious idea. He remembered when he was running up the stairs of the house that a little dog passed him on the way down. He went and found the dog, placed it in a corner of the house where a bit of smoke had damaged the wall.

He got his photographer to take a picture.

That evening the *Herald* had a wonderful story about how the barking of the family's pet dog Rover had saved the whole household from being burned to death, and placed beside the story was a fine picture of Rover, looking pleased with himself. There was a reporter with initiative. It certainly put me in my place.

You may at this stage be wondering why news editors send reporters out on so many wild goose chases. The answer is simply because of that rare breed of greedy animal – the tip-off men. These are the people who are constantly on the look-out for something unusual around town and then immediately dash to the nearest phone and breathlessly tell the news desk about what they have seen. They have more than just a casual interest in letting the paper know what has happened and the satisfaction of being involved in something out of the ordinary. No, there is a strong mercenary aspect involved in their diligence. They know they will get a tip-off fee from the paper if the story comes to anything. They always give their name and come into the office a few days later to collect their few quid. Tip-off men are usually taxi drivers, unemployed people, students, people who are constantly moving around the city and keep a sharp look-out for incidents. Because they have a chance of picking up a few quid they usually exaggerate everything they see to monumental proportions.

This gets news editors excited and they immediately send a reporter and photographer to the scene. Therefore, many of the incidents are of a minor nature and not worth giving much space to. Tip-off men were the bane of our lives in my days in the *Herald*, although they were a necessary evil, as sometimes they did come up with the goods. There was one character who used to work in a hospital and spent much of his time topping up his salary by ringing the *Herald* with stories. Every time an ambulance came in the gate of the hospital he made it his business to find out what had happened and called us straight away. The *Herald* would have the story before the injured person reached the casualty section. He used to show great enterprise, and of course after ringing us he would then call our opposition, the *Evening Press*. The hospital eventually found out about his extra curricular activities and he was dismissed.

Certainly, there was no fear of suffering boredom working on the *Herald*. It was all quite frenetic and unpredictable. The most amazing, but true story is told by Michael Hourihane, who worked on the paper back in the 40s and 50s. It was long before I joined the paper, but the story has gone into journalistic history.

Michael was sitting quietly in the newsroom one fairly uneventful day when a big strapping labourer walked into the office and stood beside him. Now this couldn't happen today because all newspapers have security personnel guarding the doors and all strangers are carefully vetted and not allowed in unless they get clearance from the top. In the old days we had every headbanger in the city casually wandering through the door with all sorts of cock and bull stories. On this occasion a big chap strolled in off the street. He told Michael he had a story to tell.

'OK, what is it?' asked Michael, not exactly madly enthusiastic.

'I've just murdered my wife,' said the man, impassively.

Reporters are used to hearing tall stories from people who should be locked up or are just looking for publicity, so Michael didn't believe him. The man, sensing that his story was being treated with a certain scepticism, added:' I'm telling the truth.' When Michael still did not take him seriously, the fellow unwrapped a load of newspapers and produced an axe with blood on it. He just wanted to give himself up. Michael contacted the gardaí and they arrived and took the man away without a struggle.

After my four years stint with Independent Newspapers I decided to move to *The Irish Times*.

Good Times at The Irish Times

I joined *The Irish Times* on a bright, sunny day in May 1969. Five of the staff had left to join RTE and they had to get replacements quickly.

It was a big exodus from a small paper. RTE was expanding its news service at the time and the appeal of radio and television work was hard to resist for many Dublin journalists. Two weeks earlier I had got a telephone call from the *Times* asking me if I would be interested in one of the jobs. They gave me 24 hours to think about it. I replied that I didn't need 24 hours and accepted on the spot.

I remember walking into the old, battered newsroom and chatting to my new colleagues. They made me very welcome and there was a nice, friendly, relaxed atmosphere in the place. From my first day in the building I loved it. It became my spiritual home. That was three decades ago and I still feel the same about the Old Lady of Westmoreland Street, even if it has moved over to D'Olier Street, a less imposing thoroughfare.

Newsrooms in those days were usually areas of chaos and dishevelment, unlike the space-age newsrooms of today with their computers, high technology and flashy desks and furniture. The *Irish Times* newsroom, however, could have taken the prize for the most ramshackle working conditions in the whole of the western world. Not that it particularly worried us: we loved it. There was a certain atmosphere about it: it reeked of tradition. Many fine journalists had written many superb stories on those old desks, with the leather peeling off the top, the handles broken on the drawers and the legs shaky, to say the least.

One woman journalist laddered her nylons off the rough leg of one antiquated desk. She was so annoyed that she put in for a new pair of tights on her expenses. She said they were the third pair she had had ruined and enough was enough. What's more, her claim was successful: it was accepted without a murmur. Take it from me, stranger things than women's tights have appeared on reporters' expenses over the years.

Ugly black telephone wires hung from the ceiling and big industrial-type pipes ran along other parts of the ceiling. There were a few big heavy, tank-like typewriters on some of the desks. When they were all in use at the same time it was like World War II. Much of the time they weren't in use or else they needed ribbons, so we were encouraged to bring in our personal portables. The place was also in need of a good coat of paint and a proper ventilation system. But details like that didn't worry us: it was a happy work environment and aesthetics didn't bother us. Besides, in those days we didn't know any better: it was the norm. As long as the paper came out on time and provided we got paid at the end of the month, life was great. My big problem when I arrived in *The Irish Times* was where to sit. The desks may have been in bits, but it was an achievement to get one.

Unfortunately, there weren't enough of them and I spent my first two years wandering from pillar to post. I used Michael McInerney's desk a lot. He was the political correspondent and spent much of his time up in the Dáil, thus leaving me free to use his space. The only problem was that it was situated beside a broken window with a fierce draught coming through. So there were always two dangers: Michael could come back early and throw me out of his place or I could get pneumonia from the draught. Complaints about the broken window fell on deaf ears. It took six months before it was repaired. If I had been anyway handy I could have fixed it myself. My solution was to stuff a few old papers in the space.

Eventually, I got a desk of my own. I really felt I belonged then. Henry Kelly had been appointed Northern Ireland editor, so I grabbed his patch the minute he walked out the door.

In my first few months I was impressed with the quiet professionalism of the place. There wasn't a series of inquests every day on how we had performed the night before. There was no bickering or recriminations and passing the buck. Everyone was doing their best and there was a quiet confidence about the system. There was a great trust placed in you. When you wrote a good story they were very generous with praise and encouragement. It made you want to do the same again. There was a lot less fire brigade action and ambulance chasing which was the bread and butter of the *Evening Herald* and *Evening Press*. The lack of an evening paper was a blessing. You didn't have to be jumping up and down all the time and shouting into the phone or at each other to prove that you were working. We had a small staff, so we were selective in what we covered. We didn't try to cover the trivia. We were, as a result, able to concentrate on a few important stories and do them well.

When I joined paper, the infamous, well-documented, bucolic days of Bertie Smyllie were long gone. Smyllie had been editor from 1934 till his death in 1954. He remains one of the legendary figures in Irish journalism. A huge oil painting of him still hangs in the editor's office. Those were easy-going days when you could get away with a lot of shortcuts and humorous pranks which would not be tolerated for later generations of journalists. They seem to have spent as much time over in the Palace Bar as they did in the office. While we still manage to hop across the road for the odd drink today, there is nothing like the massive amount of alcohol consumption that went on in those years. Today we go across the road to get away from looking into a hot computer screen. Today,

Smyllie would not be allowed to smoke his big, black briar pipe in the building. Smoking is banned and you have to go off to a special little room if you want to have a puff. Different times, different rules, Mr Smyllie, Sir.

However, I was touched by one little incident in my first weeks on the paper. It was about 9 p.m. one evening in the newsroom and things had become quiet. The paper was full and there wasn't much to do. I was just sitting there reading a newspaper. Liam MacGabhann, one of the best journalists of his era, was the news editor that night. He came over to me and said: 'Do you drink pints, Sir?' I replied that I had been known to pay my respects to Arthur Guinness on occasions. 'Well then, Sir, get out of here and wet your whistle,' he commanded, 'As long as I know where I can get you, I'm happy. I'll give you a ring if I need you.' I, of course, readily took him up on the offer. It was a nice gesture.

I know I'm prejudiced, mainly because I was in my prime, but I believe that the late 60s–70s was the golden era of *The Irish Times*. It changed from being a low circulation, minority newspaper to one with strong opinions, in-depth reporting and lots of vibrant colour writing. It provided comprehensive, accurate and impartial reporting of a high standard. The circulation rose steadily. It had found a niche for itself and suddenly there was a big chunk of the market eager to read it every day.

* * *

Douglas Gageby, editor, and Donal Foley, news editor, spearheaded the dramatic change. They laid the foundations for its reputation today as an authoritive and reliable paper. They enthusiastically wrenched the paper out of its freefall and, through a mixture of bright ideas, experiments and innovation, transformed it into a highly readable journal. Each day it provided an informative and entertaining read. The success was based on Gageby's policy of giving everyone a fair crack of the whip. Space was always found for every voice. Even the smallest group in Irish society was entitled to air their views, however eccentric. He also had the strong view that *The Irish Times* must be a paper of record. It must be fair and accurate, totally reflecting Irish life without prejudice or favour. A person should be able to go into the National Library in a hundred years time and read *The Irish Times* and be able to know that this was a true account of what was happening in Ireland in that period.

> 'I believe,' he said, 'that advocacy and passion in a newspaper must be accompanied by constant adherence to the basic ruling of our calling: that our prime function is to give as accurately as possible, the facts of what is going on – the world picture.'

Some people, including a few of his own staff, joked about the paper being a long playing record, that by putting down the full record you were filling the paper with too much waffle, wasting valuable, expensive space, space that could be better used for shorter, just as interesting stories. Many reporters complained about not getting their stories into print.

The circulation continued to rise, so he must have been right. In his first seven years as editor, 22,000 was added to the average daily circulation of the paper. In the following four years the circulation would continue to rise until it was just short of 70,000, double its 1964 circulation. This was phenomenal progress. The paper of record policy paid a healthy dividend. The *Times* carried comprehensive reports of most speeches in the Dáil, whether they were interesting or boring.

The Budget speech was always printed in full, a Papal Encyclical would get maybe three-quarters of a page, the Spring Show and Horse Show results were given huge amounts of space. This policy, while successful, put a strain on the reporters, as they had to work twice as hard as their colleagues in other papers. Our colleagues would produce a story in eight or ten paragraphs, while we would have to quarry out maybe 30 paragraphs.

Gageby also had the view that Stormont should be given the same extensive coverage as the Dáil. He felt it should be treated with the same respect. This was a view I most certainly did not hold, as I was usually the person who had to travel to Belfast to help out. I had to spend tortuous hours listening to the most dreadful debates in the North's so-called 'parliament' and then send reams of copy to Dublin. It was only a glorified county council. Yet, our circulation in the North at the time was only miniscule. That didn't deter Gageby: we had to show ourselves to be fair and impartial to the people on both sides of the border. The fact that he was a Belfast man – and very proud of it – probably also had a big part to play in it.

Before joining *The Irish Times*, Gageby worked in the *Irish Press* and, judging from some rumours of the time, he did not hold the Old Lady of Westmoreland Street in very high regard. He is said to have bumped into Smyllie in the Pearl Bar one evening. Smyllie demanded to know why he wasn't working for the *Times*. Smyllie believed that there was only one paper that counted and that certainly wasn't the Burgh Quay publication, that de Valera creation. Gageby is reported to have replied that he did not like the *Times*, didn't like its politics, and wouldn't want to work for a paper whose staff was divided into 'gentlemen and players.' Ouch.

Gageby was obsessed with journalism and loved everything about it. He lived the job. 'It's thrilling, stimulating, frustrating and demanding,' he told a public meeting shortly after his retirement. 'And, in case you get too uppity, there are all your mistakes in print, daily, for everyone to see ... including solicitors and others with an eye to litigation.' These words could be written as an epitaph on the tombstone of any reporter, as it's a profession which has huge highs and lows.

It's when you are at your most euphoric, when you have produced a run of some really excellent stories, that it is all brought crashing to the ground by the litigation factor. Too many people now feel that newspapers are easy game and lodge hopeful libel writs relating to the most innocuous matters. There are also too many gagging writs nowadays, shots across the bow, just to keep you quiet. Juries in Irish courts seem to think that newspapers are full of money, or are insured. They are now giving big awards for the most frivolous of claims. It's a new and dangerous trend, which results in self-censorship, affects confidence and, most serious of all, undermines democracy. It is time the antiquated laws dealing with libel were looked at again.

Gageby had one golden rule, and it was a rule he did not like his reporters to break. He did not tolerate reporters mixing comment with facts in news stories. This was one of the greatest sins you could commit in his eyes and all experienced reporters on the staff made sure they never slipped in that regard. He wanted hard news stories to be run straight, with the facts speaking for themselves. I remember him getting very angry when I described a rally outside the GPO after the Bloody Sunday shootings in Derry as being 'impressive'. It had, in fact, been impressive, with O'Connell Street packed with protestors, some carrying candles, and emotions were very high. It was riveting, but he did not want any emotive adjectives or comment of any kind. He did not want to know the reporters' views on it; just wanted it straight. The facts should speak for themselves.

He was a hard taskmaster, but scrupulously fair. He was a strict disciplinarian who, as leader, laid down the rules and watched to make sure that they were followed to the letter. He had an eagle eye and nothing ever got past him in the paper without him querying it. You could always detect the old army training in him: it was reflected in his whole demeanour. The staff was fully aware of his style and stuck by his policy. He was always in total command and he did not tolerate any insubordination. He sought ideas and said he was open to suggestions, but if he had his mind made up there was no point in going against him.

The few who thought they could talk back to him, question his judgement, believing they were in the right, quickly found out that it certainly wasn't worth it. You would get nowhere. This was because, like all leaders, he had a supreme confidence in his own ability, in what he was trying to achieve, and the way he was going about it. He was always known as Mister Gageby, and only those close to him called him Douglas.

He must also be given credit for knowing when to retire. He felt it was important to hand over to a younger man, to get young ideas. Many leaders are power crazy and refuse to let go. The present strong position of *The Irish Times* is due to Gageby. He put in the foundations, set the standards, and then bowed out. His work has been built on; his legacy lives on.

He was idolised in the newspaper industry. My father, who worked in *The Sunday Independent*, was a great fan of his. Back in the 60s when I told Dad I was leaving the *Independent* to go to *The Irish Times*, he was deeply upset and asked me to reconsider my decision. 'I'm begging you not to go,' he pleaded. 'It is a big mistake: if anything ever happened to Gageby the whole place would come falling down.' I didn't like upsetting him, but I needed a change and felt I had to leave Middle Abbey Street. When the phone rang and I got the offer, I jumped at it. As it transpired, Dad was wrong. Nothing happened to Gageby, who went on for years. Conor Brady took over and continued the good work. He has shown flair and courage and, as a result, circulation has been rising steadily and the paper is doing exceptionally well as we approach the millennium.

* * *

Gageby was lucky to have Donal Foley, a big, heavy, easy-going man as his news editor. Donal had a good eye for journalistic talent and hired some superb writers and excellent general reporters. It must also be recorded that he made the odd mistake: he also recruited some less than efficient journalists, but these were the exceptions. One of these exceptions was supposed to be an outstanding writer, brilliant shorthand notetaker and a fluent Irish speaker. It quickly transpired that the individual had none of these qualities. In fact, Donal was horrified afterwards when he learned that his protegé had left two libel actions pending in his previous paper and that the particular paper was only too glad to get rid of him. This individual used a tape recorder as his shorthand note and never spoke a word of Irish up to the time of his death.

The challenge of revitalising *The Irish Times* appealed to Donal, who had worked most of his journalistic life in London, but who returned to Ireland in 1963.

> 'The year 1963 was a great time to come back to Ireland as news editor of *The Irish Times*,' he wrote afterwards. 'It was a time for extending frontiers ... The role of *The Irish Times* in the circumstances was quite clear. It should be a forum for discussion, a mouthpiece for minorities as well as the majority, and a paper with a clear-cut radical viewpoint. Guided by a radical editor this was the path we took.'

Donal was a great ideas man. He had a fine inquiring mind, a natural curiosity, was constantly asking questions. He loved originality and liked to get away from the day-to-day running news stories and to suggest and get involved in feature articles. These often had an important social content. He also liked to encourage his staff to come up with ideas. He thrived on generating exclusives. He took a tremendous pride in breaking a good story or instigating a successful series of articles. He had a sharp instinct for what would make a good feature and seemed to get a bigger buzz out of a well written feature than from a strong news story. He preferred the freedom of comment and 'colour' in features than the discipline and sometimes the boredom of straight reports.

He was always on the look-out for new young talent. A lot of the writers he hired were women. When this trend was commented on, he replied that women were more sensitive, perceptive and accurate in their reporting. On another occasion though, I saw him take a different attitude. He was questioning one of the women about what he considered to be an excessive expenses docket, when she burst out crying. Donal was a very sensitive man and quickly backed off. Afterwards, he said: 'I can deal with men but I never know what to say to women.'

He was the man who introduced specialisation to the paper. It ended up that nearly everyone had some type of speciality, whether they liked it or not. I was slotted into the job of Local Government Correspondent, even though I refused to take it twice. The third time I agreed because my wife insisted and I stuck with it for a long number of years. While Donal initially believed that specialisation was a good thing, he later came to regret it. 'As soon as they (specialists) are appointed they start building their own little empires, try to become personalities and won't do any general reporting,' he complained.

Born in the Ring Gaeltacht of Co Waterford, he always retained his great love of the Irish language. Anyone looking for a job in *The Irish Times* had a very important extra string to his bow if he had the cúpla focal. As well as being news editor, Donal also introduced and wrote the Saturday Column, edited the Tuarascáil section and had great fun writing the Man Bites Dog satirical column. It may sound incredible, but there are now about ten people doing his work. And in spite of all his writing commitments each week, he still found plenty of time to sink a few pints of Guinness. He loved to sit in a pub, pint in front of him, with good conversation around him. He invariably gave the impression of being very laid-back and of doing nothing, but the paper came out every day and all his columns appeared on time. He never missed a deadline. It was quite an achievement. In fact, for someone with his hectic social lifestyle, it was a miracle.

He was the only journalist I have ever known who could not type. He used to look around the newsroom for a reporter who was not too busy and then dictate his various columns to him or her. He would have dozens of rumpled bits of paper in various pockets containing vital bits of information scribbled down during the week. No modern filing system for him. He would then start reading from them: the end result was usually something quite newsy and interesting. However, most of the staff dreaded to see him coming, to have his big shadow loom across their desk. It wasn't easy to type dictation from Donal. He was inclined to mumble his words and was constantly changing or correcting what he had just said. You had to delete what you had written and start off again.

It was quite frustrating and an unnerving experience to get caught. We used to feel sorry for Eileen O'Brien, to whom he used to dictate his Tuarascáil column. We were spared that because that column was in Irish of which most of us only had a smattering and there was no possibility of us being able to type it.

He had a wonderful sense of humour and his Man Bites Dog column always maintained a high standard of satire. During the week Donal would test some of his jokes on the staff and get their reaction before committing them to print. Most of the time they were funny, but, in all honesty, there were some that just were not amusing. But you couldn't hurt Donal, so even if it wasn't a good joke we would try to muster a laugh and give the thumbs up. Professional comedians say that one of the hardest jobs in the world is trying to make people laugh. However, Donal persevered, year after year, and the column had a big following. He never reached Myles na Gopaleen status but he entertained and amused a lot of people.

As I stated earlier, in those more leisurely days it was the custom that if things were quiet in the office you took an air break and strolled across to the Pearl Bar or to Bowes Bar and consumed the odd pint of Guinness. One day Donal was sitting at the newsdesk and suddenly found that he had no staff. They had mysteriously vanished. He had a couple of big stories he wanted done and there was nobody to help him out. Of course, all he had to do was pick up the phone and they would come running. He jokingly remarked: 'They're all across the road, talking about socialism. They wouldn't work in a fit, just talk about it.'

He died in July 1981 at the early age of 57. Caroline Walsh, a young reporter on the staff at the time, in a poignant appreciation, wrote:

> 'He was the wisest man I ever knew. He told me never to be afraid to wear your heart on your sleeve and remember that writing books and making a name for yourself is all very well, but the best thing to leave after you on this earth is children.'

Donal may have died young, but he packed more living into that short time than others would have done in three lifetimes. He burnt the candle at both ends. He wasn't the sort of guy who could have tolerated old age.

* * *

While Gageby and Foley were the leaders and the best known for the modernisation of the paper, they could not have succeeded without their deputies, two of the quietest, most knowledgeable and most modest individuals you will go a long way to find in the newspaper industry, which, outside of Hollywood, has quite a monopoly of big egos. Bruce Williamson and Gerry Mulvey were the anonymous backroom boys who worked long hours and kept a shrewd hold on the day-to-day running of operations. They carried out the tricky, difficult, worrisome tasks, making the instant crucial decisions late at night and ensuring that every story was in on time and that we had a good product on the street the next day.

Bruce was the deputy editor and a distinguished leader writer. His leaders were masterpieces, well thought-out, succinct and informative. They had style, erudition and logic. He enjoyed the quiet backroom influence which he was able to exercise to defuse the excesses of more impetuous colleagues before they made it into print. He was a tireless advocate of good, well-written and balanced journalism, with a well-tuned ability to detect and root out humbug and fakery. He was also an excellent poet and there was never any need to look through a dictionary when he was around. He had a phenomenal grasp of the English language.

He was a poet with an unfailing control of language; he had a rare and detailed knowledge of the cinema, and for some time during his time as a student in Trinity he had ambitions to become an actor. But it was as a leader writer, working in a field which, by journalistic tradition, still remains anonymous, that Bruce made his mark on *The Irish Times* for more than 40 years. His obituary in *The Irish Times* on April 20, 1991, said:

> 'To perception and style he added erudition, generosity and balance, an inexhaustible knowledge of the world and its vagaries, and, where the occasion called for it, a Swiftian anger and a lion-hearted dedication to principle.'

When he died Gageby wrote a nice appreciation of him, in which he said:

> 'As a persona within the organisation, he was, for years, the hub around which reproduction of the next morning's issue revolved. Learned, wise, indeed, he became a father figure to many and revelled in organisation life; oddly, in a way, for a poet, it may be. But he absorbed the atmosphere of the newspaper, had friends and confidants in every department, loved, especially in the days of hot metal and linotype machines, grammatical wrangles with typesetters and proof readers; never failed to hail the fellow newspaper folk who carried on the work after we, the journalists, had finished – the machine room men, the dispatchers, the drivers. For decades he was an eminence in *The Irish Times* and no one was more loved.'

If Gageby had an able assistant in Bruce, Foley had Gerry Mulvey as his back-up man. Gerry was the assistant news editor, who had long experience in journalism, a good nose for a story, and a sharp eye for mistakes or prospective libels. With Gerry vetting your copy you knew you were in safe hands. He was an astute organiser and marshalled the staff well, slotting them all into stories best suited to their ability. He knew everyone's writing strengths and weaknesses. He knew who he could send on hard assignments and who should be put on colour stories. He had unerring judgement in this regard, the hallmark of a good director of news collection. He was also – unusual for a news editor – a very gentle person with a very caring disposition. I once saw him go up to a reporter who was out of sorts, suffering from a bad flu, and say: 'Don't be in here killing yourself. You should go straight home and go to bed.' I thought it was a very nice gesture, but typical of the man. It's not the type of gesture you normally see in business or in the ruthless world of journalism, where everyone is so busy they cannot see when a person is not well.

Neither Bruce nor Gerry were ever mentioned in all the publicity and razzmatazz of the golden years; their names never appeared in any magazines, were never heard of on the trendy social whirl, or when especially successful issues of the paper were lauded. They never sought notoriety and didn't want it. They were diligent and hard-working and got immense pleasure and fulfillment out of doing a good job. The successful end result was their satisfaction. Another vital worker behind the scenes was Nigel Brown. He was a deputy news editor for over 20 years until his untimely death in July 1997 of a heart attack. He was only 54, but the years of sitting in the hot seat took their lethal toll on him. He was my best buddy in the paper and his sudden death was a major blow. He was family. A lot of superlatives are often trotted out when you are dead. Sometimes they are over the top and are total exaggeration. I suppose it is a generous Irish trait. However, the tributes paid to Nigel were genuine and sincere. The Rev William Darlinson at the funeral described Nigel as 'a man without guile, a man with no hidden agenda.' Even if the words hadn't been so eloquent, the huge crowd which turned up to pay their last respects would be testimony to his popularity. Everyone, from the top executives of the paper to the messenger boys were there to pay their respects.

He was a quiet, thoughtful and unassuming person. One could go so far as to say he was unique. Like Bruce and Gerry, in a profession where so many people seek a high profile, you would rarely see his by-line. He was one of the people in the engine room of the paper (the newsdesk), the unsung heroes, who day after day have to ensure that all the news is covered and that nothing is missed. These people experience the heaviest stress and suffer the biggest hits in the turbulent world of journalism. Nigel had a safe pair of hands. He had the good news editor's talent of being able to do six things at the one time and not get ruffled or irritable. He had a wonderful sixth sense, almost bordering on extra sensory perception. He could spot a libel out in the Atlantic and torpedo it before it reached Galway Bay. He was thorough, methodical and always right. I never knew him to make a mistake. He was always last to leave the newsroom at night.

He was like the pits chief in a Grand Prix race. He made sure the wheels were changed quickly and all the nuts and bolts were in place to ensure that the car went on to win the race. But he never wanted to drive the car. He never wanted to be a name, a commentator, a personality. And when the car flashed past the winning post, Nigel was gone. He never hung around to listen to all the self-congratulations, to see the driver crack open the bottle of champagne. Besides, he didn't like champagne: he would have slipped off for a quiet pint of Guinness.

* * *

One of the biggest stars to come out of the golden era was Maeve Binchy. Maeve had a big, cheerful personality; a truly lovely girl. Her vitality filled the newsroom during her brief few years in the Dublin office. If you didn't see her you certainly could hear her, as her hearty, infectious laugh echoed from one end of the room to the other.

She was a naturally happy, well-adjusted person. Maeve was Woman's Page Editor and tourism correspondent and general raconteur. She was always busy, invariably in a rush, going to or coming from some meeting with contacts or friends.

She produced a lively, chatty, informative Woman's Page and availed of her tourism portfolio to see the world and to widen her literary focus. She loved to travel. It was her great passion in the early days. In fact, she still travels a lot, but is now working for herself, publicising her books, which have been translated into many languages, making her rich and famous.

Despite her hectic schedule she always filled her allocated space in the paper. There were times when she worried about what she was going to use for copy. She would periodically have an enormous, intimidating blank page in front of her and not a single sentence to go into it. 'Oh, my God, what will I do?' she would screech in mock panic, but her quick creative mind would sort it out and, a short time later, her copy would be down with the printers. Another crisis averted. If she hadn't got any copy: if some writers had let her down, if what had been commissioned did not turn up on time she simply rushed over to her typewriter, shouting: 'Don't anyone disturb me for an hour.' In that hour she would produce the best of readable copy off the top of her head, writing as she usually talks, at about hundred miles an hour. Yes, she had a great gift, words simply flowed out of her. She is a natural writer and possesses a great imagination and insight into human nature. She also has a great vocabulary and never has to think or look for a word – it is always on the tip of her tongue.

Ironically, her popularity was her biggest problem. She had so many friends everyone wanted to be in her company. There was a constant demand on her time. They were very insistent, ringing her non-stop, wanting to chat, have a drink, inviting her to parties, etc. The poor girl was literally under social siege. She was being loved to death. It was fascinating to watch. It was difficult, almost impossible, for her to get her work done. People like Donal Foley and other colleagues always wanted her in their company, understandably, because she always lit up any gathering with her natural exuberance and gaiety. 'Come on across for a jar,' they would say, temptingly. 'No, no, no, I can't; I have a ton of work to do,' she would reply, imploring them to leave her alone. But she always produced the goods. She was a true professional behind all the chat and craic.

The Irish Times was her first job in journalism. She had been teaching, but decided she needed something else to give her personality and ability more expression. Those who knew her as a teacher said she was excellent at her job. Well, education's loss was journalism's gain. She took to journalism like a duck to water.

Despite her prominent position in *The Irish Times*, her meteoric rise to fame, her big readership and numerous fans, she abandoned it all to move to our London office. She worked there for quite a long time before eventually leaving the staff and became a contributor, with a column every Saturday. She probably felt under less pressure in London, far away from the hustle and bustle of the social life in Dublin. Of course she also found her husband Gordon Snell in London. By this time of course Maeve was quite a famous author, television personality and critic. She was producing numerous books, short stories and articles. Quite a one-woman literary factory, words simply spewed out of her. Every book was an immediate best-seller; she had the ability and had hit on the right formula. It was easy. I have no doubt that if she had stayed in Dublin she would never have written a book. She couldn't have; it would have been totally out of the question. The demands on her time were quite overwhelming.

Those of us left behind in Dublin can only look on her achievements with admiration and a tinge of envy. According to the newspaper reports she was one of the highest paid authors in the world in 1993 (£600,000 sterling). She has always been very generous with her money. In at least two cases I have heard of, she has given considerable financial assistance to former colleagues who temporarily hit bad times. Once she heard of the problem she had no hesitation in offering to help.

* * *

John 'Backbencher' Healy was the top political writer of the time. His Backbencher column, which started in the *Sunday Review* and later moved to *The Irish Times*, broke new ground in political journalism. He was not afraid to knock politicians, to bring them down to earth. It may be hard to understand now, but in those days politicians were treated with excessive respect and there was little strong political criticism. John waded in with his irreverent, pungent comments. He had great insight into the political mind and could get away with some outrageous opinions. He wrote articles which no other journalist would dare, or be allowed, to write.

He admired Donogh O'Malley, Minister for Education, who was one of his main sources of information on what was going on inside government. When O'Malley died suddenly at a young age of a massive heart attack, John was shattered. He rang a friend and cried and cried. His next Backbencher Column contained an imaginary telephone conversation with the dead O'Malley. I tell that story because most people did not realise that behind the gruff, arrogant exterior was a basically very sensitive person. He liked to pretend to be a tough, hard-hitting, New York kind of reporter, but to those who knew him he was really a big softie, a little boy that never grew up. It was this boyishness, of always telling you in his columns of how good he was, that showed his insecurity. He was a very emotional man who worked on instinct. He had a superb instinct for a good story and a brilliant turn of phrase, with a nice simple incisive writing style. He had a well-tuned political ear and his Dáil Sketch in *The Irish Times* always managed to pick up the choice little tit-bits of a debate. Even if it was a dreadfully boring debate he could latch on to some quote and build a sketch around it. Ironically, it was this very aspect of his writing that caused a lot of concern to us ordinary, unsung, slave journalists on the Dáil press gallery. John could pick up these nuances and throw-away quotes which we might miss in our reports.

Gageby would then start asking why we hadn't got the quotes in our copy and this caused us quite a bit of trouble. It didn't happen too often, but when it did it put us under a lot of pressure and placed too big a spotlight on our work. Eventually, I went to John and told him to work closer with us so we knew what he was going to write and to ensure that we did not leave out any quotes that he was using. He agreed to this and we had no further problems.

John and Gageby were very close friends. John was briefing him on what was happening in the Dáil almost on an hourly basis. They were always talking on the phone. Each held the other in very high professional esteem. Gageby had great respect for John's views and delighted in him 'stirring things up,' while Healy liked what Gageby was doing with the paper and his overall policy. They complemented each other very well and it worked out successfully for the paper.

Nevertheless, there were rumours that some people on the board felt the paper was carrying too much on politics, that political coverage should be cut back. This was never done, as the editorial belief was that Irish people, more than people of other countries, are infatuated by political manoeuvrings and love to read every tittle-tattle emanating from Leinster House.

John Healy became a political institution. He was the most read political writer in the land and, not being a modest man, he revelled in the adulation. He bought a Rolls Royce, mainly for notoriety, to let everyone know he had made it, that he was on top of the heap, adding jokingly 'but it's not much of a heap.' However, he eventually got rid of the Rolls. He explained: 'I didn't need a Rolls Royce to show that I was the best in the business.'

He thrived on elections and loved the cut and thrust of the campaigns. His delight when his predictions turned out to be correct knew no bounds. If he was wrong there was ... er, a loud silence. If you jokingly mentioned his wrong predictions, he just laughed and quipped 'You can't win them all.' Like us all, he wanted to quickly forget his mistakes. He was always reminiscing about the old days and he had hundreds of amusing anecdotes about politicians and their escapades. He had a great sense of humour and got a great kick out of the characters who walked the corridors of Leinster House over the years. He had great respect for politicians, be they frontbencher or backbencher, who could hold their own in the hurly-burly of the toughest business on earth. Even when he was away from Ireland he was still talking Dáil politics.

He was also a very generous and compassionate person, as he showed during the Dublin newspaper strike in the mid-sixties. He used to write a column in the *Western People*, but when the strike started he gave this over to a journalist friend who had a young family. John took the attitude that he was doing all right and had enough to get by on, so he helped out someone who was not so lucky. The strike went on for about three months.

John's big pundit image and his hard hitting, often not very diplomatic comments, allied to his Fianna Fáil bias, did not endear him to a lot of people. They did not like the partisan positions he took, especially in his later years, when he became over-confident and reckless. His balance became affected. In a small country like Ireland, that is just looking for trouble. His critics were not all among non-Fianna Fáil politicians, they were among his own colleagues too. He certainly never made any secret of his admiration for Charlie Haughey. This had a huge influence on his writing and brought accusations of lack of objectivity. He took it on himself to fight all Haughey's battles for him, to snipe at Jack Lynch and Garret FitzGerald or anyone else that was not on the same wavelength. A Coalition Minister commented at the time: 'His columns are considered so one-sided that he has lost his audience.' There was a lot of truth in that.

He could write with great feeling and sensitivity; he felt strongly about people and issues. Paddy Lindsay, the former Fine Gael Minister and Master of the High Court, wrote in his book *Memories* of an article John wrote when his (Lindsay's) wife, Moya, died. He wrote:

> 'Moya's death brought home to me my good fortune in having so many friends who were willing to help. For myself I bottled up my emotion and it was only when I read John Healy's tribute to Moya in *The Western Journal* that, sitting alone, the flood gates burst, and I wept uncontrollably.'

He reproduced the article in the book and it was indeed a truly beautiful piece of writing.

He left Leinster House and concentrated on Europe. He wrote the Sounding Off column in *The Irish Times* where he twice weekly expounded on numerous national and international issues. But much of his writing then concerned Europe, as he was a great advocate of the EU. He travelled to Brussels and Strasbourg regularly and became fascinated by the vision of a united Europe. He was full of ideas and enthusiasm for what the EU could do for Ireland. He was impatient that progress was so slow. He wanted everything done immediately and had no patience with red tape and bureaucracy.

The last time I met him he had taken a six-month Government contract to be public relations officer in Strasbourg during the Irish Presidency of the EU. We had lunch together and I could see that his heart wasn't in the job; it was still very much in Leinster House. We spoke for two hours and he never once mentioned the EU, just asked about the latest gossip from the Dáil. He carried out his work to the best of his ability but he was first and foremost a reporter and public relations was 'not his bag'.

Love him or hate him, you can't take away his place in Irish journalistic history. He was a catalyst who broke down barriers and certainly made his mark during his short time on this planet. Like Donal Foley, he died relatively young (60), but both of them packed an awful lot of living into a short time. Neither could have tolerated the burden of old age. Their epitaphs must surely read 'No Regrets.'

* * *

There was no shortage of real characters in the 60s and 70s. They are all gone now, of course. The modern high-tech newspaper industry has no room for eccentrics or non-conformists, so we will never again see another George 'Hoddy' Hodnett, the paper's jazz critic for donkey's years. From his dress, to his conversation, to his peculiar habits, Hoddy was a character. If he hadn't existed, the most brilliant fiction writer couldn't invent him. He always wore two overcoats and two jumpers, even in the middle of summer, and invariably had the remains of a cigarette somehow glued to his bottom lip. He spent his days browsing through second-hand book shops and his evenings at jazz sessions. He would always sit at the back of the hall where the session was taking place.

He told me that was the best location if he was to do a proper critique. A talented composer and musician, he played jazz piano, trumpet and zither. He was heavily involved in the activities of the Pike Theatre with Alan Simpson and Carolyn Swift and contributed as pianist and composer to the Pike's late night revues. He wrote a number of well-known songs, including 'Monto', which was a parody of 'rare oul' times' Dublin lyrics. It was made famous by The Dubliners. He was a keen conservationist long before it became fashionable and was injured when protestors were forcibly removed from houses in Hume Street in 1970. His hand was injured in this incident and he never played the piano again.

He liked to recount the story of how a march was held in his honour on the Ramblas in Barcelona during the Spanish Civil War. Somehow, he managed to send a parcel of cigarettes to a friend who was serving with the International brigades. The friend and his nicotine-starved comrades were so delighted that they marched down the city's main thoroughfare, shouting 'Viva Hodnett.'

There is also a story told that he was arrested during the Second World War years. He was down on Sandymount beach in Dublin one night playing his trumpet. This was just an outdoor practice session for Hoddy, but a policeman came along and arrested him. He was charged with spying, of sending signals to German submarines. I often meant to ask him about that, but I never got around to it. He died in September 1990, aged 72.

When he was in hospital he was worried about some money matters, but a visitor from *The Irish Times* told him that he was going to get an increase for the weekly jazz column he contributed. Instead of being pleased, George frowned. 'What's wrong,' the visitor asked, 'surely you must be pleased about that?'

Hoddy paused before replying: 'Does this mean I'll have to start paying income tax?'

Tense Years in The North

Irish journalism began to change radically from 1968. That's when the 'troubles' began in Northern Ireland. Suddenly, the North, which rarely received more than a few paragraphs in newspapers in the Republic was big news – world news. Young reporters in Dublin were straining at the leash to get up to the battle zone to see what it was all about. It was the closest any of them would ever get to being a war correspondent. You were guaranteed the front page every day for your copy. There was now a tangible buzz about Irish journalism. You were nobody unless you had served in the North for a few tours of duty. Those coming back had wonderful action-packed tales to tell over pints of Guinness. The younger, single reporters revelled in it. To see your by-line on hot stories every day was what all reporters had been led to believe journalism was all about. There was great camaraderie among the press pack as they hunted together. The icing on the cake was that the expenses were good. But you deserved them; the work was hard, with long hours and little sleep. You could spend the whole afternoon reporting Stormont and all that night out on the streets covering riots. They were exciting and memorable times.

It all started with a civil rights march through Derry on 5 October 1968. The Stormont Minister for Home Affairs, Bill Craig, wanted the march called off. The police tried to stop it and the result was 70 civilians and about a dozen policemen injured. The historic day was brilliantly captured on film by RTE photographer Gay O'Brien. His dramatic pictures of the riot were flashed all over the world. It may have been only in old black and white film but the content was riveting.

It showed terrified men, women and children fleeing from their peaceful protest pursued by baton-swinging policemen, totally out of control. One of the most memorable pictures was that of Gerry Fitt MP with blood pouring from a wound on the back of his head. In an interview with Fergus Pyle of *The Irish Times* 20 years later, in October 1988, Fitt described the march and said he knew what was going to happen. He said he had brought along three British Labour MPs to witness the inevitable events unfold.

> 'I knew before long they were going to beat us up. I wasn't going to retaliate. I wasn't going to throw stones.'

A sergeant pinioned his arms in his coat and another policeman hit him twice on the head.

'I got pins and needles and I felt the blood rushing down. I thought to myself "I'm going to let the blood run because the cameras are there."'

He was pushed, along with some of the other leaders, into a black police van and brought to Victoria Road Barracks.

'They were shouting at me to wipe my face. Did they think I was mad? The cameras were outside.'

The marchers consisted of a wide variety of people, some with political affiliations, but most were non-aligned. All had a common purpose; they wanted civil rights. The border was not an issue. There was no talk of a United Ireland. They were not led by the IRA, as Stormont alleged. The march was the result of years of oppression coming to a head. The boil had been lanced and the pus of anger, bitterness and outrage was running free. It was frightening to watch.

Things were never the same again in Northern Ireland. The sides quickly polarised and the real war began. The killings started and continued for 25 bloody years, with over 3,200 men, women and children losing their lives.

While the civil rights marches were taking place Stormont was still in existence, but totally ineffective, giving no leadership or showing any real political judgement. Bigotry and oppression was rampant. The loyalists ruled with triumphalism, while at the same time strongly denying that there was any sectarianism. The old Nationalist Party was only there to make up the numbers. It was too small and ineffective to make any impression and was going into its death rattle. It had stopped trying and had lost the will to fight.

I used to cover Stormont regularly and it was a harrowing assignment. The behaviour in the Dáil can sometimes be chaotic and pathetic, as was clearly shown during the fall of the Albert Reynolds' government in 1994, but the antics I witnessed in the Northern Ireland chamber were absolutely outrageous. The members would slouch in their benches and hurl abuse at each other, mingled with ignorant guffaws and jokes in low taste. Decorum was non-existent. It was a poor advertisement for a parliament. Most parliaments can hit low points at times. Politicians are not shrinking violets and they like to have a go at each other now and again. They will sometimes simulate anger and try to enliven debates with a bit of verbal warfare, but in Stormont there was this indescribable unpleasant undercurrent constantly present; there was something unreal about it. There was a sick, laid-back malaise, a kind of drifting, rotting corruption, permeating through the place. And nobody seemed to care. The best thing about the old Stormont parliament was its architecture. It was unfortunate that such a splendid building should host such pathetically sterile debates. The situation was probably best summed up by a Nationalist member one day when he interrupted a Minister with the words:

'For God's sake, will you stop taking yourself so seriously. You would think we were a big state, instead of that we are only a little provincial backwater.'

With the civil rights people clamouring for change, Stormont was intransigent, stagnant, unable to get out of the rut. The Northern Ireland Prime Minister, Captain Terence O'Neill called a general election in February 1969. He hoped to defuse the situation. O'Neill was one of the few Unionist politicians who had the foresight to realise that the old ways could not last much longer, that changes would have to be made and a new agenda set. I believe his intentions were genuine, but he could not bring the rest of the party with him. There were too many in the party who felt he was 'soft' on Dublin and was conceding too much to nationalists.

I was based in Derry for the election. A major upset took place – John Hume defeated the leader of the Nationalist Party, Eddie McAteer, who had held the seat for Foyle in Stormont for 22 years. Hume was one of the young leaders of the civil rights movement at the time and was becoming well known. It was a rather sad occasion really, because 'Big Eddie', as he was affectionately known, was a very likeable character whose comments were always highly quotable – an absolute dream for reporters. He was also very approachable and helpful to reporters at all hours of the day and night.

Big Eddie took his defeat with great dignity. I asked him for his reaction to his defeat and he came out with one of his usual quotable gems: 'It's a dull morning for a funeral', and added:

> 'If I have paid the penalty for moderation, it is the price I would gladly pay again.
> I leave public life without bitterness or hatred to anyone.'

I felt it was a touching epitaph. John Hume, when the result was announced, paid him a gracious tribute for his 22 years of service and Mrs Hume had tears in her eye. Just for the record, a young lad named Eamonn McCann, now a well known journalist, came third.

Over in the Bannside constituency, a controversial cleric named Ian Paisley had been defeated and was shouting 'foul.' He claimed there had been 'malpractices' during the election and was seeking legal advice on the matter. He then accused Captain O'Neill of being 'despised, discredited and disgruntled,' that he was a man who had neglected his constituency for six years and should now return his MP's salary. Even in defeat Paisley could make the headlines. The defeat did not deter Paisley. He continued barnstorming around the province, appearing at public meetings and rallies, ranting a peculiarly disturbing mixture of politics and religion, combined with a vicious sense of humour, often at the expense of the 'Republican press.'

He never let a chance go by without throwing in a few insulting asides at the reporters from the 'Papist South.' It was never a pleasant job to cover a Paisley rally. He used to build the crowd up to frenzy with his lethal oratory. A master in the use of words, possessing a wonderful vocabulary, he always had the crowd captivated, entranced, shouting for more. He hadn't a very good opinion of journalists. In 1966, he came up with the following description:

> 'They usually sport thick-lensed glasses, wear six pairs of ropey sandals, are homosexuals, kiss holy medals or carry secret membership cards of the Communist Party. Most of them are communistoids without the guts of a red-blooded Communist, or Roman Catholics without the effrontery of a Pope Pius XII. Sometimes these anonymous editorial writers are a mixture of the two: spineless, brainless mongoloids – but, because of it, as maliciously perilous as vipers.'

His opinion of the Irish Republic, as expressed in 1968, was:

> 'The dark, sinister shadow of our neighbouring Roman Catholic state, where religious liberty is slowly but surely being taken away, lies across our state ... Not only have we this enemy without, but we have a strong fifth column of sympathisers and compromisers within. The only answer to encroaching Romanism is a revived and revitalised Protestantism, believing the Bible, proclaiming the Bible and practising the Bible.'

He held himself in the highest standing. He boasted once:

> 'Show me a man of whom is said every evil and wicked slander. Show me a man who becomes the recipient of wave after wave of condemnation; who is condemned out of hand, who is accused of the most outrageous of crimes, and I will show you a man whom God has commissioned, whom God has called, who God has sent to be a prophet to his generation.'

Most of us young reporters had never been in the North before the civil rights marches took place. We knew very little about it, and because of the constant tension of the time we understandably felt ill at ease at times. Being from Dublin, and knowing the hatred of the loyalists to the South, we felt a certain fear for our safety at Paisley rallies and in many other potentially dangerous situations. We would literally keep our mouths shut for long periods at rallies or if sent up the Shankill Road. A southern accent was not something loyalists wanted to hear at a time when they felt they were under siege from the 'papists' with their civil rights marches. The world was watching and they knew it. There was always the possibility that Paisley would set some of his heavies or stewards on us. These people were always present at rallies and they often adopted a bullying attitude to the press. There was a feeling among loyalists that the press was the enemy. We knew this and always watched our step. At one rally in Derry in 1969, when the heavies began to ominously move in on us, and when it looked as though there was going to be some real trouble, Paisley made his big magnanimous gesture. He boomed out 'Leave them alone .... We don't care what they write about us ...'

Another less dangerous aspect of Paisley rallies, but nonetheless also quite irritating, was his fund-raising tactics. At every rally there was always a 'collection' and invariably the good Doctor would announce with a great guffaw that it was to be a 'silent' collection. This meant that there was to be none of your old copper or silver. No coins, all notes. The heavies loved to rush over to the press corps with their baskets, seeking a contribution, pushing them under our noses. Yes, you're right, we paid up. Cowards to the end. It was the simple, sensible thing to do in the circumstances. Some reporters put it down to experience, but smart reporters put it down on their expenses (and doubled it) and had a drink on Paisley.

* * *

The riots in Derry on 12 August 1969 after the Apprentice Boys march was the beginning of the end. We were into the famous Siege of the Bogside. The war had started in earnest. It spread across the province like a bush fire and Belfast exploded in violence. It spread to the Republic and Taoiseach, Jack Lynch, told an enraged Irish nation, which had watched the Bogside riots on television, that we would not stand by, or 'idly by' as he was misquoted at the time. The world press converged on Derry in their hundreds. Bernadette Devlin (now McAliskey) was on the barricades. The foreign press named the 21 year old a latter day Joan of Arc.

One of the first to be shot dead in the Northern troubles was John Gallagher, a 29 year old married factory worker. He was killed in the Shambles area of Armagh by the B-Specials. He died from bullets to the neck and chest and six other men were injured. I was sent to Armagh to cover the story. I can still remember the simmering tension and anger in the town after the shooting. I booked myself into a hotel on the main street and hid my car in a yard around the back. This was a practice I always observed when in the North. Use the car to get there but then avail of taxis. A Southern registration can sometimes result in too much unwelcome attention.

There was a rumour that Cardinal Conway was going to appeal for restraint and calmness at the funeral Mass the next day. I decided to go to the Cardinal's residence and see if he would make a statement on the shooting. I did not think he would see me at such short notice, but I went through the motions anyway. My luck was in and I was shown into his sitting room. I think he was just glad to get the opportunity to talk about the situation, but he was not prepared to make a formal statement. He was very depressed and fearful of the consequences of the shooting. 'This is just the start of it,' he said, prophetically. He could see it would escalate and that there would be more deaths. But even he, in his deepest pessimism, could hardly have foreseen that 25 years later there would be over 3,200 people in their graves as a result of the political unrest, with each atrocity outdoing the next in barbarism.

The Cardinal was more than depressed, he was angry. He criticised Bernadette Devlin and those on the barricades. He did not think it was going to achieve anything. He believed the repercussions could be enormous. He was mumbling, almost as though there was no one else in the room, saying over and over, 'Things will never be the same again' and expressing the hope that the 'wild men' would not retaliate. This was his really big fear. When he said things would never be the same again, he did not realise how prophetic he was being.

As he talked, he paced up and down the room. He passed the big bay window, looked out, turned quickly to me and said urgently: 'You'll have to go now; quick, quick, get out.' I was startled at this sudden change in attitude. He had welcomed me profusely when I arrived and seemed anxious to talk, now he was literally throwing me out. Then he explained: 'It's those damn politicians. They are coming up the drive. I hate talking to politicians.' He ushered me out the back door and returned to his room.

I sneaked around the side of the building, hiding behind the trees, and furtively made my escape. Apparently, the poor man did not want to talk to the Labour Party's 'fact-finding' delegation which had travelled up from Dublin to look into the worsening violent situation. The delegation included, I think, Michael O'Leary, Justin Keating, Frank Cluskey, Noel Browne and Conor Cruise O'Brien.

John Gallagher was buried in the red soil of the local cemetery. I never saw soil so red and I was quite fascinated by this. I remember mentioning it in my report of the funeral, but some sub-editor obviously felt that it did not add to the story and knocked it out. To this day I can still picture the red earth and the first victim of the North's horrific saga of violence being laid to rest. I can still see the grim-faced Cardinal standing by the grave, holding the hand of Gallagher's six year old son, John. Shortly before the prayers ended, little John collapsed and was taken to a nearby car.

As young journalists we knew we were seeing history being made. We had plenty of energy and enthusiasm and did our best to report it as comprehensively as possible, but we never imagined that it would go on for so long. A new generation has now grown up and it has known only shootings, bombings and maimings. All those young reporters of that era are now a quarter of a century older and wiser. The tremendous energy we used to have in filing copy into the small hours of the morning has seeped away. We look back on it all with nostalgia and regret that the turmoil took such a heavy toll on such a lovely people, who were always so friendly and courteous to the southern press corps.

* * *

It was absolutely tragic to watch the prevarication of the British Prime Minister, Mr John Major, after the IRA ceasefire was announced in 1994. He and the Unionists dithered for nearly two years and allowed a golden opportunity to pass. It was almost as though they didn't want peace, as though they had a vested interest in keeping the old system alive. It allowed the hawks in the IRA to get fed up and plant a bomb at Canary Wharf. The first bit of nit-picking was to spend months asking whether the ceasefire was permanent or temporary. When they got fed up with that they jumped on to a different horse; weapons should be decommissioned became the new catchphrase. All the time, Major seemed to be working on the premise that if he could stonewall for long enough, the people seeing peace for the first time in a quarter of a century would not allow the IRA to resume hostilities. This was a very dangerous game to play. Then Major began running out of time. An election was looming; he lost his majority in the Commons, and was then placed completely in the pocket of the Unionists. The IRA was totally disillusioned at this stage and it began making threatening noises and planting bombs again. The ceasefire was over.

All the good work done by Albert Reynolds, John Hume and Gerry Adams unravelled rapidly, despite desperate efforts by John Bruton and his new government to hold it together. All the signs, however, were pointing to a return to war. This was soul-destroying. There had been so much hope.

People had relished seeing peace again and were out and about again, leading full normal social lives. Business began to thrive; tourism was booming. There was a 'good feeling' everywhere. I remember meeting a delighted John Hume in Strasbourg some months after the ceasefire was announced. He had just heard that the army had been withdrawn from his home town of Derry. This was wonderfully tangible evidence that the ceasefire was working.

> 'You don't realise it down in the South, but to see the streets empty of troops means an awful lot to us in the North. When I'm at home in Derry, I can't walk down the street to get a packet of cigarettes without having to go through an army road block.'

At the same time he was celebrating 25 years in politics 'and 25 bloody tough years they were, too,' he said ruefully. John Major could have acted more decisively. Reynolds, Hume and Adams took huge risks for peace, but Major wasn't going to take any chances and hope began to fade. Peace came to South Africa and there was no question of there being a decommissioning of arms. The Palestinians and Israelis managed to come to an agreement and there was no decommissioning. The Dayton Accord was signed and there was no decommissioning in Bosnia. Major was afraid of the Unionists when he had a narrow majority, but when he even lost that he was terrified of them.

Meanwhile, he left a highly dangerous vacuum for the wilder elements in the IRA to fill. This section, who never wanted a ceasefire, were only too pleased to get an excuse to return to the bomb and the bullet. In January 1997, Senator Edward Kennedy accused the British Government of a 'grave and profound mistake' in refusing to build on the IRA ceasefire while it lasted. He said he condemned the IRA for breaking the ceasefire, but he rejected the views of unionists that 'the ceasefire itself was phoney'. The 17 months of freedom from violence were not a sham, he said.

> 'Day after day, week after week, month after month, the British Government refused to build on the opportunity for peace, the 17 month ceasefire became a historic missed opportunity.'

It should be remembered that there is a lot more than politics, political parties and vested interests involved here; we are talking about people's lives. With over 3,200 dead, Major and other leaders have a responsibility to ensure that not one more person dies from a bullet or is blown to pieces by a bomb.

January 1997 also saw the 25th anniversary of Bloody Sunday, the occasion when British soldiers killed 13 people in Derry. The people demanded an inquiry into the killings, as it was generally felt that the Widgery Tribunal had been a whitewash. John Hume said that the least they were entitled to was an apology. He said he had a letter from John Major which stated that the people shot were innocent victims.

I wasn't in Derry on Bloody Sunday, but the following Tuesday I was outside the British Embassy in Dublin when it was set on fire by an angry crowd. It was a dark miserable evening with torrential rain. Most of the large crowd were well behaved and just wanted to make a peaceful protest about the Derry outrage, but there were a few who had marched on the embassy determined to cause trouble. They stood at the back of the crowd and lobbed petrol bombs at the building. Some of the bombs fell short and dropped on gardaí who were holding back the crowd. Some of those throwing the bombs were standing near me. They had the 'bombs' (milk bottles filled with petrol, stuffed with paper on the top) in their pockets. Many others weren't quite as well prepared and threw stones. The gardaí eventually lost patience and made a baton charge. It was the innocent people in the front that took the brunt of their rage.

About 30 people, including two gardaí were injured. One of those injured was my colleague in *The Irish Times*, Jack McManus, who was hit on the head with a baton and knocked unconscious. He was removed to hospital and received eight stitches in a nasty wound. We were going to use a picture of Jack in the paper the next day but Jack decided it would be better not to.

The news of the embassy burning flashed around the world. If there was anybody out there who hadn't heard of the Derry shootings, they certainly became aware of it with the burning of the embassy. Bishop Edward Daly, who had been a priest on the streets of Derry when the killings took place, said:

> 'What really made Bloody Sunday so obscene was the fact that people afterwards at the highest level of British justice justified it, and I think that is the real obscenity.'

A general election was held in May 1997, when the Labour Government was swept into office with a huge majority. Prime Minister, Tony Blair and his

Northern Secretary Dr Mo Mowlam immediately made the north their priority. Their good work paid off and an IRA ceasefire was called in July 1997, giving great hope and optimism that something could be worked out at the Stormont peace talks. However, the Unionists were predictably sceptical and said it would not last. Again, they called for decommissioning of weapons.

The IRA ceasefire held and the British and Irish governments agreed that Sinn Féin could join the all-party talks on the future of Northern Ireland. David Trimble's Ulster Unionist Party, after some deep soul-searching, agreed to participate but Ian Paisley's and Robert McCartney's unionist parties boycotted the proceedings.

It had been a magnificent and historic achievement to get so many parties together. Expectations were deliberately being kept low-key, but there was an air of cautious optimism as the talks began on 7 October.

The Lighter Side of the North

Covering events in the North in the early days of the troubles could be nerve-wracking and dangerous, but there was also an immense amount of fun and enjoyment involved too. At least, looking back at it now I can see the funny side.

For instance, when I was in Armagh to cover the John Gallagher shooting, I teamed up with a reporter from the *Irish Independent*. We began talking about the incredible fear and tension in the town. It was quite palpable. He remarked that he had been deeply worried when driving up from Dublin. I laughed and asked him what he had to worry about; we weren't involved in anything unlawful; we were only doing a job.

'There were a lot of roadblocks on the way up,' he replied, still quite preoccupied and obviously concerned.

'What had that got to do with you?'

'I was afraid they might search the car.'

'So what if they did? They searched my car a few times and there was no problem.'

'They might have found my gun...'

'Your WHAT?'

'I always keep a gun under the front seat of my car, just in case...'

'That's a very dangerous thing to be doing. Have you a licence for it?'

'Oh, no, it's not a real gun.'

'What do you mean?'

'It's just a toy rubber gun. I carry it around Dublin in case I'm attacked when the car is stopped at traffic lights, or some other situation like that.'

There was another reporter who was so nervous during the troubles that nobody would share a room with him. He kept the light on all night. On one occasion the press corps was spending two weeks in Derry. It was a cold miserable February, with quite a lot of snow. We decided one day, when things were slack, to get out of the tension of the town and visit the nearby Inishowen Peninsula. We had been working very hard and it seemed like a good idea. Two car loads of us left that morning. We separated and visited different scenic spots. The Inishowen Peninsula can be very beautiful even when it is bitterly cold and snow is on the ground and we had a very relaxful and enjoyable trip in our newfound role as tourists.

We got back to Derry that evening, refreshed and happy, having consumed quite a few pints. We waited and waited, but there was no sign of the other car with our colleagues. Strange, we thought, maybe they had a better time than us. Maybe they had got up to some mischief? Two hours later the four missing reporters arrived into the hotel, dishevelled and covered in mud. They were some sight. Apparently, their car had skidded on the snow, tumbled down an embankment and overturned.

'We would have been killed only for the *Daily Telegraph*,' said one of the four.

It transpired that the reporter from the *Telegraph*, a heavily built man, with a handlebar moustache, formerly of the RAF, had averted what could have been a disaster.

'The minute we overturned he had the foresight to shout "Switch off the ignition," said our informant. 'If he hadn't we could have all burnt to death. The car would have gone up like a bomb.'

It was probably the man's jolly old RAF experience that had saved the day. Getting a few journalists out of a crashed car is probably only chicken feed in comparison to saving airforce personnel from a ditched aircraft. The press had nearly succeeded in making a bigger story out of itself than the one we were covering in Derry.

* * *

I always liked going to Derry. It was smaller and friendlier than Belfast and a lot easier to cover events there. One man who always made our visit enjoyable was Malachy Durnin, manager of the City Hotel, where all of the press corps usually stayed. It is now a car park, having being blown up by terrorists. He got to know our *modus operandi* and if anything happened in the town while we were away from the hotel he quickly got word to us. We were good for his business and he was good for ours. It was a nice, reciprocal little arrangement. One evening a few of us had gone to the local snooker hall to while away a few hours. We got a phone call from Malachy to say there was trouble at the other end of the town. We quickly dropped our cues, picked up our notebooks and cameras and were on our way.

This is just another skirmish or a false alarm, or so I thought. But of course we had to check it out anyway. In fact it turned out to be quite a major riot, with the two sides hurling stones and bottles at each other. There were a few hundred people involved. I started off badly by getting into a dangerous position between the two warring factions and was nearly hit by a bottle which struck the wall beside me. It is always crucial in a riot situation to get a vantage point where you can see everything without becoming involved in the mayhem. It's a trick I thought I had mastered but it didn't work that night. The Loyalists were singing

'The Sash My Father Wore.' It was the first time I had heard the song. Whenever I hear the 'Sash' now I get an immediate flashback to that bottle hitting the wall. So I can assure you, it's not one of my favourite songs. It's not just a song, it's a battle-cry.

I managed to put together a few notes and ran down the road and dived into a telephone kiosk to file the story. I was dictating away to the copy-typist in the office, delighted to have found a kiosk so fast, when I realised that the riot had rapidly spread down towards me like a bush fire and the crowd was milling around outside. The bricks and bottles were still flying. The angry, swirling crowd practically turned over the kiosk. It was quite frightening. I could hardly hear myself shouting into the phone because of the din of the abuse and explosions of the petrol bombs outside.

There I was, thinking myself a hero, getting the news through in spite of the danger to myself, when a senior sub-editor in Dublin comes on to the line. 'Yes, this is good stuff, Frank. Yes, we are going to use every bit of it. There is only one thing missing though .... What is the name of the street you are in?' Well, this particular sub-editor had a reputation for being meticulous and always ensured high accuracy in the paper, but he had no experience of reporting. I naturally hadn't a clue as to what street I was in. I simply said in the report that the riot was in the centre of Derry and that was good enough to be going on with. I hadn't gone around looking for a street nameplate with bricks and bottles filling the air. Derry is a small place and we weren't talking about New York. I wasn't going to get out of that kiosk to ask someone with a brick in his hand for the name of the street to satisfy a sub-editor's over-conscientious demands. One bottle had just missed me, the next might not. Let's say we threw a few compliments at each other, mostly prefaced with the f-word. I then banged down the phone.

There was one great character from the *Irish Press* who used to come up to the North on occasions on relief work, like the rest of us. He was a real Walter Mitty, although he never let his fertile imagination get in the way of his accurate reports. He loved to spin a yarn. He loved aeroplanes and believed he had once been a fighter pilot in the US airforce. One night in a Belfast pub he was enjoying himself telling in minute detail of one of his bombing missions in Vietnam. As he was leaving the pub that night, three US GIs walked up to him and said: 'We've been listening to what you were saying and we didn't like it. You were never in Vietnam.' My friend was a little taken aback, but only a little ... He quickly retorted: 'Of course, I was in Vietnam' and then pulled open his shirt and showed a chest covered in scars. The Yanks were highly embarrassed and apologised profusely and made a quick exit. They didn't know that my friend had been involved in a very serious car crash some months earlier. He was very lucky to survive it, but he was covered in scars as a result. Unfortunately, his luck ran out some years later and he died from cancer at a young age. A lovely colleague and a big loss.

Travelling around Northern Ireland during the early 70s was fraught with danger. However, journalists always seemed to be able to extricate their way from difficult situations. They developed a kind of sixth sense, and that, along with a bit of luck, had you back in operation again. An example of this was the incident that happened to Wee Willie Carson, the diminutive, cheerful Derry freelance photographer. Willie was on his way down to a republican march in the centre of Derry one day when three masked youngsters stuck a gun through the window and demanded that he get out of his car. They then disappeared with the car in a cloud of dust. Willie met up with his colleagues at the start of the march, looking very glum, not his usual cheerful self. The photographers present asked what was wrong. He told them his story. The photographers held a meeting to discuss this outrage. They decided on strike action. They went to talk to the parade organisers. They told the republicans that the parade wasn't going to be covered because of what had happened Willie's car. The republicans protested and said they knew nothing about it. The photographers walked away. Fifteen minutes later they were approached by a man who handed over the keys of Willie's car. One of the photographers later told me: 'I dread to think what happened the little bastards who stole the car. The lads have their own way of dispensing justice.'

One of the most unfortunate but amusing car stories to come out of Northern Ireland during this period involved Reg Cullen, of RTE, and his car. Again, the scene was Derry. A crowd of militant loyalists had surrounded the City Hotel to protest at coverage of Northern Ireland affairs by the press. Everything that went wrong was always the fault of the press. If the media went away, there would be no trouble in the North. They were extremely hostile to reporters and often issued threats. The doors of the hotel were locked and the crowd screamed abuse and insults at the reporters looking out the windows. The siege went on for quite a while.

Then, a few of the loyalists, realising the futility of their action, decided to do something more practical to get their message across. They tried to push a big white Mercedes car belonging to one of the Dublin journalists into the nearby river. They huffed and puffed but they could not budge it. Nowadays they would just set it on fire, but they were less bloody minded then. Having failed to get a move out of the Merc they went to another car, a lighter model. This belonged to Reg Cullen, who looked on horrified as it was pushed into the River Foyle. A great cheer went up from the loyalists, who dispersed shortly afterwards.

A shocked and distressed Reg went down to the RUC station to report that his car had been shoved into the river. 'They did not believe me,' Reg told me afterwards. 'They weren't a bit interested or sympathetic. I didn't like their attitude at all.' He eventually managed to convince them. The river was dredged but, amazingly, there was no sign of the car. The police were then really convinced that the car had not gone in. We joked about this at the time and said that a special warning should be issued to shipping to watch out for an underwater car.

'I wouldn't mind if it was my own car,' said Reg, 'but I just borrowed it from the garage.'

He explained that RTE had asked him to go to the North at short notice. His own car was being repaired in a garage in Dublin. The garage owner refused to lend Reg a car while he carried out the repairs. Reg pleaded with him on bended knees, so he eventually agreed to give him one of his spare models.

'He wasn't too pleased when I told him what happened,' said Reg.

'I'm sure he wasn't,' I laughed.

When I met Reg recently we chatted about the incident and he said that garage owner had never lent another car to anybody since that day.

The Dáil

I have spent a large chunk of my working life covering the Dáil, that nerve centre of political life and hive of gossip and intrigue. It is a fascinating place to work and not all the news is taking place in the chamber. There are always plenty of plots and little dramas going on behind the scenes. At times you don't know what to believe. Politicians love intrigue and are always plotting and scheming and fixing things.

They are a breed of people who never relax. Even if there is nothing happening they will still be hyped up. Rumours are two a penny and you have to be very careful and take much of what is being said with a grain of salt. John 'Backbencher' Healy, who thrived on the Dáil atmosphere, always said divide by four anything you hear in the corridors of Leinster House. He was right. But the rumours and the gossip just add to the buzz of the place.

In the old days only the most experienced middle-aged or elderly reporters were trusted with this assignment. It was looked upon as the most important job on the paper and you had to produce reams of verbatim, accurate and concise reports every day. The Dáil was treated with the utmost respect and about two pages of the paper were allocated to it each day.

We used to write masses of copy. Every deputy, including the smallest, most insignificant backbencher, even if he was talking utter rubbish, which he usually was, had to be given a couple of paragraphs, to show that he was present and doing his job. It was also for the purpose of increasing our circulation in his constituency. The Dáil pages in those days were avidly read by the public. People were much more interested in politics. The reporters took the job seriously – far too seriously, in fact, and rarely missed a sneeze or an off-the-cuff remark. Fortunately, all the reporters from the different newspapers and radio worked together, which made it a lot easier to get through the morass of words.

The system we worked was a half hour on the gallery taking notes and an hour transcribing them on battered and much abused typewriters. I always liked being assigned to the Dáil even though it was very hard work at times. Nowadays, some reporters, particularly the young ones, hate going there: they believe it's dull and frustrating and will make up any excuse to get out of it. There can be a great snobbery in journalism and in journalistic terms now, it is looked on as a totally archaic place. However, I have never felt that way about it. I liked the atmosphere there, the feeling of history that permeates through the corridors of that fine old building. You will meet some of the finest, most experienced and reliable journalists in the country there. Whenever I worked in the Dáil I had the strong feeling that this was the nerve centre of the State. It was here that the law was laid down, the country was being run from here. It was certainly very educational and gave me a tremendous knowledge of the workings of the State. Admittedly, on many occasions it could be boring and frustrating, but overall it was where the big stories were. I enjoyed listening to the debates and watching legislation evolve, watching the government trying to push through its policies and the opposition picking holes in it.

* * *

There have been many riveting and dramatic Dáil debates over the past three decades, but none to equal that night in May 1970 when the Taoiseach Jack Lynch announced to a hushed House why he had sacked government ministers Charles J. Haughey and Neil Blaney for the alleged importation of arms and ammunition. I will never forget Lynch, pale and gaunt, nervous and trembling, reading out his speech explaining why he sacked the two Fianna Fáil heavyweights – a decision which shocked the nation. Kevin Boland resigned his ministry in protest. The press gallery was packed, with many reporters having to stand (reporters are no longer allowed to stand in the gallery and this has reduced the capacity by about 50 per cent).

The previous night, 6 May, the head of the Government Information Service, Mr Eoin Neeson, telephoned newspaper offices and asked how long the papers could be held for a major story. He would not indicate what the story would be. A short time later a Fianna Fáil TD arrived in the Irish Times office to say that Mr Haughey and Mr Blaney were resigning and another Minister, Mr Kevin Boland, was resigning in sympathy with them.

The Dáil debate was highly acrimonious, with accusations and allegations being hurled back and forth with reckless abandon. Never had there been such a heated debate in the House. Voices were raised amid constant calls for order by the chair. Deputies snarled across the floor at each other, hatred written all over their faces. The tension was quite palpable. The debate went on for three days, non-stop. Rumours abounded in the bars and restaurants. There were even scuffles in the corridors between rival factions. You had to pick your words carefully. The most simple remark could be wrongly construed in such an electric atmosphere.There was talk of a general election, talk of a chaotic cabinet meeting taking place in another part of the building, where fists banged the table, some ministers stomping out and slamming the door after them, talk of a possible civil war, an invasion of the North ... the rumours ranged from the absurd to the ridiculous.

Mr Haughey was in hospital throughout the drama. A press statement said that he had fallen off his horse. Some deputies maintained that this was untrue, that he had a heart attack, that he had been beaten up. It was heady stuff and emotions ran very high.

Some conversations among deputies, press and hangers-on nearly resulted in fisticuffs. Because the debate had gone on for three days, with nobody getting any sleep, and because so muck drink and gossip had been circulating during this time, feelings had built up to a dangerous level.

Michael Mills, the former political correspondent of the *Irish Press*, wrote a series of articles reminiscing on the occasion. He said: 'That week was the most bitter and divisive I ever experienced in Leinster House. Friends fell out and never spoke to one another again; colleagues who had worked together for years called one another ugly names. Deputies who had sat at the same table were told to find themselves another table. The people in the middle who did not know what it was all about until the details gradually leaked out in the following days took sides more or less along the lines of the 1966 succession race. As the debate wore on, deputies thought it safer to stay around Leinster House rather than go home – for fear the Dáil might collapse in their absence. They slept in chairs and on sofas and even, sometimes, within the Dáil chamber.'

Former Taoiseach, Dr Garret FitzGerald, who has written an account of his own years in office, asserts that 'much of what happened in and around the Arms Crisis remains puzzling, and may never be sorted out.' Certainly, both Mr Haughey and Mr Lynch have always shown a reluctance to talk about the subject. It is the one real big taboo subject in Irish politics. You can talk about the civil war or the machinations between politicians and the hierarchy, or any other sensitive matter you like, but the conversation that always goes nowhere is the Arms Trial. There has been speculation over the years that both of these men would write their memoirs but this has not transpired and does not look now as though they will. Dr FitzGerald is probably right when he says that the facts may never be revealed. Mr Haughey has always refused to answer any questions relating to the matter and if any reporter raises the issue, the interview is immediately terminated.

As a journalist, it was exciting to have been there to see the drama unfold. The pressure on reporters that week was the worst I have ever experienced. The papers wanted every line of the debate and we hadn't time to draw breath. The occasion was not without its humorous side. Late on the first night of the debate, the phone rang in the press room. At the other end of the line was this voice speaking in broken English. It was Pravda, the Moscow newsagency, asking if there was any reporter there who could give them 'a report on the coup d'etat?' We had all heard of the *Skibbereen Eagle* keeping its eye on the Czar of Russia, but this was ridiculous. At that time, there was little or no contact with Russia, and to get a telephone call from behind the Iron Curtain heightened the excitement of the occasion. Years later, Pravda appointed its own correspondent to Dublin.

The saddest reporter in Leinster House during the arms crisis debate was Ned Murphy, the political correspondent of the *Sunday Independent*. A week earlier, Ned had all the details of the story for his paper but they wouldn't use it. After the story broke in the other newspapers, the editor of the *Sunday Independent*, Mr Hector Legge, explained that they hadn't carried the story because they wanted to act 'responsibly' and not destabilise the country. That was a pretty lame excuse for a newspaper with the biggest scoop ever on its hands. So Ned Murphy, who lived to be 82, and worked up to the day he died of a heart attack, will go down in history as the man who had the greatest scoop never used. His contacts within Fine Gael were excellent and the information was spot-on but the story was spiked.

* * *

One of the great advantages of working in the Dáil is the club atmosphere, the satisfaction that you are far away from 'the office', without having news editors breathing down your neck and dreaming up more work for you every few minutes. The working conditions are good and the facilities are excellent. The same people work there all the time and have built up a good relationship with each other and the politicians. One of the big perks is that you have the most prestigious and safest parking space in Ireland for your car; not to be sneezed at in this day and age when you can rely on getting your car vandalised or broken into at least twice a year on average.

You also have the luxury of the Visitors' Bar, where you can adjourn when you are finished your stint on the gallery. This is where the real life of the Dáil takes place, where the big deals go down, where the representations are made, where the nod is as good as a wink, where the gossip is passed as fact, where the hangers-on try to influence decisions. There is always a great buzz, a great vitality about the bar. There is always great conversation and information being passed.

Everyone is always looking for the latest news on the issues of the day. It is a veritable rumour factory. Much of what you hear can be taken with a grain of salt, or a pint of Guinness, although the pint there is not the best, according to the connoisseurs, myself included. About 15 years ago, there were some complaints about the lack of privacy in the bar, too much ear-wigging going on political opponents and reporters listening in on some big deals being made. It was decided to look into the matter and it was eventually agreed to introduce taped music into the hallowed hostelry to 'neutralise' the conversations. This lasted for only a short time and then fell by the wayside. If you are discussing something confidential now, you just lower your voice and make sure there is nobody around to hear what you are plotting.

One big drawback about Leinster House is the central heating system. For some reason they don't seem to be able to control the thermostat and at times it gets unbearably hot. There have been a lot of complaints about this. As a result, many TDs and staff can often be seen walking around the grounds, trying to get some oxygen. It also works up a big thirst and drives many people into the bars. Others don't need that excuse. I don't know if they have resolved this problem yet, as I have not been in the building for a few years, but it certainly caused major problems in the past. However, it is not as bad as the European Commission's building in Strasbourg, which also has a dreadful air conditioning system and after spending a few hours there you can really feel ill and dehydrated.

About 10 years ago a heavy fog fell on Dublin and the mist somehow filtered into the Dáil chamber, probably through the ventilation shafts. This cold mist was so bad that one deputy said he could not see the Minister across the floor. It was quite a boring, late-night debate and it was eventually decided to adjourn in the hope that the fog would be gone in the morning. There have been many nights since, when debates were at a very boring level, when we fervently prayed for fog. However, fog and smog are a thing of the past since Mary Harney TD did her clean up of Dublin when she was junior Minister in the Department of the Environment.

One of the funniest incidents I can recollect taking place in the Dáil had Garret FitzGerald at the centre. Garret had served in the Senate before getting elected to the Dáil. While in the Senate he was irrepressible, could not remain silent, was constantly interrupting, and was deeply involved in every debate, regardless of the subject or its importance. He just loved talking. And talking fast ... too fast most of the time. Eventually, the stenographers had to approach him and ask him to slow down so they could get a note of what he was saying. If the official notetakers could not take him down verbatim there was no chance for the rest of us, whose shorthand would not be as good. He apologised to the stenographers and promised them that he would slow down. But he couldn't and it was no time before he was off again spewing out words like a machinegun.

When he was elected to the Dáil, he was made Fine Gael spokesman for finance. But that was not enough for the young FitzGerald. He thought he was still in the Senate and constantly intervened in every debate. He was just bubbling with enthusiasm, full of ideas, determined to express his view. This used to annoy some deputies who felt he was monopolising the time of the House and they were fed up listening to his views on life.

It all came to a head one evening when an independent, west of Ireland deputy, who had been having a few pints in the Members' Bar, wandered into the chamber. Garret was doing his usual thing, jumping up, making points, asking questions. This was too much for the weary deputy to take. He shouted across the floor: 'FitzGerald, will you sit down, for God's sake. You're up and down like a whore's knickers.' The chamber erupted in laughter and, it may only have been my imagination, but Garret was that bit more careful afterwards when timing his contributions.

Another amusing Dáil incident involved two of my colleagues, members of the press gallery. The two – the late Ned Murphy, the doyen of the press gallery (a great prankster) and a young reporter, Peadar MacGiolla Cearr, who later died tragically – were down in the visitors' bar having a few pleasant drinks on a boring day in the chamber. Ned was in one of his mischievous moods. He bet that Peadar couldn't drink half a bottle of whiskey, or some such heavy amount, in the one swallow. Peadar said he could and placed a bottle to his head and knocked back the required amount. The only trouble was that shortly after this the two intrepid reporters had to go back up to the gallery and take over their stint covering the boring proceedings. During this stint Peadar began to feel decidedly fidgety and unsettled.

Below him in the chamber, a Fianna Fáil backbencher was droning on and on and on. Peader was beginning to feel the effects of the drink and the excruciating boredom of the speech was getting to him. Then the TD, for what must have been the hundredth time, started off another sentence with 'I remember the time ...' This was too much for Peadar who immediately began to sing the song 'Memories.' There was consternation as his song wafted across the chamber. There are very rigid rules and regulations governing the behaviour of members of the press. For a reporter to burst into song and to interrupt the business of the House and make fun of a TD in the middle of his speech was unheard of. Members of the press gallery rushed over to Peadar and hustled him out the door.

Dáil Antics and Personalities

Watching a lively debate in the Dáil can be better than any theatre. There is drama, tension and humour present. Some of the best drama is provided by the more extrovert, independently-minded deputies. These are not ministers or big names; they are the backbenchers and the 'characters' who have something to say and are determined they are going to get their view across. It is not easy for the independent or the ordinary backbencher to get time allotted to them under the rigid rules of the House. This causes great frustration and anger, but it doesn't stop the more boisterous and ingenious members who are determined to be heard at any cost. They jump up angrily, interrupt the proceedings, ignore all appeals to resume their seat, and shout their protest across the chamber. This may result in them being thrown out of the House for misconduct and being suspended for a few days. Nevertheless, if the deputy has been able to get his message across before being thrown out, he doesn't mind. In fact, being thrown out is a bonus. It means his name gets prominence in the papers the next day and the people back home in the constituency knowing he is working hard. Not only that, but he is doing it so well that he has been 'victimised' and thrown out of the Dáil for his determined efforts. That goes down very well with the punters. They feel he is the person to fight their corner and of course he is the person to vote for the next time around.

This used to be a popular ploy with some volatile deputies who demanded to be heard. It is not used as much today and you don't hear of many being ejected for 'disorderly conduct.' As a tactic, it seems to have been abandoned. There is also a more discerning public today who sees through these stunts.

In the old days never a week went by without someone being shown the door. This used to enliven many a boring day for both deputies and reporters. Invariably, the introduction to the story went something like this: 'There was uproar in the Dáil yesterday when Deputy X tried to raise the surprise closure of such and such a factory with the loss of fifty jobs.' There was always a grudging admiration for the man who could simulate rage, go beetroot in the face, bang the bench in front of him and demand to have his constituents' grievances aired. Of course, they were the bane of every Ceann Comhairle, who was trying to abide by the rules of procedure.

The master at getting himself thrown out of the House was Fine Gael's Gerry L'Estrange, who was a bundle of energy and full of mischief. He was for many years the party's chief whip and could always be seen scurrying around the building looking for truant deputies, pulling them out of restaurants and bars, warning them, cajoling them, joking with them. He simply never relaxed. In an interview in the *Sunday Press* before his retirement, L'Estrange said he couldn't think of anybody who could come anywhere near his record of being expelled from the House.

However, he was never vindictive or malicious, and even though he was a major thorn in the side of Fianna Fáil ministers, he still maintained a good relationship with them. His antics were all simply for public consumption. Just part of the game of politics, which he loved. He was a born politician. The life was food and drink to him. I have never seen any politician revel in the job as much as Gerry did. He was very popular with politicians of all parties. He laughingly described one infamous incident when he was asked to leave the chamber:

> 'I remember I was put out after a fierce row with Neil Blaney over the price of heifers, and we nearly came to blows in the chamber. I met him in the corridor later and I stopped and said "No hard feelings, Neil" and he looked at me and said, "The same to you, you fucking hoor".'

He tells a hilarious story about a meeting in Ardee to protest over a factory closure. Sean Lemass was visiting the town for an election meeting and Fine Gael was determined to make trouble for him. 'Gerry Sweetman got me dressed up in an old coat, with cow dung all over it, and tied a bit of twine in the middle. I had a cap and an ash plant and Sweetman asked me to question and keep roaring at Lemass.' He performed the job so well that the meeting ended up in chaos and a garda sergeant warned him that if he didn't shut up he would have him arrested. Gerry admitted in 1986 that none of the present crop of TDs were adopting the same belligerent tactics in the Dáil. Being 'shown the door' was always the best way in those days to ensure getting on the front page. Times change.

While this type of behaviour was always good for a chuckle it naturally annoyed the quieter, more serious minded, less extrovert deputies who felt their bellicose colleagues were stealing a march on them with their histrionics. But politics is not a game for the faint-hearted. It is a tough, ruthless business and the name of the game is survival at all costs. It is an arena containing a fascinating combination of brilliance and ignorance; peopled by the good, the bad and the downright ugly. Politicians are always seeking compromise and a lot of principles are thrown overboard to meet this aim. The end always justifies the means. The maxim that politics is the art of the possible is true, but to reach that point you have to bend a lot of truths and whip a lot of reluctant people into line. Democracy in action is a strange beast indeed. Watching politicians up close for the past 39 years never ceases to amaze me. Just when you think you understand them they will do something new to confound you. They go from the sublime to the ridiculous. You will never know what way a politician is going to jump; in fact, he or she may not know themselves until minutes before they make a speech coming down on one side or the other; there is always soul-searching up until the last second.

Their hypocrisy can be astounding. Some politicians find no difficulty whatsoever in saying one thing publicly in the Dáil chamber and an hour later state the exact opposite down in the bar or outside in the corridors. Conscience doesn't enter into it; it is the end result that counts. Conscience can sometimes be a major handicap in politics. There is also the collective survival syndrome – when a party is in a tight corner and the whip is put on. In this situation, it doesn't matter a damn what you think, you just do what you are told. The whip is on and you troop through the lobby and vote as you are directed. It's totally irrelevant that your conscience or constituents want something different. The beauty of this is that if one is wrong then all are wrong, the whole party is wrong, but if they judge it right, they are all in the clear and they have won bonus points against the other side. If they miscalculate, they are all in trouble. Survival is essential because they all know how hard it is to get re-elected. It is so easy to lose your seat. Always know which way the wind is blowing. If you are a good political yachtsman you will survive. After all, the public can be very fickle and the road to Leinster House is littered with political corpses. If they make one slip there are dozens of young aspirants queuing up to fill their shoes, many of them masquerading as your best friend.

* * *

Watching politicians from the press gallery every day is like having a permanent seat in the front row of the Abbey Theatre. I should correct myself here: the drama in the Dáil is light years ahead of our national theatre. Politics is a lot stranger than fiction and the esteemed members of Equity have a long way to go before they reach the acting heights of some public representatives. Nowadays, deputies are even trained in how to present themselves to best effect in debates on television, radio, in media briefings, and are well versed in how to emphasise a point. If that isn't show business I don't know what is.

I've referred to the vociferous backbenchers who are determined to be heard even to the extent of being thrown out of the House for misconduct. There are also those who are very philosophical and have deeply thought-out ideas of how society should be changed. They are always worth listening to. They provide many hours of interesting and educational debates, but the simple fact is that nobody really wants to know. Even the most brilliant ideas are rarely taken up by the Government and I have seen some excellent ideas sink without trace. The record shows that Irish people don't want their TDs holding fine ideals and making constructive speeches. They want them in the realm of the messenger boy, getting things done, pulling strokes. Most of what they want could be adequately handled by a county councillor or a secretary.

Our lack of political sophistication and our dependence on political parochialism was clearly illustrated in the 1970s when the Labour Party put some of the country's best intellectuals into the Dáil. They made a solid and constructive contribution to debates, made some brilliant speeches, put forward intelligent amendments to various Bills, and generally performed their role in an excellent manner. It was a pleasure to sit in the press gallery and listen to so much common sense expressed so eloquently. Great stuff, but they were wiped out in the next election. They were politically naive and did not pay enough attention to 'potholes' and 'putting tiles on roofs.' They were annuals not perennials. They bloomed brightly for a short time and then vanished.

The most talented of these intellectuals was David Thornley, who had an impressive track record in the academic world and had been a presenter on the RTE current affairs programme, Seven Days. He was a brilliant lecturer, a gifted polemicist, a broadcaster of penetrating ability, but he could never get to grips with Irish politics. Labour made him shadow spokesman on education. He revelled in this portfolio and made numerous incisive contributions to educational debates. But it was frustrating for him. In Irish politics unless you are in the Cabinet you are just voting fodder. This was not a role which someone as intelligent as Thornley could accept. I remember him becoming very emotional one day when he was getting nowhere in a debate. He had been putting forward numerous bright suggestions, but was getting no response from the then Minister for Education, who sat there with a bored look on his face, letting it all wash over him. Thornley suddenly paused and said wistfully to the Minister: 'I would give my right arm to be Minister for Education in this country, to be sitting over there where you are.'

Before going into active politics, Thornley – small, rotund, with a quick smile – was asked by the late Mr Gerry Sweetman to join Fine Gael.

> 'I was offered a safe seat in Dublin South West and a Parliamentary Secretaryship, but I turned it down because I am a socialist. I didn't want to join a party that had still too much of the blood of Blueshirtism running in its veins.'

As a teenager he was briefly a member of Fianna Fáil 'before I knew better.' He received an offer from the Labour Party in 1969 and was elected in Dublin North West. During the ensuing years in the Dáil, he tried to maintain his independence as an historian and broadcaster but he found it difficult. He disagreed with his party colleagues on many issues. He said he believed that the right to divorce, contraception and abortion were fundamental human rights and did not agree with a Catholic state for a Catholic people.

'If I were Dr Ian Paisley I would have nothing to do with the Republic of Ireland until it was made clear to me that my civil rights were guaranteed by the regime in the Republic.'

When he entered the Dáil in 1969, he thought he was going to change the world, just like a lot of other enthusiastic TDs before him, but unfortunately they soon became painfully aware of the facts of Irish political life. Thornley said after his short period in the Dáil:

'I always felt that deputies should be above the parish pump mentality, that they should concentrate on passing good legislation and making the country a better place to live in.'

That was the mistake he made. He lost his seat and he died shortly afterwards, at the early age of 42.

Paddy Lindsay, the former Fine Gael TD and Master of the High Court, would agree with Thornley's views on what the role of a member of parliament should be. Lindsay, an articulate man with a mischievous sense of humour, and a brilliant criminal lawyer in his day, stressed that the primary function of a TD should be to make good legislation. He had little time for clientelism – 'the tendency of the TD to present himself as the possessor of influence which he hasn't got.' He maintained that this goes 'a long way towards undermining the integral parts of the State, including the courts.' He added: 'I did the usual constituency work, but I must admit that I hated it. Imagine the frustration of getting a letter, as I did, saying 'Please write to Dr Kelly and tell him to send me on my tablets.''

The Dáil in the 60s was very much a gentleman's club; very easy going with a predictable smoothness about the business in hand. Many deputies were part-timers. No serious business was tabled until 5 p.m. when the barristers finished their work in the Four Courts. They would then come into the Dáil, make big speeches, which would be fully reported, and the public naturally thought they had been in attendance all day. The opposite was in fact the case; they were treating the national parliament with contempt. The public never knew, or if they did, they did not seem to care. Fine Gael was the biggest offender.

The former leader of the Progressive Democrats, Des O'Malley, entered the Dáil in 1968. He described the experience very well in an article in the *Sunday Times*.

'One of my earliest memories as a young deputy is of being regaled in the members' bar one evening by an elderly gentleman's account of the number of Black and Tans he had shot and the circumstances in which he had shot them. That deputy, I have no doubt, felt the elimination of the Black and Tans had been his major contribution to Ireland. Certainly he had come through about ten elections on the strength of it. The Dáil at that time still had figures who had played a prominent part in the war of independence and in the civil war. For some of them, the civil war had never really ended. The conversation was often backward-looking and historical events excited them more than current topics.'

The whole parliamentary system, based on the old British system, was quite Dickensian. However, in fairness, it has been changing over the years, but only slowly. The almost revolutionary decision to allow television cameras into the Chamber has shown the public how archaic the place actually is. If the public had seen how it operated 25 or 30 years ago they would have been appalled. There is still a lot of room for improvement. There have always been calls for change by some progressive deputies, but the maxim that 'big wheels move slowly' certainly applies to our national parliament. The few changes that were introduced only took place after years of tedious negotiations, with large numbers of deputies totally opposed to any divergence from the old trusted formula.

The setting up of Oireachtas Committees was also resisted for years. The deputies did not want the extra work load. Provincial deputies did not want to spend longer in Dublin than they had to and claimed that committees were placing an extra workload on them. They wanted to be with their families and doing their constituency work. They also wanted time to attend their local county council meetings. The fact of the matter is that they should not be holding a dual mandate and should leave local politics to the councillors. When a recent Local Government Bill was being drafted which would have prevented members of the Oireachtas from being members of local councils, there was such uproar that the idea was quickly dropped. Instead, it was just stipulated that ministers cannot be members of local authorities and TDs cannot in future hold the chair or vice-chair of such authorities. One of the reasons there was such opposition to television cameras being introduced to the chamber was because they were afraid that some determined deputies would hog the limelight. It was felt that television might increase the likelihood of more histrionics from some of the 'characters' who never let an opportunity go by without making their bid for self-advertisement. They were afraid of the deputies who manipulated the system and contrived to get themselves thrown out. However, as it transpired, the fears were totally groundless. There aren't as many simulated rows now. There is certainly more maturity about the Dáil than heretofore. Maybe they are growing up at last. It is a change for the better and, in fairness, they must be complimented for this.

* * *

If Gerry L'Estrange was one of the most volatile politicians in the Dáil in my time there, certainly the most conservative was Oliver J. Flanagan, Knight of St Gregory, who was a TD for 43 years up to his retirement in 1987. He once told me that he had kept a diary for every one of his years in politics and he jokingly asked me if I would like to write his life story. Oliver had plenty of stories to tell.

However, I did not pursue the matter and never got to see the diaries. While his public image was that of a blinkered Catholic politician trying to stop progress, he was in reality a likeable character, with a good sense of humour and a quick wit. He was nobody's fool and was well able to look after himself even when the other politicians and the media were attacking him. In fact, he revelled in teasing the public and the media. He was highly suspicious of the media generally and never missed an opportunity to hit back at them. He once told a group of reporters at Leinster House that they were 'the lowest of the low.' They were so low, he asserted, that they 'could go out between a duck's legs'.

The 'Father of the Dáil' – as he was in his latter days in the House when he was the longest serving deputy – defended Charles Haughey when the new Fianna Fáil Government came in in 1982. He said Mr Haughey had survived a campaign of disgraceful vilification by the media.

> 'I too was a victim of vilification by the media after the Locke's Tribunal in 1948. I was the victim of media vilification on my appointment by Mr Cosgrave as Minister for Defence. I survived it, but it is only right when a new Government takes office that it should be made very clear that it is this parliament and the government who run this country, not a group of journalists or penpushers.'

He was never far away from controversy, but he enjoyed it. He worked on the basis that there is no such thing as bad publicity. As long as the media spelt his name right and put his picture on the front page, he knew that everything was fine with the world. The wily fox could see his vote growing by the minute. Oliver was one of the truly great characters of the Dáil. He was always worth listening to, even if you didn't agree with a word he was saying. It was something about the way he presented his case. He fervently believed in what he was saying and he could express himself very well in a debate on any subject. His commitment and determination was seen in his final dramatic act in the Dáil. The last time he was seen in the Dáil he was very ill and came from hospital, pale, feeble, thin, especially to cast his vote in a vital division. When he completed his vote, he waved to the members of the House. They gave him a standing ovation. That was the last time he was seen in the chamber. He retired from the Dáil and died a few months later in April 1987. Certainly the Church appreciated his work on their behalf. There were 45 priests present to concelebrate his requiem mass.

* * *

One of the most enigmatic politicians in the Dáil during the 60s and 70s was Noel Browne. Most of the work for which he is now remembered took place in the Government of 1948–1951 and when I came to report him he was a backbencher with no power. He was very much a loner, a voice in the wilderness and seemed quite frustrated. He was brim-full of ideas, but once you are not in a political party or in Government your chances of getting any of your proposals translated into legislation are almost zero. He used to make long speeches severely criticising the Government, the Church, the establishment, censorship, semi-state bodies, various organisations, foreign governments: all got the lash. He was fascinating to watch in action, although sometimes he could become quite tedious with his repetition. Yet, I knew I was looking at a political legend and I followed the end of his active political career with great interest.

Browne had practically been canonised for the trojan work he had done while Minister for Health in fighting rampant TB in Ireland. He had also stood up to the Catholic Church at a time when it held a dictatorial dominance over the people. He deserved all the praise he got for this and it is something that should not be forgotten, even though it was a long time ago. It is an important part of our history.

Nevertheless, he could not have succeeded without the backing of a fully committed Government which gave him every support. There was also radical reform under way in the Department of Health at that time through dedicated public servants like Padraig O Cinneide and Dr James Deeny. He never really gave any credit to his ministerial colleagues: in fact, all they got was some vehement and personal criticism. The most recent of this was in his autobiography, aptly titled *Against The Tide*, published in 1986. While marvellously well written, it was staggering in its venom against former colleagues and those he disliked. He was obviously a man who did not make friends too easily or have close acquaintances.

While many of the views I heard him express in the Dáil were sound and compassionate, even courageous on occasions, he was far too impatient, often with people who might be trying to achieve the same goals. Yes, 30 years ago we were a backward country in many respects, but so was Britain, Europe and the US. All of the western world was conservative and changes were only coming slowly. Anybody living through those years could see that everything wasn't right, but sensible politicians know that change only comes slowly. You don't change views and opinions overnight. Browne, because of his enthusiasm and impatient nature, wanted us to run before we could walk. Yet there were other good politicians who were quietly and efficiently changing society over those decades. The results are there to be seen today.

Watching Browne over the years, I came to the conclusion that he was his own worst enemy. His turbulent, crusading spirit did not leave any room for discretion. He always took the direct path, straight ahead and never tried to walk around the obstacles in his path. He wanted all society's ills remedied immediately. While it gave him a justifiable reputation as a great reformer, it also made him a lot of enemies among his political colleagues. If he was cuter and more patient he could have got more of his ideas accepted and implemented. But I suppose it was not in his nature to compromise and he just went battling on. The *Magill Book of Politics 1981* said:

'Browne's career has been full of contradictions and inconsistencies. He has probably damaged the cause of progressive politics in Ireland by his failure/refusal to work within a party structure. In spite of all this, however, it must be acknowledged that almost alone among Dáil members over three decades he has spoken out on behalf of the poor and deprived in Irish society. He has been virtually the only voice of radical dissent in Irish politics. He was reviled and scorned for several for several years in Dáil Eireann, though nowadays he has attained a position of eminence and respectability. This has been largely because of his dogged obeisance to parliamentarianism, a feature which has quietened a great deal of his radicalism.'

Browne retired from politics in 1983 and went to live in a cottage on the shores of Galway Bay. There was a proposal in 1990 to make him the Labour Party's candidate in the presidential election. However, the party decided instead to put forward Mary Robinson and the rest is history. Instead he had a long and peaceful retirement in Connemara where he relaxed for probably the first time in his long life. When he died in May 1997, Professor John A. Murphy, Emeritus Professor of Irish History at UCC and a former senator, wrote in the *Sunday Independent:*

'Noel Browne has been described (even by sympathetic critics) as a loner and a maverick who disregarded advice and who found it difficult to work harmoniously with any association or political party. Clearly, he was regarded as a nuisance by his Government colleagues in 1948-'51, some of whom were obviously glad to get rid of him. The truth is that he was a visionary, an unhappy warrior, whose tortuous odyssey through so many parties and organisations was a futile attempt to discover the political mechanism which could make his vision a reality.'

Summing up, Professor Murphy said Browne would be remembered as the first great social-crusading politician in independent Ireland, who uniquely pushed out the frontiers of political discourse.

* * *

One of the wittiest and most constructive speakers the Dáil in recent decades was John Kelly, a former Minister for Industry and Commerce, Attorney General and chief whip for the Fine Gael party. Any time Kelly stood up to contribute to a debate there was a flurry of excitement and an immediate feeling of expectancy. Even reporters, who are generally fed up listening to speeches, slipped into the press gallery when Kelly rose to speak, hoping to hear something 'different'. He could always be relied upon to provide some interesting copy. He also had an impressive way of delivering a speech, a fine style of oratory and an enormous vocabulary. He was never stuck for a word. Cutting through humbug in a short sentence or two, he could regale the House with his incisive wit. He relished his role as the orator, the successor to James Dillon. He liked to talk and he got great satisfaction out of putting together a good script for use either in the House or outside it. He was not slow to contact the newspapers if they 'played around' with his carefully constructed speeches.

Luckily, I escaped this treatment but I know of others who suffered his wrath. Sometimes he was right to complain, but other times he just showed too much sensitivity.

There was a certain arrogance and eccentricity about him. He was never a real politician, as one understood a politician to be. He was very much an academic, a philosopher, a man who stood back and took a panoramic view of Irish politics. He was constantly making sweeping generalisations about the way in which the country was run, containing very strong views on quite a number of subjects. It was always presented in a very dogmatic fashion, with an aura of ex-cathedra about it. It could range from the absolutely brilliant to the utterly naive. He had a firm belief that his opinions were right and he would deliver these views in a highly articulate manner, almost daring anyone to contradict him. He had a fine intellect, but he always gave the impression of being very much the academic who wandered into the chamber for the day to express his views on political life. He used to boast about not holding 'clinics.' This was one of the many political practices which the other TDs carried out diligently, but on which he looked with disdain. His big strength was his knowledge of the law. A qualified barrister, he was fascinated by constitutional law and human rights.

He was appointed Minister for Industry and Commerce, but he had no experience of either industry or commerce. His spell in this portfolio showed his political shortcomings. He would have been much more effective in the Department of Education or in Arts and Culture. But it wasn't his fault that he was placed in a ministry which did not suit him.

I remember him leading a trade delegation to New York in 1981. It was organised by Coras Trachtála and was one of the biggest 'Sell Ireland' packages ever to be undertaken. A battalion of reporters accompanied the trade mission. One morning we were to visit the famous Mayor Ed Koch. When we arrived at City Hall, Koch was delayed, so we had to hang around for half an hour. Kelly then saw a man wearing red robes and a gold chain of office around his neck. He went up and said, 'Hello Mayor Koch, pleased to meet you.' The man got the fright of his life and turned the colour of his robes with embarrassment. He was a mayor alright, but it was Paud Black, the Mayor of Cork, who also happened to be on the delegation. Not only did Kelly not know the Mayor of New York, but he didn't even know the Mayor of Cork, who was accompanying him on the trip.

It was a very embarrassing moment. It was an amazing mistake because Koch was one of the best known politicians in the western world at the time. He was one of the most popular politicians ever to be mayor of that city and possessed a great sense of humour. Later, when Koch saw Paud Black with his robes and chain, he said: 'That's a valuable bit of gold; don't wear that in the subway'. I was standing nearby and immediately filed the story to *The Irish Times*. When Kelly got home and walked into the Dáil, Charlie Haughey could not resist saying:

'Here comes Mayor Koch.' Every opportunity he got he used to taunt Kelly with the Koch jibe.

Kelly could have had other ministries later in his career, but he did not want to be a minister. He declined other offers and made it clear he wanted to be unfettered to express his views from the backbenches on the numerous subjects that interested him. That showed his eccentricity in Irish politics. Every politician who enters Leinster House dreams that some day they will become a minister, even a junior minister. But not John Kelly. It was as though he did not want to accept responsibility. He wanted to be on the outside telling the others what to do. Yet, the only way you can get anything done in this country is to be a minister. Always entertaining inside or outside the Dáil, he had a brilliant, if sometimes vicious, sense of humour. His numerous contributions to debates added style to the Dáil. He made many excellent suggestions and observations during his too short reign. He retired in 1989 and died in January 1991 at the young age of 59. At the time of his death there was speculation that he would stand again. Certainly his party wanted him to stand, as he was a top vote-getter.

* * *

There has always been a great debate among politicians and journalists about who was the best orator in the Dáil. The accolade is usually given to James Dillon. I remember hearing him make a number of eloquent speeches in his latter years in Leinster House and he was certainly very impressive. He was a superb parliamentarian and a man of great integrity. However, sometimes he was inclined to be very woolly, talking for talk's sake. This was as much a fault of the system as the individual. Often there were a few days allocated to Bills that could have been disposed of in a few hours. This meant that deputies had to come in and stonewall for long periods. Dillon was able to dramatise his speeches with long pauses and sweeping gestures. He liked to throw out pertinent questions and then pause, dramatically glaring around the chamber in theatrical fashion as if to say, 'How could any government minister in his full mental faculties make such a terrible mistake?' He would never use one adjective where he could use three, or use one sentence when he could stretch the same point to a lengthy paragraph. There was always a lot of hot air involved, but that's nothing new in political speeches.

I heard one amusing story about Dillon which was supposed to have happened when he was a minister. A senior civil servant came into his office with the short list of the names for some big job that was coming up. Beside three of the names was a little red mark. Dillon asked what the red marks meant. The civil servant explained that those names were members of Fine Gael, Mr Dillon's party. The story goes that Dillon was outraged and bellowed that the person best qualified for the job was to be appointed and he would not tolerate nepotism. He sent the civil servant scampering out of his office. Years later, a Fine Gael TD jokingly told me it was that type of attitude that had kept his party in the wilderness for so long. He stressed that type of 'naiveté' would never happen again. He was right. Fine Gael are now as good as Fianna Fáil at rewarding their party workers. There is no political party in Leinster House backward in this particular area now.

In my opinion the best orator in the Dáil during the past 30 years was Conor Cruise O'Brien. While not agreeing with many of the things he said in the House, he certainly knew how to make his point. He was a dream for a Dáil reporter. He was highly articulate, with each sentence having a beginning, middle and end. He knew how to make his case and expressed it concisely. No waste, no waffle. He got his message across. When you came off the gallery and sat down at your typewriter, every sentence read perfectly. He really had a wonderful gift. Most politicians are not good speakers and they can go on for hours waffling on some Bill or local issue, invariably jumping from point to point, often getting confused and not making sense at all. The reporter has then to battle to summarise the speech. The end result often makes the TD's speech look brilliant. In fact, journalists don't get credit for this. I have often heard TDs make statements and then say to the press, 'That's it, you put English on it.'

The days of the orator are long gone. Oratory is basically irrelevant, something from a bygone era, now languishing in the universities and the Four Courts. There are fewer long-winded speeches in the Dáil today, thank God, and few deputies want to speak at all. They are just interested in getting their spake in during the cut and thrust of Question Time and then getting out of the chamber as quickly as possible. The front benches do most of the talking. In the old days a speech could go on for three hours. Deputies were told by the Chief Whip to go in and 'hold the fort' because all their other colleagues were otherwise engaged. So they just went in and talked, and talked and talked .... I have seen deputies come in with books of statistics and read huge monotonous chunks of it to the annoyance of everyone, particularly to the Dáil stenographers who had to record everything for posterity.

Being a TD today involves a lot more than making fancy speeches to a half empty chamber and a few bored reporters. Most of the TD's job is now outside the chamber and it doesn't matter a damn about how good he is at making flowery speeches. The media rarely cover Dáil speeches now unless an issue of major news value is being debated. Back in the 60s and 70s it didn't matter what rubbish the TD came out with he always got a 'mention,' just to show he had turned up and was making an effort. Fifteen reporters used to work on a shift basis, taking down every golden word. Those days have disappeared and so have the reporters; the 15 reporters have been cut down to about six. Older deputies are constantly complaining about not getting their names in the paper. They should realise that those days are gone.

Jimmy Tully

Jimmy Tully was a politician I got to know quite well when I was covering local government affairs in the 70s. He was the Labour Party's Meath TD and Minister for Local Government in the 1973–1977 Coalition. He was regarded as one of the hardest working Ministers in that government, a formidable political street fighter. He was a great man to smile – always smiling – but just because he wore his famous smile did not mean he was happy or relaxed. He was the most paranoid politician I have ever come across. He seemed to spend most of his life looking over his shoulder at real or imagined problems or enemies. He was full of energy and got through a phenomenal amount of work, but there was always that fast-running undercurrent of restlessness, like a volcano waiting to erupt. Yet, he was one of the most fascinating politicians I ever met. Despite his faults and the many battles we had I admired the man and his turbulent ways.

He was happy in Local Government (now the Department of the Environment) when everything was going well. He was in his element when there was plenty of money in the kitty to build houses, construct roads and keep all the various sectors of local government ticking over smoothly. But when the money started to run out, when the complaints started to flow in, when the Opposition was on his back, when the press reflected all of this ... well, Jimmy was inclined to get very upset. Unlike other politicians he was not good at hiding his feelings. Criticism became a media plot in his mind, cleverly set up by Fianna Fáil or some other enemy. He flatteringly described me as one of the 'more honest young lads around' when he was getting a good press, but when things started to go wrong for his image in the media, when I criticised some of his decisions, I was quickly branded 'just as bad as the rest of them.' I have never known any politician, especially one as experienced as Tully, to be so sensitive to the media.

I did an extensive interview with him after his first year in Local Government. I thought I had done a fair and accurate report and it got a good show in *The Irish Times*. However, Jimmy thought otherwise and was on to the editor like a shot, claiming I had misquoted him. The interview related to the abolition of domestic rates, a highly controversial issue at the time. He kicked up quite a fuss. It was arranged that I would go to meet him in his Dáil office and iron out the problem. When I arrived, Jimmy – all smiles as usual – said: 'Well, Frank, I suppose you'll put in a correction tomorrow.' I replied: 'No.' He became quite agitated. I said there would be no correction because there was no mistake. He insisted that he had been misquoted. I was just as adamant that the report was accurate. When he continued to demand a correction, I played my trump card. I switched on my tape recording of the interview, which showed quite conclusively that he had used the words I had quoted in the article. As his voice on the tape wafted around the room, he turned pale and fell back in his seat, wiping his forehead with the back of his hand.

'How could I have said that?' he asked, incredulous. I said I hadn't a clue why he made the remark, but the fact was that he had. I also told him I resented him going to my editor complaining about my report without speaking to me first. I was very fortunate to have had the tape recorder with me, otherwise it would have been my word against his. And with the fuss he made about the matter there was no doubt who would come out on top. Tape recorders were not too common among journalists at that time, so I was steeped to have had one with me. It is always easy to question a shorthand note, but once it is on tape it is game, set and match to the reporter.

'What are we going to do about it?' he asked, deeply shaken. 'What do you mean we,' I answered. 'You have made the mistake, not me. You'll have to sort it out yourself.'

'What could I have been thinking of?' he mumbled. 'I don't know,' I replied, 'but whatever it was, what appeared in the paper was what you actually said.'

We chatted for a while and then I tried to do a deal with him. I suggested that I would write another story about domestic rates and make sure his view was contained in it. This would clarify his remarks in the earlier article. It would get him out of a hole. In return, I asked him to tell me what his decision was going to be on the planning application for the Dublin civic offices at Wood Quay. In those days it was the Minister for Local Government who made planning decisions. To put it mildly some of the Ministers abused their position and gave many outrageous permissions, which stand around the country today as monuments to their expediency. The planning application for the civic offices was a highly contentious issue and I was very anxious to find out what the Minister was going to do. It would have been a great feather in my cap if I could get a scoop on the decision. But Jimmy wouldn't budge on the matter. He said that was a matter for the Cabinet to approve and he was not going to break a confidence. I was disappointed, but I must say I respected his view. I knew there were a lot of other Ministers who were not so honourable and were leaking regularly. I told him that at the time, but it made no difference. He wasn't going to leak. Anyway, even though I didn't get what I was looking for, I decided to write another article to clarify his views on the rates situation. So all ended well.

We had a few more differences of opinion in the years after that. On one occasion he stood up at a building society dinner and said the editor of *The Irish Times* should sack me for a story I wrote on house-building standards, which reflected badly on him. This proved very embarrassing to all the building society chiefs present, who had to sit there listening to a tirade of abuse thrown at me, but diplomacy wasn't Jimmy's strong point. He called a spade a spade; what another politician might say about you behind your back he would have no hesitation in saying it to your face, even if there was 100 people in the room to hear it. He had a ferocious temper and whenever he exploded politicians and civil servants dived for cover. I remember him verbally abusing a very senior civil servant in front of me, which was extremely embarrassing. Afterwards, the equally shocked Department press spokesman, remarked:

> 'You saw something today that I have never seen happen before and it wasn't nice. A Minister never attacks a civil servant in front of a member of the public, especially a journalist.'

While I had a stormy relationship with the man, I also had a grudging admiration for him. He had energy and courage, not a lot of finesse, but plenty of enthusiasm and determination. His main ambition was to build as many houses as possible, to set house-building records. That's what he wanted to be remembered for. I think he did set the record before leaving office. As well as attacking the press, he was a hard task-master on his civil servants and often criticised their attitude. 'They are a funny breed, civil servants: they live in a world of their own,' he told me one day, not in anger, but sort of bemused. Civil servants had to be pushed all the time, he explained. He proudly boasted to me how he managed to introduce votes at eighteen years of age.

> 'I told them I wanted votes at 18 introduced immediately. They said it would take twelve months, but I got it in in six.'

Pondering on this, he added: 'They're nice people really, but they're too cautious.'

On another occasion, when I was interviewing him in his Dáil office for a wide-ranging article on all aspects of Local Government, the division bells rang in the chamber and he had to leave to cast his vote. Before he left, he handed me a file and said:

> 'Read that when I'm gone. It's a civil service briefing document. It lists out all the questions Mr Kilfeather might ask me and the answers I'm to give you. They must think I'm very stupid. Funny people, civil servants ...'

In his more tranquil moments he liked to philosophise on political life. I remember him ruefully telling a story against himself, or a story of how he came out of a situation badly. Apparently there was talk for a long time about building a housing estate in a town in his constituency, but nothing ever happened. Jimmy didn't believe in talk; he wanted action, and as a minister he could make things happen – quickly. Within a couple of months of being appointed a minister he had harassed the civil servants, cut through all the red tape and had the housing scheme built without delay (about 30 houses). He was as proud as punch of his achievement. These were the things that politicians were elected for; this was what politics was all about; this was why it was so important to become a Minister, especially for Local Government, and be able to do it. His joy knew no bounds.

However, the sting in the tail was: 'After all my efforts,' said Jimmy, half way between laughter and anger, 'guess how many votes I got out of that estate?' Not waiting for a reply, he bellowed 'Three bloody votes. Who'd be a bloody politician?' But he loved being a politician. He revelled in the cut and thrust, the challenge of taking on the opposition head-on, and of routing them. He was at his best when in a corner or with his back to the wall. A very tough individual, but far too sensitive, anyone who dared to criticise him was treated with contempt. And he never forgot a slight, whether real or imagined. He had a powerful memory and critics were carefully filed away in his mind so that he could be wary of them in future. He always labelled his critics 'begrudgers,' a favourite word of his.

Even though he was a doughty fighter, he did give up eventually. He declined to stand for election after serving in his second Coalition as Minister for Defence. Announcing his decision, he described his time in the second Coalition as being 'sheer hell' and he had no intention of going forward for election again. He had a long run in politics and had a good retirement before dying at the age of 77. Not a bad span for a man who always seemed to be on the verge of a heart attack anyway. But it was his open hatred and suspicion of the press that fascinated me. He once confided in me that a 'young fellow from the *Sunday Independent*' had been 'snooping around' his home village of Laytown, looking for information on him, 'trying to do a hatchet job on me'.

Coincidentally, I just happened to know the reporter involved and I knew he was just there to do a straightforward, harmless profile on Jimmy. I said nothing and let him continue with his tirade. Anyway, the outcome was that the 'little bugger' was sent packing by the local people who were 'loyal' to Jimmy and wouldn't see him hurt. He told this story with great pride. I stressed that there was no point in attacking the media, saying that there was good and bad in every profession. He should be able to roll with the punches. After all, he was no shrinking violet himself. If he felt injured by some reports he should take legal action. His scornful response to that was:' That's a joke: did you ever hear of a politician winning a case against a newspaper?' Well, until he tried, I said, there was no point in constantly whingeing about the press.

Since then quite a few politicians have won libel actions. A former Taoiseach, Albert Reynolds, has had a few out-of-court settlements in cases against newspapers and radio stations, amounting to about £150,000. However, generally speaking, many of the libel claims that land in the newspapers' legal offices could be resolved with an apology, a correction and a donation to charity.

In a speech to a Bar Council seminar on press law in 1994, the editor of the *Sunday Independent*, Mr Aengus Fanning, compared payments in libel cases to payments in personal injuries cases. In one instance, he cited the payment for a libel which was four times what the same person would have received if he had lost his wife or child in a car accident. He said:

> 'There is a widespread view that newspapers are financially fair game. Newspapers in this country face a plethora of actions for libel – some serious, some not so. Behind a large number of cases is a belief – shared by plaintiffs and lawyers alike – that a libel action is the legal equivalent of three stars on a scratch card.'

Most politicians I have spoken to believe they should not sue, unless it is for something truly vindictive or malicious. Many have told me they have been tempted on a few occasions to sue, but after calming down have let it slide. As one said: 'We are sticking out our neck every day of the week, so we should be able to take the odd heavy hit'.

Jimmy was a great man to tell a story. He used to enjoy describing how he was nearly killed during the assassination of President Sadat of Egypt in 1982. Jimmy, who was Minister for Defence at the time, was on the platform with a number of other dignitaries as Sadat was reviewing his troops. Suddenly, a hand grenade was thrown at the platform. It didn't go off and almost immediately a second was thrown. He graphically described the scene:

> 'I had spent six years in the army in this country and while I was not the first one to hit the ground, I was very little behind the first man down ...'

In spite of his quick action, the assassins then began machine-gunning the platform and Jimmy was shot in the jaw. He was taken to a hospital run by Italian nuns. An elderly nun offered him a large glass of brandy, but he declined.

> 'She was very disappointed when I wouldn't. I don't take alcoholic drinks and I'm afraid showing her a pioneer pin in my coat did not make any sense to her either.'

Jimmy made a quick recovery and was back in harness in a few weeks as though nothing had happened. It took more than a bullet in the jaw to stop the little Meath man.

Who'd Be a Politician?

'Did you ever think of standing for election, Frank?' the young candidate asked me during a general election about ten years ago. He was in the middle of his campaign and was flushed with excitement and enthusiasm. There is always a great buzz about politicians during election times, whether they be running for a seat in the Dáil or on the county council. They are pumped up to an incredible degree and seem to think that everyone has the same feverish interest in politics. It's a wonderful game to them, but the public generally hasn't got the same all-consuming interest in the subject.

My reply, to put it mildly, was unprintable. It wasn't quite the answer he had expected and he was a bit deflated. But I was deadly serious. In my opinion, anyone who goes into politics is crazy. Having watched politicians in action at all levels over the past 39 years, I never cease to be amazed why anyone would want to take on what must be one of the toughest, most thankless jobs in the world. You start off full of idealism; you are going to change the world, get things done, not like the guy before you: after all, he was incompetent. You are convinced that if the public gives you a chance, you will make things happen. However, after a few years in the job you are a different person. You are compromising your principles daily, you are harassed every week, you see enemies everywhere. You develop a sense of paranoia. And you are right .... There are enemies everywhere, and the most dangerous are those closest to you, in your own party, waiting for you to make a mistake. In politics you have to develop a very thick skin, which most do, but you still take some very heavy hits. Your family suffers dreadfully. It's not a normal vocation. The casualty rate is very high. In addition, many deputies are also members of county councils. Being a local councillor must be the most soul-destroying occupation of all. You are the local messenger boy or girl for every menial job imaginable. Why any intelligent man or woman would bother is beyond me.

You are trying to get potholes filled, put tiles on roofs, get land for a football pitch for the youngsters, pushing for a house for so and so, trying to pressurise for a planning permission for Mr X, who happens to be one of your best constituency workers, trying to improve the water supply somewhere else, etc. You have to take on council officials who may have other priorities. You also have to watch your opposite number who is trying to do the same thing. If he succeeds before you, it's your neck on the line in the next election.

As a TD you are constantly under pressure. Your home is not your own. The phone never stops ringing. There is always someone at the door. You can't walk down the street without getting buttonholed. You can't go into the pub without having to buy a round of drinks. You are expected to contribute to every charity and jumble sale. As a TD, you must always be available and highly visible. You have to patiently listen to all of the whingeing and complaints of your constituents. You then have to show sympathy and promise action when you know it is just another impossible crank request, but you don't dare say that or the 'client' will move to another deputy. I knew a very good, hard-working TD who always told it 'as it is.' If a person had no chance of getting a house or a grant, he explained that. He was being honest. He lost his seat in the next election, of course.

It's a dog's life. TDs will be the first to admit it. They will agree one hundred per cent with what I have said about the job. Nevertheless, they love it. They are this world's truly great masochists. As soon as election time comes around, they are out again on the trail, knocking on doors, attending every meeting, pushing out the propaganda, listing their achievements .... They suffer, their family suffers, their friends suffer, but they press on regardless. They push on even though they know the voters are fickle; voters will say one thing to your face and another behind your back.

I remember meeting a TD at a reception in Dublin some years ago who was drinking a big glass of milk. Everyone else was downing whiskies and brandies. I asked him when he gave up the drink. He replied that his doctor had diagnosed an ulcer, and that, along with his weak heart, meant he would have to be careful in future. Looking at his frail, battered figure, I presumed he wouldn't be standing in the next election. 'Not at all: of course I'll stand again ...' was the emphatic reply. I was told that he had been a TD for 15 years and he wasn't going to bow out now, just because of an ulcer and a dicky heart. Well, he was re-elected but died two years later.

Then there was the case of the TD – a very prominent politician – who developed cancer. It wasn't a serious cancer. It could all be sorted out with a little operation immediately. However, he couldn't have that. He was a very busy man, wasn't there an election looming and wasn't he having trouble with a running mate. He kept putting it off. The cancer got worse. The TD died, but political life went on. He was a good TD, but nobody is indispensable. He had impeccable political judgement when involved in running the country, but he was not capable of making a crucial decision on his own future. He ended up with no future and nobody remembers him today.

You certainly won't get rich in politics. Some people say that TDs are in it for the loot, but there is very little money in politics, unless you are a member of the European Parliament. I remember a bank manager telling me that he had worked in many towns but had never known a politician, whether TD or councillor, who was not seriously deep in the red. They will make a few bob on expenses, especially if they are on enough committees, or if they live a good distance from the Dáil or council offices, but that's about it. When I worked in the provinces, I used to see maybe four or five councillors arrive in the same car to save themselves a few quid. While the expenses, mileage and subsistence, have increased considerably since then, none of them are making a fortune. Yet, they are accused by the public of being there to line their pockets, of being corrupt, of being only interested in looking after themselves.

Because of the frustrations and humdrum nature of the job, councillors are always on the look out for a good junket as compensation. That's what makes it all worthwhile. A few trips to foreign climes with your colleagues to attend conferences on building, housing or roads can work wonders for the morale. The TD, on the other hand, has the opportunity of getting Dáil junkets as well as council junkets, something that is resented by the councillors. Every time a council receives an invitation to a junket ... er ... I mean a conference, the excitement is palpable. The jockeying and canvassing, the wheeling and dealing, gets into full stride. They become like children at Christmas time. They know that to get away on one of these trips, all expenses paid, and plenty of hospitality laid on, is a real perk. The only cloud on the horizon is the press. The press will splash the story and reveal who is going on the junket, what it is going to cost, pointing out that service charges have been increased that year because of the alleged shortage of money. Publicity about junkets infuriates councillors. 'Totally exaggerated,' they claim. 'Conferences are important. We are going to learn something which will be of benefit to the locality. Yellow journalism.' One councillor once suggested that the press should go along with them. 'That will reduce the criticism,' he added. In recent years, some councillors have agreed to produce reports on what they learned on their trips to show that they are not going away to enjoy themselves. Of course they are going away to enjoy themselves at our expense. Many councils don't discuss invitations to junkets at their meetings any more because of all the controversy the subject generates. Instead, they decide in private whether to accept the invitation, how many should go and then decide on the names. Generally, all parties co-operate in sharing out the trips. While in public, political parties, like barristers, will knock spots off each other, once they get away to foreign climes or into a bar they are the best of friends.

While many junkets are fairly ordinary affairs, there are some which can be to far away, exotic countries, where the hospitality is quite lavish. Many taxpayers feel that the politicians are 'feathering their own nest.' They say that if politics is such a tough job, why do they keep going forward for election? That is a good question, but to get an answer you have to understand the mind of a

My father, T.P. Kilfeather, a journalist of the old school. He was political correspondent in the Irish Press *and later became chief feature writer and television critic for the* Sunday Independent.

John McDonnell, editor of the Drogheda Argus *when I joined in 1958, one of nature's greatest gentlemen. Few other editors would have tolerated my shaky beginning in journalism.*

At work. Above interviewing Garda Commissioner Edward Garvey after his removal from office and below in New York in 1978 with mayor Ed Koch. Also present are journalists Terry Keane (Sunday Independent) *and Michele McCormack* (Sunday World).

Four of the most interesting political characters I knew from my time in journalism.
Clockwise from top left, Noel Browne (Ind.), Oliver J. Flanagan, Gerry L'Estrange
and John Kelly (all F.G.)

Dr Tiede Herrema poses, after his release, with the bullet given to him by his kidnapper, Eddie Gallagher.

A victim is taken away after the Dublin bombings in 1974. It was one of the most harrowing stories I have ever covered.

Jimmy Tully with then Labour Party leader Brendan Corish. Tully was probably the politician to whom I got closest. Although often quite paranoid, Tully loved the political life. Building local authority houses was his greatest obsession. He also has the distinction of being the last Irish minister to have been shot – at the assassination of President Sadat of Egypt in 1982.

Two political legends, Charles J. Haughey and Brian Lenihan who were close friends and allies for 30 years until Haughey sacked Lenihan after the Duffy Tapes controversy during the 1990 presidential election. Lenihan was a remarkable man, both politically and personally in that he made no enemies throughout his political life. He died in 1995. Two of his sons are now TDs. The enigmatic Haughey's idyllic retirement was brought to an abrupt end with the revelation that he received £1.3 million from supermarket tycoon, Ben Dunne.

Irish Press workers demonstrate after the closure of the Press titles. The "Great Enterprise", founded by Eamon de Valera, died a slow lingering death. Irish journalism is much the worse for its passing.

councillor and that, as I made clear at the outset, is not an easy thing to do. They don't make any money by going on a junket. In fact, even with expenses, they still find themselves out of pocket afterwards. The real perk is that they are basically getting an almost free holiday to a place which they normally probably could not afford to go, where the majority of their constituents also cannot afford to go. There was once a councillor who mortified his county manager and colleagues by stuffing his pockets with sandwiches at a reception in a certain European capital. He was unemployed and liked to grab whatever came his way.

Reporting council meetings can often be quite boring. You sit there for hour after hour while the councillors battle away on some minor matter which is only of importance to a handful of people and of no news value to anybody else. You need great patience to sit through all the waffle, but every now and again a good story does surface. You are like a pearl diver. These divers spend hours throwing themselves into the deep and searching through the muck at the bottom, hoping to find a pearl. It's a tough life, but every now and again they come up with that elusive pearl, which is great reward for their endeavours. I have managed to dredge out the odd, nice little story out of some of the most dreadful verbiage imaginable. A journalist builds up a good rapport with councillors over the years and you get to know their favourite soapbox subjects. You are aware of what they are going to say before they say it. They often glance over at the press bench to see how their speeches are going down. When debates were extremely dull I used to sit back and smoke my pipe. They could see that it wasn't a very newsworthy item and they would move on to the next matter on the agenda. When the reporters in the press gallery started writing they knew they were on the right track. A kind of body language, you might say.

There was an old and experienced politician in Wicklow 35 years ago who was very good at journalistic public relations. He knew how to grab the headlines. One evening I met him going into a council meeting and he said: 'Have your pencil sharpened tonight, Frank: I'm going to make one hell of a revelation. It's going to be a great story.' I was excited and full of curiosity. Well, the meeting went on and on and on ... but there was no sign of my man opening his mouth. Just when I had nearly given up, he jumped to his feet, feigning rage, banged the table, and started making all sorts of serious allegations about certain business people in the town. He ranted and raved for about ten minutes and I ended up with a very good front page story. He put on a great act. All those present thought that his actions were spontaneous, but he had been able to tell me hours earlier what he was going to do. It's all in the game.' If you want to be an effective councillor, it helps to be a good actor.

Nowadays, councillors have very little power. Ever since domestic rates were abolished, local authorities simply have not got the money to carry out all the projects they would like. The local authorities have been heavily dependent on the Exchequer for finance. The Exchequer, of course, keeps a tight rein on the disbursement of funds and most local authorities are barely surviving as a result. Service charges were brought in to fill the gap, but these proved extremely unpopular. This was galling for councillors, who are full of big ideas and have numerous plans for spending money, but discreet officials pat them on the head and explain that the money is simply not there. End of story.

* * *

Most council meetings are eminently forgettable, but there were many meeting of Dublin County Council in the 70s and 80s which were absolutely outrageous and have left a bad taste in my mouth. While councillors may have very few powers left, one of the big strengths they do have is making the County Development Plan and thereby the zoning of land. Land is designated (zoned) for a particular use, e.g. amenity, agricultural, residential, etc. By rezoning agricultural land (cheap land) to development land (expensive land) they can make a fortune for big landowners. Dublin councillors have also passed numerous Section 4 motions and made several material contraventions of the development plan, appalling behaviour in flagrant disregard of the best professional advice. Section 4 motions force the county manager to take action on something which he does not think advisable. Land rezoning is all very well when it is needed, but when there is sufficient land zoned for development and councillors press to double or treble that amount against good expert advice, that is wrong. That was what Dublin county councillors, or at least a large number of them, were doing in the 70s and 80s. In fact, I see this practice has come back again recently and the Minister for the Environment, Mr Michael Smith, has quite rightly strongly criticised it and appealed for restraint. He said that land zoning in County Dublin had become a 'debased currency', with many of the decisions indicating 'a frightening degree of irresponsibility' – particularly when it means, as it usually does, that the public has to pick up the tab for providing the expensive services, water, sewerage, roads, etc.

Reporting Dublin County Council meetings in those days was a disturbing experience. To have to sit for hours listening to some councillors advocating a rezoning was upsetting and annoying. They never made any reference to the fact that there was already plenty of land zoned for housing and that it was serviced. They pressed for rezoning and the taxpayer paid for the servicing of the newly-rezoned land. If you were an ordinary citizen and wanted planning permission to extend your house they would not fight as hard for you.

They used make the most plausible arguments for rezoning. They would stress the amount of employment it would give to the building industry, the much-needed houses it would provide, emphasising the promise of the builder to provide, free gratis, a public park or a golf course. This just showed what huge profits they were making. They would say the green belts were 'only fields,' to which the public had no access, and farmers were not able to farm being so close to housing developments. It was the same old tune, played over and over.

Brought down to basics, it was sheer greed. It wasn't pleasant to watch and at times it became quite depressing. On many occasions I can remember walking down O'Connell Street, on my way back to the office, feeling almost physically ill. I can remember thinking, if this is democracy it is being totally abused. It certainly wasn't being done for the people, because all the local residents' associations were strongly opposed to the rezonings. Every time councillors call for more powers, I can only say 'No' and hope that they never do get increased responsibilities. They don't deserve it.

Their arrogance and double-think back in the 70s, and I understand it is still going on, was absolutely incredible. I used to sit there and ask myself if this was really happening. They could even convince themselves into thinking they were doing good by rezoning as much green space as possible, even though the local people were totally opposed to it – and the councillors claimed they were representing these people.

Before each monthly meeting, they would buttonhole me in the foyer and admonish me for my last report on their rezoning antics. They would accuse me of all sorts of misrepresentation. 'You would think we were all crooks from the way you are reporting these meetings,' one councillor remarked, as he showered abuse on me. I kept a diplomatic silence. Then they would flatter you to knock you down: 'I thought you were an accurate reporter until I started reading your reports of our rezonings.'

There was one unsavoury incident which happened in the 70s. It still rankles, but it showed the mentality of some of the Dublin councillors at the time. Every Christmas, after their monthly meeting, the councillors traditionally go to a nearby pub for a few seasonal drinks. I was invited to go along on one occasion by a certain politician who was a prominent land rezoner. I declined, pointing out that I had to get back to the office, and as much as I would enjoy a drink, duty came first. In addition, I have a reputation for being a bit of a loner and don't allow myself to get too close to politicians generally. I believe it is always better to keep a healthy gap between the two professions. We need each other and we use each other but it is possible to have a good relationship without getting too close. Well, this individual was adamant. He continued to insist that I go along. Then, when he was convinced that I wasn't going, he pretended to shake hands with me and placed a fiver in my hand. I was astounded at his audacity. I went to give it back to him, but he ran away. I was absolutely furious. It was the mentality of a small-town politician trying to buy votes or make friends. I found the incident deeply insulting. I walked down O'Connell Street in a daze, fuming at his arrogance. I didn't know what to think I was so annoyed. As I reached the GPO, I heard a choir of school children singing Christmas carols. I walked over and put the fiver in the collection box. The look on the face of the woman holding the box will always stay with me. In the 70s, a fiver was a lot of money. The little woman probably thought I was the last of the big spenders. In retrospect, I suppose it was the best thing that prolific rezoner has ever done for Dublin.

However, while rezoning and expediency were the downside of covering local government, there were also good times. I enjoyed seeing at first hand the big controversies and of witnessing the decisions on the rebuilding of Dublin. For instance, the civic offices at Wood Quay and the Central Bank controveries were fascinating sagas and it was wonderful having a front seat to watch these dramas unfold. Every time I walk around the city now and look at the various office blocks, apartment blocks and roads, I think of their backgrounds. I was privileged to have seen history being made. Good and bad decisions were made, but the buildings are now standing and are part of us. They will be there long after we are gone. In fact, a lot of the personnel involved in some of the biggest controversies have passed on, but their achievements, or sometimes their sins, live on after them.

* * *

While many Dublin City Council debates could be excruciatingly boring, they were invariably more constructive than that which took place in the neighbouring county council. Despite the boredom, there were quite a few lively and witty discussions. This was mainly due to the 'characters' who knew how to enliven a flagging debate with some jocose remarks or sharp observations. The best of these old-timers were Paddy 'The Bishop' Burke, Frank Sherwin, who boasted that the only political machine he had was his bicycle, Dickie Gogan, who was constantly asking me: 'Frank, how can you listen to this stuff?' Sean Dublin Bay Rockall Loftus and Ned Brennan.

Ned Brennan, a north Dublin city councillor, a postman by occupation, was depicted in the media as being a philistine because of the outrageous remarks he made at the cultural committee meeting of Dublin City Council. However, much of this was carefully calculated, tongue in cheek stuff. He worked very hard on the ground and in fact topped the poll with 3,513 votes in one election. The controversy which catapulted him into national prominence was his criticism of the Gay Sweatshop play 'We're Guilty Because We're Filthy' about 15 years ago in the Project Theatre. Ned lambasted the play and claimed it was the most scurrilous thing to have ever been allowed onto an Irish stage. Gay Byrne, always on the look out for a good controversy, invited Ned on to The Late Late Show to talk about it. During his appearance Ned took a bit of a hammering for his anti-cultural views. Coming near the end of the programme, it looked as though Ned was cornered. Gay asked him how he could criticise a play he hadn't seen? There was a brief pause, and you could see that Ned was in big trouble. Then he came out with the immortal lines: 'I didn't see the crucifixion either, but I believe it happened'.

During the centenary of the birth of James Joyce, one enthusiastic group applied to Dublin Corporation for permission to erect a plaque of Joyce in the city centre. Ned wasn't impressed.

> 'The ordinary man in the street never heard of James Joyce,' he said. 'The ordinary man out there is only interested in bread and butter issues and doesn't want to be bothered with this kind of thing.'

Ned, whose greatest ambition, never fulfilled, was to be Lord Mayor, used to boast:

> 'We have to stand up and be counted. There is a real world out there. People always know where they stand with me.'

Yes, you always knew where you stood with Ned. He livened up many a long, hard night at city council meetings for me. May he rest in peace.

Brian Lenihan

When Brian Lenihan died on 1 November 1995, tributes rolled in from every sector of Irish life. He was universally loved, a man with no enemies. The obituaries simply showered praise on him and editorials were extremely generous and highly complimentary. There wasn't even a hint of criticism. Quite remarkable; but he was a remarkable man. He will always be remembered for his cheerful personality and affable manner. He was a good guy to be around. He lifted you with his infectious humour and eternal optimism.

Usually when a politician dies you get people coming out of the woodwork, piously saying what a great person he was, what a great loss to the nation, etc. Sometimes the hypocrisy can be quite nauseating, especially when you know the players involved and are familiar with the background. However, I suppose it is an Irish trait that you never speak ill of the dead. The big difference with Brian was that all the tributes were true. It's very rare for a politician to be liked and respected by everyone, including the opposition parties. He had political opponents, but no political enemies, nor was it a question of praising him just because it was the thing to do. There is plenty of this in Irish society, especially in the political world, where you can expect to get verbally mugged behind your back on a regular basis in those great gossip haunts – the Dáil bars and restaurants.

Political gossip can be quite cutting and frightening for those who don't understand it. It is a tough, vicious game: certainly not for the fainthearted.

Yes, political opponents could have their differences with Lenihan across the floor of the House, but that's where it was left. Outside, with the show over, it was back to respect and comradeship. It was an amazing feat to spend so many years in the Dáil – first elected in 1961 – and have no political enemies. Generally the longer you are in the Dáil the more enemies you make. It worked in reverse with Brian. He treated everyone with respect, from ministerial colleagues down to the most insignificant backbencher. That was probably the secret of his incredible popularity. He could get on with people. That is an important asset for most politicians, but he had brought it to perfection. It was sad that such a decent person should have had to suffer so much physically and politically in his last few years. His dreadful illness, the Duffy Tapes controversy, the defeat in the presidential election and being sacked from the Cabinet by his friend Charlie Haughey, were major blows, but he took them stoically and with his typical good humour. People used to laugh when Brian used the expression 'no problem,' but he meant it. Nothing was ever a problem. He had a tremendous capacity for putting difficulties behind him and getting on to the next challenge. He was intelligent and experienced enough to know he was operating in a tough profession where you had to take the rough with the smooth. He had a lot more ups than downs. That was because he could react to changing circumstances faster and better than most.

I remember when he lost his seat in Roscommon/Leitrim in 1973, a major surprise and a huge blow to the young Lenihan. He did not, as most losing candidates do, immediately look for excuses, castigate his opponents for dirty tactics and his own workers for not trying hard enough. There was no self-pity. He did not look for pity or condolences. I remember him coming into the Dáil bar, his usual chirpy self, and saying: 'Well, it's back to the auld law practice again'. It is not generally known, but if he had stayed with the law he could have been very successful and have made much more money than he did in politics. But politics was in his blood; he was an absolute political animal.

I was told by a colleague who was at the 1973 Roscommon/Leitrim count that after the result was announced Brian told his supporters to 'cheer up', peeled off his jacket, rolled up his sleeves and vaulted behind the bar to serve the drink. His shattered workers were amazed at the way he was able to hide his feeling and get on with life.

He had a tremendous zest for life and lived it to the full. After working a sixteen-hour day he loved to have a few drinks with friends or constituents. He could stay drinking until the wee small hours of the morning. He loved people; he enjoyed the chat. He was great company and always drew a crowd around him. He also drew plenty of freeloaders, eager to avail of his unfailing generosity. The porter of a well-known Co. Kerry hotel tells the story of Brian attending a high-powered conference. Brian addressed the conference in the afternoon, made a speech at the dinner that night, and started drinking with colleagues at 11 p.m. and went on into the small hours, till about 3 a.m. or 4 a.m. Yet, says the porter, he was up again, bright and breezy, at 7.30 a.m. and being driven to a meeting in Dublin. The porter couldn't believe his eyes. 'I didn't think anyone could shift that amount of drink, stay sober, and then be able to get up so early in the morning,' the porter told me afterwards. Brian had the constitution of an ox. He couldn't pack enough hours into a day. However, even the strongest cannot continue to burn the candle at both ends. When he began to get the liver trouble, his face got thinner and became a frightening yellow colour. He used to get angry and say to friends 'Why are they looking at me like that?' He didn't realise how bad he looked. He basically felt all right, but the story was written on his face for all to see. He was not a well man. I must say I found it distressing to look at him.

He was advised to give up the drink. It was a big decision, but he accepted the good advice and immediately gave it up. A year later, he remarked:

> 'As for alcohol, it is out. Many people have asked me if I miss it; the answer quite truthfully is that I don't. I still enjoy company over a drink, except that now I'm on mineral water. It doesn't upset me when I see other people drinking when I know I can't. In fact I get a vicarious pleasure from the presence of friends who are enjoying a drink. Anyway, it is a small price to pay for being alive and healthy.'

His strength and courage before, during and after his operation in America was incredible. The day after his heavy operation he was up and walking about. The doctors in the Mayo Clinic in Rochester had never seen anything like it. Nor have they seen it since. His wife, Ann, described in her book *No Problem – To Mayo and Back* arriving at the hospital after the operation: 'When we got there his bed was empty and my heart sank.' A nurse told her he had been moved back to his old room.

'We couldn't quite absorb what had happened,' said Ann. 'Brian had gone from intensive care, within 24 hours of his operation, when I had been told he could be there for anything up to a week.' It showed tremendous strength and power of recovery after just undergoing an exceptionally heavy seven-hour operation.

A lot of people at the time wondered how much such an operation cost and how, knowing the figure was astronomical, Brian could afford to pay it. The average cost of a liver transplant at Mayo varies from $150,000 to $300,000, but can be much higher depending on complications. Mayo requires proof of ability to pay the costs of the operation prior to surgery. After the operation, Ann wrote: 'In our case the VHI were agreeable to making a contribution towards the cost. A group of friends made up the balance for us.'

Brian was told he would have to spend a few months recuperating. However, a general election was called unexpectedly in Ireland. This threw him into a quandary. This was the last thing he wanted, but there was no question of him retiring. He sounded out the political situation back home and then offered to stand in absentia. His family, workers and friends rallied around and ran a good campaign. Incredibly, he topped the poll.

There has been a lot of talk about Brian being a 'warm-up man' for Charlie Haughey at Ard Fheiseanna. He would go out front and build the delegates up to a pitch of hysteria. They would lay down their lives for Fianna Fáil when Brian was finished with them. He was a brilliant orator. Like many politicians, he was also a good actor. He knew how to play a crowd. They were like putty in his hands. Sometimes I used to wonder how the attendance could be so gullible. They never questioned anything he said. If Brian said it, it was all right. Afterwards, Brian would sidle up to a few friends and say, 'How do you think it went?' He knew it had gone well and he was happy at having pulled off another successful job for the party.

Brian was the man who replaced Erskine Childers as the respectable face of the party. He was the man who was wheeled out when cracks appeared and had to be papered over, when appeals for calm needed to be made, when the party needed to be straightened out. No matter how big the crisis, Brian could put the best face on it and have the faithful ready to make a new start. He never objected when asked to perform these many dirty tasks. His loyalty knew no bounds. He took it as part of his duty to the party and never feared that the repercussions might rub off on him. A lot of people felt that he should not have allowed himself to be so often put into the front line in difficult situations. They were afraid it could damage his own reputation. They did not see why he should always be the one to mend fences which he had not been responsible for breaking. They feared that by appearing on TV and radio so regularly to resolve crises that some of the dirt was bound to stick to him. It never did, though, and he got by unscathed.

Many of his close friends believed he was never properly appreciated for this type of dedication to the party. They were particularly incensed when Haughey fired him after the Duffy Tapes controversy. They could not understand how Haughey could turn around and dump an old friend and colleague so callously. This was deeply hurtful to Brian. Having fought off bad health and in the midst of a turbulent campaign for the presidency, he felt he was being hung out to dry. It was probably his darkest hour.

Yet, he handled the aftermath of the crisis quite well. Charlie McCreevy TD wrote: 'His political professionalism ensured that he bore no enmity to Charles Haughey, who had to sack him. He realised that the Taoiseach had no option if he was to prevent a general election. But funnily enough, Brian never understood or appreciated why Des O'Malley went so far in insisting upon it. I recall him saying: 'Sure, O'Malley is a friend of mine; didn't I work in his by-election.'

Nevertheless, despite his defeat, Brian came back into the mainstream of political life. While he never again held a major political post, he did regain a lot of influence in the party and was very actively involved in the few years he had left. A lot of publicity has been given to the 'survival instincts' of Haughey and how he, like Lazarus, always came back. Lenihan's struggles were literally life- threatening, and he came back with the big smile on his face, looking for the next challenge. Many commentators tried to paint Brian as a kind of a bull and bluster merchant, a kind of political clown, a nice guy, with a good sense of humour, but lucky. Nothing could be further from the truth. Having watched him for 30 years, I know he had exceptional ability. He was one of the best politicians we have produced. While a lot of people might not agree, I believe he was one of the finest politicians to have ever walked through the front gates of Leinster House. It may sound hackneyed but we won't see his likes again.

After his death in the autumn of 1995, *The Irish Times* editorial summed him up accurately. It said:

> 'Brian Lenihan was a complex man. He almost made a virtue of concealing the sharpness of his intelligence and his great grasp of detail. He preferred to put forward an image of bluff cheerfulness, unencumbered by too much that might appear cerebral or reflective. It was not the real Lenihan. He loved company, he loved politics, he loved to be involved with issues. But he had a deep insight into the social and political questions of the day and he was, at his best, a powerfully effective Minister whose impact was always tempered with compassion.
>
> He was denied his last remaining political goal, to move to Áras an Uachtaráin as President of Ireland, through a combination of bizarre and unfortunate circumstances which were largely traceable to his illness.
>
> But great as his sense of disappointment may have been, it was again a measure of his generosity that he never hesitated to acknowledge the huge success of Mary Robinson in the presidency.'

Yes, he would love to have finished off his political career as president. It would have been a worthy end. However, in retrospect, it was asking a lot of the electorate to put in a man with such a medical background. During the presidential election campaign, one journalist asked PJ Mara, the government press officer, if there was a medical report showing Brian's fitness for the job. It was a legitimate question at the time and something the electorate was entitled to get. He was told 'Fuck off, and you can quote me on that.'

Brian's gaffe over the Duffy tape was a clear indication of a man who was not a hundred per cent fit. He believed he was fit enough for the job and was determined to get it. Once he got an idea into his head it was hard to deflect him. Such was the case concerning the presidency. More cautious political people felt he should have given the presidential campaign a wide berth.

Ironically, Charlie Haughey was against Brian standing for the presidency. He was concerned that Fianna Fáil would not win the by-election in the unpredictable Dublin West constituency if Lenihan became president. The Government's tiny majority was at risk. Haughey, like many other people, was also concerned about the health factor.

After Mary Robinson won against all the earlier predictions, Brian set out to explain his defeat. He wrote a book titled *For The Record*. He was convinced that if the tapes fiasco had not arisen he would have been safely ensconced in the Aras. The main thrust of the book was his personal analysis of the controversies of that election.

Having watched and spoken with Brian for over 30 years, I don't want to give the impression that he was a saint. I don't want this chapter to look like an eulogy to the man. There are no saints in politics. They wouldn't last a week. No, like everybody else, he had his faults. I was particularly disappointed by his performances when he became a member of Dublin

County Council. After losing in Roscommon-Leitrim, he got on to the council which he used as a base to get a seat in Dublin West. His attendance record wasn't good and when he did turn up his contribution was invariably poor. He was never properly prepared and his speeches were just a string of clichés. He did not seem to be on top of the local issues. He just wasn't interested. It was obvious that local politics bored him, but he was going through the experience to get his Dáil seat back. It was a legitimate attempt to keep his name in front of the electorate and build up a launching pad.

Another aspect of him I didn't like was the way he would put people down in the Dáil when they became vociferous about some controversial issue. He would put on his mock shock expression and begin tut-tutting and wagging his finger. In school-masterish fashion, he would shout across the floor 'Come, come, please behave yourself.' Often adding 'Please have respect for the House. This is outrageous behaviour.' There was something pathetically sanctimonious about it. I didn't like it. He was well able to mix it himself when he wanted to. His own deputies were just as rowdy. Every other week there was a row. It wasn't anything new, but Brian could put on this insufferable pompousness which could be quite infuriating. It was all an act, of course, but it was a tactic that did not become him. It was an effort to try to demean his opponents.

Basically, Brian liked to operate on a higher plane. He loved being Minister for Foreign Affairs, rubbing shoulders with world leaders and playing a part on the bigger stage. Foreign Affairs is the plum ministry. If a senior politician cannot become Taoiseach, the next best portfolio is Foreign Affairs, especially since we got into the European Union. You just have to look at how Dick Spring revelled in the office. It is the one ministry where you feel a real sense of power and influencing world affairs. Brian was a very effective foreign minister.

Because of his bubbly personality and infectious good humour he had a lot of close friends in many world governments. He enjoyed the buzz of the world stage. It was a major blow to him when, in 1988, he had to undergo his liver operation and relinquish Foreign Affairs. The portfolio was naturally too much for a man recuperating from major surgery. Although he did continue as Tanaiste, second in command in the government, he was transferred to the Defence portfolio, which isn't too onerous. When he died on 1 November 1995, Lenihan had been a Dáil deputy for 34 years, a Minister for 17, and a central political figure through the political events of three decades.

His will, published a year after his death, clearly exploded the myth that politicians are in business to feather their own nests. He left £246,942 in his will. The bulk of his estate was made up of the valuation of his home and its contents, £150,000; statutory death in service benefit of £51,000 and £50,000 private Dáil Group Life assurance policy. He transferred property he owned in Co. Galway to his widow, Ann, in 1992. She was the sole beneficiary of the will.

The Dublin Bombings

'What was that?' asked a startled Noel Carroll, Dublin Corporation's public relations officer, at the other end of the telephone line. 'It sounds like a bomb, but it couldn't be,' I replied in disbelief. I was sitting at my desk in *The Irish Times* newsroom, as the booming sound echoed in the street outside.

It was 5.27 p.m. on Friday, 17 May 1974, and a series of car bombs in the centre of Dublin and Monaghan left 33 dead and 100 badly injured.

Three bombs went off simultaneously in Talbot Street, Parnell Street and South Leinster Street in Dublin, leaving a trail of devastation and horror. The Monaghan bomb went off outside a pub in Church Square, Monaghan.

It was the most horrendous, saddest and deeply disturbing story I have ever covered. Even today, looking at the old yellowed press clippings of the bombings in my files, I still feel upset when I think of it. The sheer barbarity and inhumanity of such an insane act, the wiping out of so many innocent people and the maiming of others physically and mentally for life, still makes me angry and bitter.

I had hardly put the phone down when the whole newsroom was swinging into action. Gerry Mulvey, the assistant news editor, said: 'One of them has gone off in Talbot Street, Frank. Get up there as quickly as you can.' He added: 'Bring Geraldine (Kennedy) with you, but look after her.' This amuses me now. She was more than capable of looking after herself, as she has proved in the years since. We ran up O'Connell Street and into Talbot Street. After that we got separated in the general chaos.

The first sight we came across was a dead paper-seller lying on the ground. The papers he had been selling minutes before were used to cover his badly shattered body. The papers were also used to cover a number of other dead people in the vicinity. Talbot Street had received the worst blast and the bodies were all over the place. The injured were bleeding and screaming for help, ambulance sirens were blaring incessantly. The street was littered with broken plate glass and bits of debris from the shops. The scene was one of total devastation and chaos. The gardaí were trying to keep control and divert the crowd away from the scene. It was quite eerie. A garda warned me that I was entering the area at my own risk, as another bomb could go off at any minute.

I had never seen such devastation before or since. I remember being quite numb from shock. I was, in my innocence, annoyed that they were leaving the dead bodies lying on the ground and not doing anything about them. I mentioned this to a garda and he said:

'Look, son, we have more important things to do. They are dead and we can't do anything for them. We are trying to look after the injured.'

He was right, of course: they had their priorities. They were doing a good job. I just continued floundering around the area, the glass crunching under my shoes. A young reporter from the *Independent*, who was only wearing a pair of canvas shoes, got a sliver of glass up through his foot. He had gone out to cover the story but ended up being another casualty.

I then moved up to Parnell Street, where the situation was nearly as bad. The full horror of the tragedy was coming into focus. An eye-witness said: 'We saw blackened objects in a store move slightly and it took a few numbed moments to appreciate they were human beings.' It was like a war scene. The injured were moaning with pain and the onlookers were crying, helpless to do anything, just watching the scene in total disbelief. People were warned to get out of the city in case further bombs went off. They had to go home by train or car because there was a bus strike at the time. However, gardaí believed that this was a blessing in disguise. The final death toll could have been higher if double decker buses, loaded with rush hour passengers, had been in use when the blasts occurred.

After spending half an hour in Parnell Street, I decided to go down to Jervis Street Hospital. The injured were being brought to Jervis Street and Richmond Hospitals' casualty departments. There were about 15 ambulances parked outside Jervis Street hospital when I arrived. If the scenes of the bombings were harrowing, what I saw here was absolutely heart-breaking. I have never seen such stark grief, such shock and fear.

People seemed to be helpless, listless with fear and foreboding. The dead – there must have been about ten when I arrived – were brought to a special section of the hospital. The injured were quickly examined by doctors and given labels to work out a system for priority treatment. The most poignant scenes, however, were to be seen in the rooms where friends and relatives waited for news of the injured – or to be told a member their family was dead. Nurses moved silently among the shocked, weeping and white-faced people, asking for information which might be of help in identifying the dead, or to see if there was a relation of an injured person present. There were middle-aged people looking for sons and daughters – husbands looking for wives, wives looking for their husbands, friends looking for friends. Everyone spoke in whispers. A heavy pall of despair and disbelief hung over the place. This sort of thing only happened in war. When a dead person was identified the relations were quietly steered away to a sideroom to be consoled. I saw this happen three times and I will never forget the look on those faces as they were ushered away. Their loved ones had left home that morning for work, fit and well, not a care in the world, and now they were no more, blown to bits by shrapnel from bombs planted by imbeciles.

Over at Pelican House, the blood donation headquarters in Leeson Street, hundreds of Dubliners arrived to offer blood. Eventually, the staff had to stand on the steps and turn away dozens of conscientious people anxious to help. About 500 units of blood were taken that evening. A spokesman said that all the hospitals' needs up to that time had been supplied and there had been no difficulties about rare groups.

'We have come to the point when it would not be proper to take any more blood until we assess the hospitals' requirements again,' he said.

When I got back to the office, I was just as shocked as any of the people in Jervis Street. Gerry Mulvey asked me what I was going to write. I could hardly talk I was so upset. Never in my life had I seen so much horror within such a short space of time. No violence I had reported in the North had been anything like this. One of our reporters who had covered the story got ill and had to go home. I sat for a long time at the typewriter before I could get the first few lines down on paper. I remember saying to Gerry: 'How can any words describe this atrocity?' And I meant that. There was a kind of futility about writing. It appeared so pathetic and so inadequate. I managed to write two stories about the events in Talbot Street and the scene at Jervis Street hospital, but I did it in a kind of daze.

Somehow we managed to get the paper out. Everyone worked heroically in spite of the dreadful depression. I still have two copies of that paper to remind me of that terrible day. What I saw that evening, I never want to witness again. The next day, an elderly neighbour came up to me and started talking about the bombing. Like everybody else she was outraged and said: 'I hope they find those who were responsible.' I was still feeling quite shook at the time, in fact it took me three days before I fully recovered. I remember being annoyed by this remark. It did not matter a damn whether they were caught or not. It would not make any difference; it would not bring back the dead, or heal the injured or take away the mental scars. What had happened was horrific callousness on a grand scale. Catching the criminals and putting them away for life sentences would be absolutely useless. They could not conceive the magnitude of what they had just done. Maybe I'm naive, but I don't believe that any human being in their right mind could prime those bombs. If they were in full control of their senses and realised what the results of their work was going to be, they could not have done such a despicable thing. You can only feel sorry for those who commit mass murder.

A compensation system – the Criminal Injuries Compensation Tribunal – was established to help the injured and next-of-kin. By comparison with subsequent tragedies, such as the Stardust disco fire in 1981, the payments to the bomb victims were paltry, absolutely derisory – an insult. One man who lost his wife was awarded £1,900; an elderly woman who lost both legs received £2,000.

One of the highest awards went to a man who suffered severe ankle injuries (£35,700).

A solicitor who was on the original compensation tribunal said some years later that the tribunal had been set up specifically to deal with the 1974 bombings, if another similar bombing happened, there would be no such compensation because it was a non-statutory scheme of ex-gratia payments. Furthermore, as no organisation ever accepted responsibility, no one was charged, civil legal actions would have been unsuccessful and he was 'almost a hundred per cent certain that none had been taken.'

It is now more than 22 years since that terrible event: no one has been charged with causing the blasts. Most people have forgotten that they ever happened. But those who lost loved ones, or those who have been maimed and still carry around the scars, won't forget. Those ambulance and hospital workers who had to deal with the effects of the blasts won't forget. Reporters who were there won't forget.

An investigative television report in 1993 raised the matter once again and named the people in Northern Ireland whom it claimed had carried out the atrocity. The reopening of the issue caused quite a flurry at the time, with more outrage expressed. Relatives and friends of the dead and injured claimed with a certain amount of justification that they were the 'forgotten people'. The scar had been opened again. The gardaí were urged to take some action, to get in touch with the programme makers and there was strong criticism of the inadequacy of their original inquiries by both public and politicians.

The outlawed loyalist paramilitary group, the Ulster Volunteer Force, claimed that it planned and carried it out. It was also alleged that the British secret service was implicated because the UVF was not capable of detonating such sophisticated bombs at that time; it hadn't the equipment or the know-how. Rumours abounded, but very few facts emerged.

The gardaí began a new investigation of the files relating to the bombings, but nobody is too optimistic about the outcome. The trail is now ice cold and it is said that most of those involved have died or been murdered. On the twentieth anniversary of the bombing in 1994, a special Mass was held in the pro-Cathedral which was attended by President Mary Robinson; government ministers; the archbishop of Dublin, Dr Connell; members of the diplomatic corps and many dignitaries. The memorial stone unveiled in Parnell Square four years earlier was unveiled again in the more central location of Cathal Brugha Street, but this was stated at the time to be only a temporary measure pending the erection of a larger monument bearing the names of the victims.

Up to the time of the twentieth anniversary ceremonies, relatives and friends of the victims felt that the tragedy was being ignored by the authorities. They pointed out that it was the worst mass killing since the Northern Ireland conflict began, yet they believed that no genuine effort had been made to bring those responsible to justice. It was, said one of the organisers afterwards, a great relief to have their suffering officially acknowledged after years in which the authorities seemed almost embarrassed by what had happened. Father Dermod McCarthy, head of religious broadcasting in RTE, who had been chaplain at the Richmond Hospital 20 years earlier, said:

> 'I feel that as long as the facts remain hidden and as long as the investigation is not progressed and the facts not made known to us, there will be public disquiet about this event. There will be a question mark hanging over the whole event, especially for the families of the 33 victims. If I was the father or son of someone who had their leg blown off I would like to know who did it before I died.'

In July, 1997, six relatives of the victims decided to take legal action in the European Court of Human Rights. As 'indirect victims' they have lodged a complaint with the European Commission of Human Rights. This is the necessary preparatory step to taking it before the European Court of Human Rights.

Article Two states that everyone's right to life shall be protected by law. This, it is argued, requires the proper investigation of all suspicious deaths. The case is being taken against the British Government because of the failure of the RUC to take all necessary steps to investigate the bombings and to trace and prosecute those responsible.

In their complaint they list 15 specific failures on the part of the RUC, including that it failed to establish a murder inquiry and failed to allocate sufficient resources and personnel appropriate to the investigation as warranted by the seriousness of the offences. Although the complaints happened a long time ago, they claim that the matters complained of, the failure of the RUC to investigate, have only recently come into the public domain through television programmes and they could not have acted sooner.

The Herrema Kidnapping

The kidnapping of the Dutch industrialist, Dr Tiede Herrema, in October 1975 had all the ingredients for a major international story. It captured the imaginations of news editors all over the world. It involved money, industry, crime, politics and sex. Hundreds of reporters converged on the little village of Monasterevin in Co Kildare, where Dr Herrema was held for 17 days by Eddie Gallagher and Marion Coyle in an upstairs room in 1410 St Evin's Park. Here was a story that had everything. The victim was the managing director of the Ferenka factory in Limerick, one of the biggest industrial plants in Ireland at the time.

The Government was concerned that the adverse publicity would mean the end of international investment in Ireland. The kidnapper was a young Donegal man whom the police could not, after eventually locating him, persuade to give himself up, despite adopting many subtle ploys. And of course there was an attractive woman involved – Marion Coyle – who was quickly adopted by the media as 'Maid Marion'.

It was a real peach of a story and a very impatient media vigil was mounted outside the house. The tabloids and the evening newspapers were straining at the leash, determined to produce some new angle every day, whether it was there or not. They grasped at straws; they interviewed everything that moved, anything that would make a line to build a story around. News editors were watching Monasterevin just as diligently as the gardaí were watching Number 1410. It was making the lead story every day in the newspapers, radio and television.

There was an unfortunate Garda superintendent appointed as public relations officer for the occasion. He held a press conference each day to give the latest developments, which usually amounted to very little. Gallagher was well dug in and was going to stay there till hell froze over. The unfortunate superintendent used to get the third degree every day, as he was mercilessly pressurised to reveal more of what was going on. He would stonewall stoically. He was only relating what he had been told, which was very little, and the rest, the bulk, was being withheld for security reasons. Try telling that to a pack of baying journalists. The superintendent was eventually given the assistance of a spokesman from the Government Information Service, but he did not fare much better.

The press left no stone unturned and if there were no morsels available, they speculated. Some of the most hair-raising stories ever published came out of Monasterevin in those seventeen days, as excited reporters let their imagination run riot. Rumours were everywhere; some of them incredible. How they started is a mystery, but every single one was chased with dedicated enthusiasm by the news hounds. It was cold, wet and miserable in Monasterevin in October 1975. Each newspaper set up a rota of reporters to cover the kidnapping. The facilities were minimal, practically non-existent.

Each paper would have a reporter watching the house during the day and another at night. The night shift was the worst. It meant hanging around a bonfire in the press compound on a waste piece of ground about 300 metres from the house. Each evening we scouted around and tore branches from trees to make firewood. One or two of the reporters had brought their guitars and played a few songs. No disrespect, but some of the music was pathetic. It did give us a laugh, though. The house was lit up by garda search lights. Neither Gallagher nor Coyle ever came near the windows, which were watched by detectives with rifles. The press compound was located far away from the house, where reporters would not be able to see too much.

The cameras could only cover part of the scene in front of the building. The windows were at too acute an angle for anyone appearing at them to be seen, and a wall obscured the lower front of the house as well as the front door. It ensured that there could be no sighting of Dr Herrema unless he was allowed to put his head out the window. Chief Superintendent Laurence Wren had stated that the earlier press positions were 'hampering the garda operation.' A Government Information spokesman assured photographers that arrangements would be made for them to cover the final moments of the affair when the time arrived. Trucks were to be arranged which would take them closer to the scene when the garda operation was finished. Later that evening, four army lorries drew up and parked beside our compound. Tickets were passed out to one photographer and one reporter from each news organisation entitling them to board the lorries, which would approach the house when the siege ended. What was required during the vigil was patience. Gardaí have more patience than journalists, particularly in a case where they had their quarry cornered they were in full control of the situation. The press weren't in control of anything and the facilities in that field were dreadful. The press had deadlines to meet.

The gardaí only had to wait for the kidnappers to make up their mind to come out. There was no question of them escaping. During the cold nights our mood went from amusement, to boredom, to frustration. We wondered if it would ever end. The nights went tortuously slowly. While facilities at the scene of the siege were deplorable, away from St Evin's Park the situation wasn't much better. There was only one hotel, the Hazel Hotel, which was really only a newly-built roadhouse with about six bedrooms. It has since been developed into quite a large premises. These rooms were snatched up within minutes and every other reporter had to travel many miles to find the next hotel. It was very unsatisfactory. However, one evening Dick Grogan, of *The Irish Times*, was having a drink in Monasterevin, when he got chatting to this elderly gentleman. He was a local businessman and when he heard that Dick worked for *The Irish Times* and was down covering the kidnapping, he offered us the use of a small caravan in the grounds of his house which was located near St Evin's Park. He said there was no heating or real facilities in it, but if we wanted it we could have it free gratis. He would not take any payment for it, as he was just pleased to help out. He enjoyed reading *The Irish Times* and was glad to be able to assist. We were delighted and made the best of it. We slept in the caravan and ate in the pubs and in the Hazel. It wasn't exactly luxury and was quite cold at times, but it was a big help. After about two weeks of the siege the Dublin newspapers and foreign media all hired large mobile homes and placed them in a field beside St Evin's Park. We got phones installed. We felt at this stage that Gallagher would hold out for months. We were quite pleased with our new facilities and were now living in the lap of luxury, compared to what we had been putting up with. We did not care how long the siege lasted. Things were starting to look up. Unfortunately, a few days later, Gallagher decided to surrender.

Reporters who were not on the late shift used to spend most of the night in the Hazel, drinking till the small hours. It was turned into a kind of press club, packed to the rafters, full of good cheer and banter. Many a fine ballad session took place. The drink, of course, flowed non-stop. Each night a tall foreign young man used to join our company. I think he was Dutch. He used to just stand around, smiling, watching everything and not really getting involved in the journalistic speculation about the kidnapping.

I became curious about him and asked a colleague who he was. 'Oh, he's one of the foreign reporters over to cover the story,' I was told. I didn't think he acted much like a reporter and was suspicious. If it had been in Belfast in the 60s or early 70s I would have put him down as an undercover RUC man. Somebody spying on us. The RUC liked to keep a careful watch on the press and listen to what we had to say while 'off duty'. The quiet guy at the end of the bar with the big ears twitching and staring into space was invariably the RUC plant. We knew them a mile off. I felt just as uneasy with this Dutch man. An even blacker mark against him was that he never bought his round. However, I soon forgot about him and went about my business. It was not until six months later that the matter of the 'mystery reporter' came to my attention again. I was sitting in Bowes pub in Fleet Street when a colleague, Mickey McConnell, came up to me with a big grin on his face. 'Frank, remember that fellow you were suspicious about in Monasterevin?' he asked. 'Sure,' I replied, not knowing what he was getting at. 'Well, he was a psychologist studying journalists' behaviour under pressure,' Mickey revealed. 'He has a big thesis on us in a prestigious international magazine this week.' I knew he wasn't a journalist, but I never dreamed he was a psychologist. Just goes to show you that George Orwell was right. Big Brother is always watching. Funnily enough, I never saw a copy of the magazine to find out what he thought of us. Not much, I presume, certainly if he was going by our antics in the Hazel. Watching a slightly under-the-weather reporter trying to play the guitar and 15 others making an attempt at singing can't have been a very edifying spectacle. It wasn't really pressure, we were just letting off steam. When the siege ended Donal Foley, my news editor, a very generous and compassionate person, made efforts to try to pay the man who so kindly lent us his caravan, but he again refused to take any money. Donal was determined, as were all the reporters who covered the siege, that we do something for him to show our appreciation. Eventually, an assistant news editor was sent off to Monasterevin one Saturday morning with a big bouquet of flowers and presented them to Mr Holmes, I think that was his name.

* * *

After his release, Dr Herrema said he did not hate Gallagher and Coyle: 'I have children of the same age, and I see them as children that have a lot of problems. I must say, that if they were my own children, I would do my utmost to help them.'

Dr Herrema posed with the bullet given to him by Gallagher, and again when he showed his tooth which had been knocked out by his captor. He said he had been repeatedly threatened, Gallagher often warned: 'We'll kill you'. He demonstrated how they gave him instructions to do things with the gun at the back of his head. He felt the police had 'done well' by staying away from him and his captors. At times Gallagher had been very aggressive. 'He hit me with the gun on my head.'

Asked about possible escape attempts, Dr Herrema said he had thought along those lines, but there had been no possibility of success. The window where he was kept was too small, and there was a cement parapet outside it. The police had invited him to jump, but it was impossible. His captors had held his feet and he had a gun in his back. During his captivity he was forced to record a message. The message was that his captors demanded the release of three prisoners Kevin Mallon, James Hyland and Bridget Rose Dugdale. Dugdale was Gallagher's girlfriend, who later gave birth to his son, Ruairi, in Limerick prison in December 1975. He said he advised Gallagher and Coyle at different stages to give up.

'I think that Eddie Gallagher was more inclined to give up than she was, but finally she also agreed, and I remember that she gave the message to the police.' Dr Herrema hasn't been allowed to forget his ordeal in Monasterevin. Every time there is a major kidnapping on the Continent, he is inundated with inquiries from journalists, eager to revive all the old memories. His view on this:

'I'm no expert on kidnapping. Every one is different. I'm a bit like a man who gets pushed into a pool and manages to clamber out, and then people start coming to me looking for swimming lessons.'

Eddie Gallagher, who was sentenced to 20 years for the kidnapping, has since been released after serving 14 years, and is now living in his native Co. Donegal. He runs a youth hostel with a pony trek/riding school attached. In an interview in the *Sunday Tribune* in March 1993, he said:

'I regret that somebody who really shouldn't have been drawn in was made to suffer, himself and his family. I regret that we were caught. And I regret that we were trying for too few prisoners. I regret those aspects of it. But I don't dwell on it ....'

Dark Days

At 9.30 p.m. on Tuesday, 13 November 1984, I was sitting in *The Irish Times* newsroom thinking about going home. The paper was full and most of the evening's activity had come to a stop. The usual helter-skelter was over. The news editor, knowing that in a few minutes he would have no staff, came over to me and said: 'Hang on, Frank, don't leave yet ... there's an unconfirmed report that a small plane has crashed with Irish people on board. There mightn't be anything in it, but hold on for a few minutes anyway.'

Fifteen minutes later, the report was confirmed. Nine people, including four leading Dublin journalists, were killed when their light aircraft crashed in east Sussex on its way to Paris to take in the annual Beaujolais wine race. The four journalists were Kevin Marron, former editor of the *Sunday World*, Tony Hennigan, reporter and columnist with the *Irish Independent*, John Feeney, columnist with the *Evening Herald*, Niall Hanley, editor of the *Evening Herald*. I was devastated. I knew three of the lads very well. The fourth, Niall Hanley, not so well, but still had shared a few pints with him in earlier days, coming back from soccer matches in Dalymount Park. It was a horrible moment. I could not believe that four of the brightest and most talented people in the business were gone. They were so full of life. They were too young to die.

The aircraft was half way across the channel and was being handled by French air traffic control at Orly Airport when the pilot decided to turn back towards the English coast, a spokesman for the British Civil Aviation Authority said later that night. The plane had not re-established contact with the British Air Traffic Control at West Drayton when it crashed shortly afterwards at Jevington in Sussex. Eye-witnesses spoke of seeing a plane flying low over Eastbourne seafront, apparently in difficulties. A farm worker saw it circling over the village of East Dean in Sussex and then disappearing in a ball of flames.

Later that night, I noticed Joe Kennedy, the *Evening Press* columnist and a former editor of the *Sunday World*, in the newsroom. He was very pale and seemed to be going around in a daze. Apparently he had been due to go on the flight, but then told his editor, Sean Ward, that it was more a news story than something for his column. Mr Ward agreed. 'Mr Ward's decision saved my life,' said Joe. The seat then went to Kevin Marron, his friend, and the man who had replaced him as editor of the *Sunday World*. He was understandably in deep shock.

'Kevin took my place and it could have been me ... I'm still shocked ... He was one of my closest friends and we worked very closely together over the years. This has not really hit me yet. I just don't know how I feel.'

said Joe.

* * *

Kevin Marron was in my class in Blackrock College in the 50s. He was the last one you would expect to go into the hurly-burly life of journalism. He was quiet and reserved. He was in fact quite shy. He didn't participate in anything outside the classroom and never played any sports, as far as I can remember. He always seemed to be standing outside of life, looking in. He later went into a seminary, but gave it up after a week. He exchanged the pulpit for a typewriter as a means for getting his message across.

While Kevin rarely opened his mouth in his schooldays, he was, nevertheless, very observant. He turned out to be a natural journalist. He got his all-important provincial work experience on the local paper in his home town of Dundalk before joining the *Irish Press*. He then went on to become editor of the *Sunday World* and the country's best television critic. He was a superb satirical writer, with a great repertoire in one-liners. He liked to make his point with good humour and never lowered his standards to be malicious. He wasn't one of those critics who like to show how smart they are to the detriment of some actor or television personality. He had a big following; many people bought the *Sunday World* just to read him. To all intents and purposes, he had it made. However, life can be so unfair at times. Just when he was at the peak of his career, when everything was going so smoothly, he suffered a severe brain haemorrhage. For a while it looked as though he would die. But, with great courage and determination, he pulled through. The setback meant he had to reduce his workload. He relinquished his job as editor but continued with his television column. He re-established himself in the front line of Irish journalism and everything was back on the rails again. Things were looking up. Or were they? Two years later his plane fell from the sky. His young life was over.

He always found it easier to express himself on paper than in conversation. A perfect example of this was given by Father Brian D'Arcy, a friend of Kevin's, who wrote after his death:

'I am writing through a haze of tears and a fuzzy brain. I still can't believe Kevin is dead. And I know that nothing on this page can describe how much Kevin meant to me. So perhaps you'll forgive me if I use some of his own words. A couple of years ago, a friend of ours lost a baby a few days after birth. I had tried to say some comforting words to the parents. I knew Kevin was upset too, but he kept in the background. Then, a few hours later, he dropped a typed note into the mother and sped off. That letter brought inestimable consolation to the mother. And no wonder. This is what Kevin wrote to the mother in her hour of tragedy:

"If we knew what was ahead of us, we'd turn back.

If we try to figure out the meaning of it, we would go mad.

There are only two certainties in this life. That your child is already where the rest of us are making such a mess of getting to. The times pass and as they pass, they heal.

My pathetic prayers do not carry much weight in that place where prayers queue up to be heard. But for what it's worth, you are in mine and Margaret's at this time".'

He was 41 when he died. His death was a huge loss to Irish journalism and to his many friends. He is survived by his wife Margaret and two children, daughter Micheline, and son Conor. Sam Smyth, the *Irish Independent* journalist, wrote: 'He will be missed most by those who took the trouble to know him.'

* * *

Tony Hennigan was the opposite to Kevin: an extrovert, full of fun and wit. A wonderful story-teller, a great raconteur, extremely well read. He was a gentle man without an ounce of guile. He was the son of Tommy Hennigan, who used to write a column in the *Evening Herald*. Tony showed the same flair and wrote the James Mulcahy social column in the *Irish Independent*.

I remember the day he joined the *Independent*. He was 18 years of age, just out of school, full of enthusiasm, looking forward to his first job and wondering what the future held. He was in the business because of his father, whom he admired and wanted to emulate. He arrived in the newsroom dressed like a diplomat, wearing an immaculate navy blue three-piece suit, a dazzling white shirt and a light coloured tie. He kind of made the rest of us look scruffy.

Brian Barrett, the group news editor, asked me to look after him and 'show him the ropes.' I introduced him to the staff and gave him a run down on our chaotic *modus operandi*. He appeared in awe of the chaos before him. He asked if he could smoke. I thought it funny that anyone should look for permission to smoke. If he had been relaxed enough to look around him he would have seen half a dozen pipe-smokers and the rest were chain smokers. He was addicted to smoking, but he thought he was still at school. 'Of course, you can smoke,' I replied.

He soon settled down and became very popular. You couldn't help liking him as he had a truly wonderful personality, exuding happiness, damn good company. When he was younger he had ambitions to become a professional actor. He had attended the Brendan Smith Academy where he was very promising, way above average. He could easily have made a successful living out of the theatre. He had parts in a few plays and a small film. He was a member of the Sundrive Players and was well-known on the amateur drama circuit. He won an award for best actor in the RTE Drama Awards in 1981.

He was a brilliant mimic. One day, when there was a lull in the newsroom, he began to mimic the *Herald* news editor, Bill Shine. Bill was one of the old school and a very hard taskmaster, who drove the staff relentlessly. You were expected to go beyond the call of duty to get a story. If you didn't come back with the story you were made to feel about two foot tall. Tony was doing an absolutely hilarious imitation of Bill and we were all doubled up with laughter. However, he failed to notice the door open behind him and Bill quietly walked in. Tony, totally immersed in the part he was playing, didn't realise that we had all stopped laughing and had begun to busy ourselves. Then it dawned on him that something was amiss. He turned around ... I will never forget the look on his boyish face. Instead of getting an Academy award for a great performance he got one hell of a dusting down, interspersed with a lot of sarcastic remarks. Poor Bill himself died tragically a few years afterwards in a traffic accident. Des Rushe, who used to write the Tatler column in the *Irish Independent*, wrote a nice tribute to Tony after the crash: 'He was a gentle person of infinite mirth and of high sensitivity. He was a totally lovable human.' Only 36 years of age, there is no knowing what heights he could have achieved. Instead, his death left a young widow, Cecily, and five young children, the eldest only 10.

* * *

John Feeney, it is fair to say, was a legend in his own lifetime. He was 35 years of age and at the top of his profession when he died. For one so young he had achieved a lot. He had made an outstanding success of his social column in the *Evening Herald*. It was highly controversial and readable. He used all his personality and sharp, mischievous flair to build up a huge readership. The circulation was rising like never before. John had become a well-known Irish personality. Not being a modest man, he would fully agree with that assessment. He had real charisma and was truly a great character, a character in a business which doesn't produce many colourful eccentrics any more. Nowadays, journalists are inclined to take themselves too seriously. They are too busy taking on the world single-handed to indulge in any Feeney-like behaviour.

Earlier, he had been a radical student leader. During his college days he got into every scrape imaginable, but always managed to extricate himself unscathed. He was never boring and his name was always to the forefront of any campaign that happened to be in vogue at the time. He had incredible energy and intellectual ability. He later joined the *Irish Press* as a sub-editor before going on to become a researcher on the prestigious RTE programme 'Seven Days.' In February 1973, he resigned from RTE because of what he described as 'threatening supervision' from the then Fianna Fáil Government. He always revelled in the bit of political drama. He became editor of the *Catholic Standard*.

It was a remarkably brave appointment by the Church at the time. To put someone as unpredictable as John in charge of the mouthpiece of the Catholic Church was an amazing decision. Still, he had a comprehensive knowledge on all religious matters and when he was in UCD, had edited the radical Catholic magazine *Grille*. The views he expressed in the *Standard* frequently incurred the wrath of Catholic conservatives. However, this did not worry John. He never set out to please people and realised at an early age, that in journalism it is always more profitable to go against the tide. His business was to inform and entertain. There is no percentage in sticking with the status quo. People don't want to read what they already know.

He found his final niche in the *Evening Herald* and his Ad Lib column gave him full scope for his particular type of reporting. He loved to exaggerate and twist stories, infuriate people, start controversy. He was a wonderful journalistic catalyst. Some of his stuff was clearly off the wall and he stood on many sensitive toes. There was never any shortage of complaints to the editor. Solicitors' letters were always flying with gay abandon. As far as I know, only one libel action was successful. But the stuffy legal profession and a few sensitive readers weren't going to upset him. He thrived on it. The more feathers he ruffled the better.

He was more than just a good journalist, he was a highly literary person. He wrote several books, his first being a biography of the Archbishop of Dublin, Dr John Charles McQuaid, which was critical, but showed some admiration for his subject. In 1974, he wrote a novel called *Worm Friday* which had a background of television journalism and, in 1977, he published a collection of short stories under the title of *Mao Dies*. In fact, for a time he ran his own publishing company, appropriately called The Egotist Press, and he was involved also in the Irish Writers Co-operative.

John would have been looking forward to that France trip. He was a fluent French speaker and loved to visit that country. Joe Kennedy, while reminiscing on how he nearly came to be on the ill-fated flight, said:

> 'One of John's closest friends was Francois Schelbaum, a truly lovely man. (He also died in the crash). We planned, the three of us, to 'do' all the pubs mentioned in *The Sun Also Rises* and end up in the Place du Contrescarpe, certainly not in a fasionable area today, or ever ... and have a glass of wine as the sun came up.'

* * *

After the crash I carefully filed away the newspaper reports. They are all yellowed and crumbled now. It has been a poignant experience reading them again, reliving the tragedy for this book. It has been sad looking at the young faces peering out from the front pages. It is hard to believe that they are all dead and that it was so long ago.

The Lighter Side

Journalism is a frantic business, full of chaos, dramatic moments, deep tension, plenty of rows and acrimonious inquests. It is dominated by deadlines. That is what causes all the pressure. The best story in the world is no use if you can't make the deadline. You cannot recall the trains and the vans that carry the newspapers to the readers. This can be tough on the blood pressure at times, but it can also provide many hilarious moments. The number of amusing stories and cock-ups are legion. Probably no other profession in the world can produce as many truly funny incidents and have such a big laugh at its own expense. As the old maxim says: 'All human life is there'.

It is only in recent years that the newspapers have begun to produce Corrections and Clarification columns. This provides an important service for the newspaper, the reporter and the public. It immediately rectifies the mistake, mollifies someone screaming at the other end of the phone, and keeps the story accurate for posterity. It can also stave off the odd libel action. The Corrections and Clarifications column sometimes carries the most incredibly embarrassing howlers. Reporters cringe when they see some of their mistakes in the 'sin bin'. However, the whole nature of the business makes this inevitable. In fact, the amazing thing is how we manage to get 99 per cent of our reports accurate.

Here is an example of some of the corrections we have made in *The Irish Times* in recent years. It gives a good idea of what can happen when you are rushing against a deadline and things haven't been checked properly.

> 'A profile of John Walker, one of the Birmingham Six, in yesterday's editions, said he had six sons and a daughter. In fact he has six daughters and a son.'

> 'In yesterday's report of the Merriman Summer School, Professor Denis Donoghue was quoted as seeking an openness to the 'otherness' of the self. This should have read the 'otherness' of the Other.'

> 'A caption in yesterday's editions referred to Ms Teresa Carr as wearing an Ian O'Shanlen. She was, of course, wearing a Tam O'Shanter.'

> 'The report on the conference on rural development in yesterday's editions referred to the de Valera notion of 'food and comfort'. This should have been 'frugal comfort.'

> 'In the Property Supplement on October 24th, Longford was inadvertently placed in Co. Westmeath.'

It is very easy to make a mistake or find yourself in an invidious situation, through no fault of your own. An excited West of Ireland correspondent found himself in such a corner many years ago and provided me with a good laugh. Unfortunately, he was in an impossible position. That is the trouble with journalism, one man's embarrassment can provide another with a huge belly laugh. Yes, it's a cruel life. However, no doubt the correspondent recovered to have his day at someone else's expense.

It happened in the mid-60s, when I was working in the *Irish Independent* newsroom. The correspondent, who was from one of the remoter parts of the West, rang and excitedly told me about the story of five men who nearly drowned. The men had been out fishing in a small boat when it capsized after being hit by a big freak wave. They managed to swim to the safety of the nearby rocks and were none the worse for their ordeal. Our correspondent gave a graphic description of the event. If he was reporting the sinking of the Titanic he could not have been more graphic. When he was finished he said 'How about that for the front page?' I could hear his brain ticking over and saying to himself 'This is at least worth a fiver.' In those days correspondents got paid about three pence a line.

I did not want to be a spoilsport and deflate him too much, but I had to make the point that he had left out the most important part of the story. He hadn't put in the names and addresses of the five men who had escaped a watery grave. 'Oh, Jesus, I can't do that,' our man in the West exclaimed.

'Why?' I asked. 'You know we can't use a story like that. Without names and addresses it simply can't be used. I mean, anybody could make up a story like that. I'm not saying that you have made it up, but there are no hard facts in it.'

He dug his heels in. He was absolutely determined that he was not going to give the names of the men, so I said I'd have to speak to the group news editor, Brian Barrett, about the matter. As I expected, Barrett insisted that we be given the names. I went back to my friend on the phone and gave him the sad verdict. He was distressed and started to mumble about this causing 'problems.' He probably had a vision of his fiver going down the drain. But he remained adamant. He wasn't going to give the names, and that was that.

'Why can't you?' I pleaded with him, wanting to get the complete story and also trying to ensure that he made a few quid.

'Well, it's like this,' he moaned, 'if I give the names, I'll be in trouble locally. All these guys are unemployed and are drawing the dole. If it's discovered that they are also making money fishing they will lose that dole. My life won't be worth living...'.

Stifling my laughter, I told him I'd inform Barrett about his predicament and see if he would make an exception in this case and run the story without the names, although I knew damn well that there wasn't much chance.

Brian Barrett, red-faced, roared: 'Ask him does he want to continue working as a correspondent for Independent Newspapers Ltd?'

After conveying this ultimatum, there was a sharp intake of breath at the other end of the line and he mumbled the immortal lines: 'Well, OK, I'll give you the names, but just remember ... if anyone asks you ... you didn't get them from me.'

When I suggested to the correspondent that people might think he had made up the story if he did not give the names, I was quite serious. It was not unknown for the odd renegade correspondent, with a good imagination and a sharp nose for making a few quid, to fabricate a story which could not be checked out. I remember once working with such an individual on a provincial paper. He was quite a genius really, with an impressive writing style and a wonderful imagination. He was also very fond of Jameson whiskey and needed to be producing a lot of copy to feed his hobby. He used to come into the office with obituaries of 'highly respected' farmers who died in remote mountainy areas who were 'deeply mourned by all and sundry'. Nobody ever heard of these dead farmers and the reason they hadn't was simply because they never existed. He used to dream up their names and then run a list of clichés about their lives. He was eventually found out when his love for Jameson got to such a stage that he had to increase the tally of dead farmers. It was then apparent what he was up to and we did not accept any more copy from him. He took his sacking stoically: he knew he was going to get caught some time. He often dropped into the office afterwards for a chat and a good laugh about his 'stiffs' that never existed. The reason for his visits was usually to ask for a loan, which was actually more of a grant because it was never given back. He lived on the dole and went on to reach a good age.

Whenever reporters come together for a pint and a relaxing chat, they invariably talk shop. They will discuss the latest news and, as the evening wears on, laugh as they recount the legion of cock-ups which have happened over the years. They will invariably get around to the classic story of Maurice Liston and the Reverend Mother.

Maurice was one of the great characters of Dublin journalism in the old days. A big, heavy Limerick man, with a ruddy face, he worked for the *Irish Press* for about 30 years as a general reporter, doubling as agricultural correspondent at times. One day he was told to go out to cover what was believed to be a big fire. They were holding a space on the front page for it.

About an hour later the news editor walked into the Scotch House pub and lo and behold there was Maurice sitting comfortably on a high stool giving due respect to a ball of malt.

'I thought I told you to cover the fire in the convent?' the news editor bellowed.

'Relax, relax,' said the always laid-back Maurice in his inimitable Limerick gutteral accident, 'Sher, I was out at the convent.'

'Well, where's the story?' asked his angry boss. 'There is NO story,' said Maurice calmly.

'You must be joking,' said his boss, astounded, haunted by a big white hole on the front page of the *Evening Press*.

'I was speaking to the Reverend Mother ... and she said there's fuck-all in it,' Maurice explained, emphatically putting an end to the inquisition.

When Bill Shine was news editor of the *Evening Herald* he made an urgent telephone call to one of his reporters who was on an assignment in Derry. He wanted to get the reporter to go over to Donegal to cover a story which had just broken. It was very early in the morning, about 8 a.m., and the reporter had had a very late night and was not anxious to go anywhere. He kept making up excuses as to why he should stay in Derry. Eventually, the exasperated Shine gave up and said: 'They are now putting men on the moon and we can't get a reporter to Donegal.'

About 35 years ago a reporter in the *Irish Press* strolled up to the Gresham Hotel to cover the annual dinner of the Licensed Vintners Association. This was a plum job for any reporter who was fond of the drink. The efficient reporter arrived on time, button-holed the president of the association, and obtained a copy of his speech. He then got on the phone and gave the president's words of wisdom in full to his office. Everything was running according to plan. This job was, as always, a piece of cake. He then rejoined the vintners for a night's heavy drinking. He later recounted the story to me, with tears of merriment running down his face.

> 'The next thing I remember was waking up in this lovely bedroom, with pink curtains and beautiful furniture. I didn't know where I was and I had a terrible hangover. Then, there was a knock on the door and this attractive woman came in with breakfast on a tray.'

The woman opened the curtains and the sun poured in, torturing his bleary eyes. 'Where am I?' he asked ruefully. Then the full story came out. She told him that after he had telephoned his copy to the office, he had joined their table and had been drinking with them all night. At the end of the night they were all in good spirits and they put him into her husband's car and drove to Wexford. 'Jesus Christ, what time is the next bus back to Dublin?' asked the shocked reporter.

Michael Mills, the former political correspondent of the *Irish Press* and later Ombudsman, reminisced on the time he was a young journalist and theatre critic. Addressing a meeting of the Dublin Jewish Students' Union on the theme 'Limits to Free Speech,' he told how he once attended a play which was all about a man who had undergone a sex change. The man had gone to America to have the operation. 'Naturally, I couldn't in those days (the 50s) say he went to have a sex change. So I thought about it for a while ... then I wrote: 'He went to America and came back a changed man.'

Some newspapers will take shortcuts to make sure they make their deadlines. One of the classic cock-ups of all time has to be the *Evening Herald* front page story on the 1970 Budget. The *Herald* graphically described the then Minister for Finance, Charlie Haughey, walking slowly across the Dáil floor to his front bench seat, watched by a full chamber of deputies and a hushed public gallery. It wrote of Mr Haughey opening his briefcase and taking out his budget speech, describing every move Mr Haughey made in flowery prose. It was all highly dramatic. Very readable stuff.

Unfortunately, there was a problem. Quite a big problem, in fact. Haughey wasn't in the Dáil. He never delivered the speech. He was in hospital, seriously injured after falling off his horse at Kinsealy.

How could such a dreadful mistake be made, you may well ask? Well, first of all, the Budget speech usually begins about half an hour before the evening papers put out their final editions. It is therefore only possible to get in a flavouring of what happened on the day.

Realistically, all you can do is write a colour story. It is not too difficult to write a Budget colour story. It's the same procedure every year, plus the picture of the Minister with his briefcase held aloft.

The *Herald* decided to take some harmless poetic licence and build up the atmosphere for the 1970 Budget. That is what the public want and that is what they got. Basically, the Budget story is really for the morning papers.

When my father was a young reporter in the West of Ireland 60 years ago, he was approached one day by a judge after a Circuit Court sitting. The judge was, to say the least, a bit under the weather and had not been able to follow the case he was presiding over as efficiently as he should. He asked my father if he would come over to his hotel and read back his shorthand note of the proceedings so that he could give judgement the next morning. Dad spent about two hours diligently re-reading his notes to the now nearly sober, worried judge.

His Lordship assured him he would be paid for his stenography work. Dad was happy – an extra few quid and all he had to do was keep his mouth shut. The next morning the judge went into court and gave a superb lengthy assessment of the case, full of brilliant quotations, and then delivered an impeccable judgment. Little did anyone know how he managed to do it. Months went by, but there was no sign of a cheque payable to T.P. Kilfeather. Disappointed, Dad made a few approaches to His Lordship, who insisted he would get him the money. Eventually, six months later, a cheque arrived for ten shillings, with a covering letter explaining 'for payment of ostler's fee.' Dad didn't know what an 'ostler's fee' meant. After making a lot of inquiries he discovered that the ostler was the poor devil who looked after the judge's horse in the old days while the court was sitting. He used to get paid an ostler's fee.

Dad enjoyed telling that story. 'Can you imagine how much it must have cost having a bevy of civil servants running around trying to find a pretext for paying out that cheque. A lot more than the ten shillings they gave me?' he chuckled.

He said he would have liked to have framed the ten shilling note and hang it on the wall, but he just couldn't afford to at the time.

One of the classic humorous stories in American journalistic folklore involved Samuel Crowther, of *Journal-American*, a man well-known for his love of alcohol.

An escaped convict took a family hostage in Rhode Island. The news editor, Eddie Mahar, told Sam to get an interview with the convict. Just like that. News editors always expect you to do the impossible.

Sam went off and looked up the address of the family in the telephone book. A few minutes later, he rushed over to Mahar and said: 'Eddie, would you believe it, the convict himself answered the phone and talked with me. He told me that if the police don't get out of there and give him a chance to escape, he's going to kill the family one by one.' Mahar was ecstatic. He shouted 'That's fantastic. Great work, Sam, terrific.'

The interview was splashed in a banner headline across the first edition. Everyone on the staff was excited because this was real old school journalism at its best. The occasion is described vividly by William Randolph Hearst, Jr, in his book, *The Hearsts, Father and Son*.

He wrote: 'About an hour after our story hit the streets, the police closed in, crashed through the doors of the hostages' home, and shot the convict to death. He was identified as so-and-so ... a deaf mute.'

The story had come into the *Journal-American's* wire room from the news agencies. A furious Mahar shouted for Sam and handed him the copy and said slowly: 'Read that'. Sam scanned through the story and turned pale when he read the convict was a deaf mute. His moment of glory had gone. Never a man to be stuck for words, he mumbled: 'Gee, Eddie, the guy never told me that.'

* * *

One of the enjoyable and satisfying aspects of journalism is that you come across a lot of interesting characters and quite a few unusual human interest stories in the course of your work. This is what makes the job so worthwhile and different from other professions. These are the stories that fascinate you, impress you, or amuse you. You come to admire and respect certain people; you come across amusing stories that give you a good chuckle. Covering politics, tribunals, courts, divorce and abortion referendums can be heavy going, quite wearying, so it is always a pleasure to come across a nice human interest story.

These are the encounters I like to think back on, the stories I got a kick out of doing. Rikki Shields most definitely came into this category. He was one of the most committed and determined individuals I have come across.

Rikki Shields was the best lobbyist I ever met. Newspapers are constantly being lobbied by individuals and organisations looking for publicity for their campaigns, but Rikki must rank as one of the best I have come across. He was an Australian aboriginie who arrived in Ireland in February 1990 on a very enthusiastic, if unusual, mission. He wanted to repatriate the 150-year-old preserved head of an aborigine warrior which was in the possession of the Royal College of Surgeons in Ireland. The Tasmanian warrior, known as Shiney, was a bequest to the college over a hundred years ago.

Like most Irish people, I had never heard of the head until this tall, bearded, sincere and committed aborigine arrived into the newsroom and told me of the strange tale of Shiney. At first I was inclined to disbelieve it, but the longer he talked the more I could see how deeply he felt about his mission. He said he would not return to Australia until he got an assurance that the head would be handed over to the aborigine people. He wanted it brought back to Tasmania immediately to be given a sacred burial:

> 'I challenge the college's right to keep the head. Nobody can own somebody else's head. An Irishman cannot own the body of an aborigine from Australia. The college say they got it quite legally. They are using white man's law which was inherited from the British.' He stressed that the head could not die until it got a sacred burial.

You get used to hearing crazy, off-beat stories in the newspaper business, but this one certainly put everything else I had ever come across into perspective. Rikki, who had come to Ireland with some aborigine friends, was not the type to take no for an answer and he had a well defined plan as to how he was going to succeed in getting the head back. He and his friends lobbied politicians and influential people. They even wrote to the Taoiseach and President Hillery. They arranged meetings, they made numerous telephone calls, they wrote letters, they visited Leinster House, they travelled the length and breadth of the country. They wanted the safe return of all other sacred objects and paintings which might be in Ireland.

> 'The British stole these objects, but the Irish are perpetuating the crime. As a matter of goodwill, I'm sure the Irish will agree to give everything back.'

Rikki told me.

Shiney, a nickname given by white settlers is thought to have survived repeated attacks on aboriginal settlements during the mid-1800s that reduced their numbers significantly. Few survived, only those who worked for or co-habited with whites. It is said that Shiney was murdered while working on the Hobart docks and, instead of being buried, his head was preserved and sent to Europe. Rikki said he had never been given the traditional aboriginal ceremony to rest his spirit. 'With our tradition this must be done. His spirit is still crying out in his tribal area, seeking the return of his body for burial.'

The appearance of the aborigines in Ireland demanding the return of Shiney, proved a major embarrassment to the Royal College of Surgeons in Ireland. A spokesman said there had been some requests from the Australian Embassy some years earlier. The college had not agreed to this, as the head had been given to the college through a bequest a hundred years earlier and they had to honour that trust. The head was kept in a safe place and was not on public display because of the controversy surrounding it. I asked the Royal College of Surgeons in Ireland spokesman if he knew how deeply the aborigines felt about the head and if he was aware of the religious traditions of the aborigines, that the head would not die until there was a proper sacred ceremony. The spokesman said they were aware of that. Their view was that scientific research was being served by retaining it.

Eventually, the pressure paid off and the RCSI agreed to hand over the head. The council of the RCSI made its decision after considering a formal written request from the Australian Ambassador to Ireland, Mr Brian Burke. Rikki and his friends were naturally delighted at their success. Rikki sent me a nice letter afterwards, thanking me and *The Irish Times* for our 'sympathetic story'. He added that the college had to comply 'with the will of the Irish people, who, like the Australian aboriginal people, had suffered oppression by the British.'

* * *

Another fascinating and unusual story was the discovery of the body of a big black bear – as large as two men – in the Liffey below Chapelizod, at Longmeadow, in April 1993. The news editor thought it was a bit of a joke when I first mentioned it. In fact, I thought it was a joke myself when I got the tip-off. After all, it's not often that a fully grown bear, dead or alive, is found in the Liffey. You will find plenty of interesting rubbish and get a terrible smell from the Liffey, but bears rarely turn up, dead or alive. The unfortunate animal was discovered floating in the water by a surprised member of the public out walking his dog. After convincing himself that it was in fact a bear, he rang Dublin Corporation.

Corporation officials are used to people ringing them with all sorts of strange stories, and they naturally take some of them with a grain of salt. After the initial scepticism and hesitation, they accepted that the story was true. A team from the Corporation's cleansing department went to the scene. Sure enough, there was the bear. Not as big as King Kong, it nevertheless was a real bear and it was very, very large. 'We have no idea where it came from; it's a mystery to us,' said Noel Carroll, the Corporation's public relations officer. 'We don't find bears in the Liffey every day.'

The Corporation team, after a lot of tugging, managed to get the body ashore. It was levered on to a lorry and taken to the local tiphead where it was buried. One theory was that the bear might have belonged to a circus. It could have died and been thrown into the river, or it could have escaped and fallen in. The owner of a well-known circus which had last been in the area said they had no bears and he did not know where it had come from. The mystery was never resolved.

Another amusing animal story I enjoyed reporting involved two lions who escaped from their circus trailer. It started off badly. I heard the story on RTE's Morning Ireland programme while still lying in bed. Two fully-grown lions escaped from Chipperfield's Circus in Wexford in October 1984 and residents were warned to stay indoors while the search went on for the animals. An hour later my phone rang and I was asked to rush to Wexford to cover the escape. I wasn't exactly pleased to be sent on this assignment. Morning Ireland had covered the story in great detail. As well as having all the facts, they had some graphic eye-witness accounts of the lions roaming around the road and in the nearby gardens. It was great stuff. The evening papers would already be at the scene and I would be arriving after it was well and truly flogged to saturation point. There would be nothing new to report. No reporter likes to be put into that situation. But ours is not to reason why, so I did what I was told. Sure enough, when I arrived the lions had been captured and the circus had moved to Kilkenny. The eye-witnesses had also disappeared. The lions had escaped from their trailer as the circus was leaving Wexford for Kilkenny. It was not known how the lions had escaped, but gardaí were not ruling out the possibility that it could have been someone with a perverted sense of humour who opened the bolt on the trailer.

I wandered up a boreen near the part of the road where the Great Escape had taken place. I went into a small farm yard and asked a man there if he knew anything about the incident. He burst out laughing and told me how 'Sandy', a year-old donkey he had bought that week, was asleep in the field when one of the lions emerged through a hole in the hedge. Nobody had told Sandy that he was supposed to be afraid of the lion, the King of the Jungle. All he knew was that this strange creature was trespassing on his patch. He took a run at the lion and chased it into the next field.

I couldn't believe my luck. Here was a harmless little young donkey putting a big jungle beast to flight. This was a great story. Morning Ireland and the evening papers didn't have that. His owner told me: 'He is only a little donkey, but he wasn't afraid. You might think he would be afraid, but the roles were reversed. The lion didn't wait around; it jumped on to the timber lying against the hedge and ran away.'

I rang the office and told them to tell the photographer to call to the farm to get a picture of the donkey. The next day there was a three column picture of Sandy on the front page of the paper and a story with the heading 'Lion in the Donkey's Den.'

A local Garda said: 'They were fourth generation lions. They were tame. They were bred in captivity. Still, you never know. Maybe, if they got hungry. ...'

* * *

One of the funniest stories I have covered was the case of Dublin Corporation, amid ferocious controversy, buying a 'blank' painting for the Hugh Lane Municipal Gallery of Modern Art. The city councillors had reluctantly agreed after a number of heated debates in January 1981 to buy what some described as the 'blank' painting by Jose Louis Fajardo entitled 'Limit 1980' for £3,500.

After making the purchase, on the recommendation of the curator of the gallery, the councillors went along to the gallery to see the bargain unveiled. They would see for themselves what a fine painting they had got.

The curator, Ms Eithne Waldron, in an address to the gathering, said she hoped 'the controversy will now fade away', now that everybody had seen the paintings in reality (instead of in the ROSC brochure). That was wishful thinking. Councillor Alice Glenn said the exhibition had vindicated the councillors in their earlier criticism. She said the Fajardo was a blank and the public could see it for what it was. Councillor Michael Keating added: 'It is well titled. It is the limit.' In fairness to the councillors, they did try to understand. They were prepared to make the effort to be converted. They diligently stood in front of the painting and looked and looked and looked. But nothing happened. Then they looked at each other and grinned, as though to say 'What in the name of God is this thing called Art?'

'Someone told me,' said Councillor Ned Brennan,

> 'that when he looked at the painting he got a feeling of tranquility. Well, for a few thousand quid I would be looking for something more than tranquility. I don't think this is going to be a major attraction. I'm speaking for the man in the street. It's just for elitist groups and the gin-and-tonic brigade.'

Councillor Frank Sherwin was also in a state of total confusion.

> 'Some people can see things in this, but they should tell me what I'm supposed to see. If I can't understand it, how can the man in the street, who I represent. If you look at a Rembrandt you can see what you see.'

A former Lord Mayor, Billy Cumiskey, looked hard at the painting and came to the conclusion: 'It's an insult to the intelligence of the public.' The Lord Mayor, Fergus O'Brien, said:

> 'I don't see any artistic merit in it, but I'm not an expert on modern art. I would not hang it in my house, but that does not make it bad.'

In his official address, Mr O'Brien said:

> 'I believe that much of what passes for modern art today stretches the imagination
> to the limit, and maybe that is exactly what it should do – stretch the imagination
> to the limit. Some feel that our imagination does not need stretching, but it does.'

He said no generation of artists were entitled to the last say, no more than a particular generation of politicians were entitled to the last say.

> 'It is absurd to accept that the art of Michaelangelo or Van Gogh or Picasso as the
> ultimate, as it is to accept the politics of Plato or Lloyd George or Charles Haughey
> as the ultimate. There will always be something new to be said by the artists and
> politicians.'

* * *

In 1982 there was a lot of concern among Dublin city councillors that the north city was being turned into one big 'rodeo.' It was becoming a status symbol among youngsters to own a horse. There were horses running around every bit of waste ground, every green patch; big horses, small horses, nondescript horses, many running wild. The councillors said the situation had gone 'beyond a joke.' They warned that the horses were a danger to the public. It was like a gymkhana on the weekends – races were held in public places and football pitches had been churned up, especially in the Finglas, Cabra, Artane and Kylemore areas. According to one councillor: 'The children are bringing them to school and tying them up to good Corporation trees.' The horses were so popular that they were being given as Christmas presents.

A politician from Finglas said he was 'blue in the face' complaining about horses. 'Every night there is racing going on. These are not itinerants' horses; they are privately owned and they are kept in back gardens. We have been told the Corporation has nobody trained to catch horses. We have also been told that we are to get a pound to keep the animals in, but that hasn't happened either.'

One diligent member of the council who was a bit too vociferous in his criticism of the horse craze, woke up one morning to find the four tyres of his car had been slashed. 'So much for being a public representative,' he muttered ruefully to me a few days later, begging me not to publish the story or they might do it again.

There was great excitement in August 1982, when one of the horses died in the back garden of a terraced house in Cabra West. The horse used to be brought through the front door, into the hall, into the kitchen and left in the back garden at night. When the family found the horse dead they did not know how to move it. This meant they had to disclose to the Corporation that they were in total breach of the tenancy rules, as they were keeping a large animal on the premises. An SOS was sent to the Corporation, whose officials addressed themselves to the problem. There did not seem to be any way that the beast could be moved, short of demolishing the house.

Then somebody had a brainwave. An enormous crane was hired and driven to the area. It parked outside the house and the huge arm reached over the building. Chains were tied to the horse and it was lifted high over the house on to the road and placed on a refuse lorry. There was prolonged applause from the large crowd of interested by-standers. 'It was some sight,' said the Corporation's public relations officer, Noel Carroll. 'The horse was brought over the building at about 130 feet up in the air. It was quite an achievement.'

My disappointment was that he told me about it afterwards. If I had known beforehand, a photographer could have got an award-winning shot of the horse being hoisted through space. It would certainly have won one of the annual photographic awards. It's not every day one sees a horse – dead or alive – 130 feet up in the air coming across the roof of a terrace of houses.

* * *

Dublin City Council and Dublin County Council always provided interesting off-beat stories. About 15 years ago, the County Council was trying to sort out what to do when seagulls were polluting the Dublin water supply in the reservoir at Leopardstown. It provided quite an amusing sequel. The Council contacted the airport authorities and asked them how they dealt with seagulls. They were informed that there were three ways of frightening off seagulls: a falcon; a repeater gun; or the sound of a wounded gull.

The Council, after much soulsearching, decided to go for the third option and got the sound of a wounded gull. They were quick to point out that they did not run out and strangle an unfortunate seagull and record its last hours. No, they went abroad and got a tape from the British Department of Agriculture. Clever.

So everything was then fine?

Well, not quite. While the tape solved one problem it created another. Local residents – like the seagulls – were disturbed by the amplification of the weird, whining sound of the dying gull, and quickly lodged their complaints. While it did not operate at night, the noise of the gull's agony played over and over, day after day, was enough to drive the residents to distraction. It was no joke sitting in your garden that summer trying to get a tan and hearing a poor seagull giving out his last shrieks. The residents claimed invasion of privacy and threatened all sorts of things on the Council if the infernal machine was not taken away forthwith.

The Council, the servants of the people, always anxious to meet the electorate's wishes, assured the complainants that they would do something about the problem. They made a raft and put the machine on it and towed it out to the centre of the reservoir to see if there was any improvement in the situation.

There were no further debates on the matter. It must have solved the problem, although I always thought that sound travelled even faster on water.

Journalists and Gardaí

There has always been a healthy wariness in relations between the gardaí and the press. Because of the nature of our roles we come into contact a lot. Sometimes this works out happily and satisfactorily, other times it can be a very frustrating experience. The main problem is that reporters are looking for news and the gardaí often don't want to give it. They sometimes feel that if they give out too much news it will hamper their investigations. Journalists become a bit of a nuisance. Naturally, journalists don't agree with this argument and want to get as much information as possible. This usually results in a lot of cat and mouse situations.

I got caught up in one of those ridiculous situations back in 1966. It was the 50th anniversary of the 1916 Easter Rising, an exceptionally busy time in the newsrooms of the Dublin newspapers. Throughout 1966 there was a strong atmosphere of republican nostalgia and numerous events were organised to commemorate the Rising. They were well attended and passed off without serious incident. However, there were a few minor incidents, explosions and demonstrations, carried out by a few extremists which raised the temperature.

A strong undercurrent of tension prevailed. We had more crank calls than usual, promising all sorts of dastardly deeds unless the British got out of Northern Ireland. Thankfully, none of it ever came to anything; it was just armchair republicans giving vent to their impassioned views. Nevertheless, there was always the fear that something major was going to happen. The memory of 1916 was still very much alive in 1966 and all reporters were more or less on red alert, expecting the worst to happen. There was a great buzz of excitement. Every day was full of expectation.

It was against this background that I was sitting one evening in the *Irish Independent* newsroom, listening to the shortwave radio, from which we could eavesdrop on the movements of the gardaí around the city. We weren't sure if this was legal or illegal, but it was a great help in following the movements of the gardaí in run-of-the-mill kind of incidents, such as small robberies, traffic problems, rows and general disturbances. It was better than an army of tip-off men and it was particularly useful for evening paper stories.

Whenever a garda or detective had reason to drop into the newsroom for one reason or another we used to make a dash to turn down the volume of the radio so that it wouldn't be noticed. We didn't want to be told to get rid of it, although a lot of reporters wouldn't have minded seeing it thrown into the Liffey because of the amount of work it sometimes gave us.

However, one evening, as I was sitting quietly half listening to the various instructions being drawled out in heavy provincial accents, there seemed to be a greater urgency than usual in the voices. It was all centred around Kingsbridge station, now renamed Heuston station.

Every patrol car in the city seemed to be converging on the area. 'Will Tango 2 go to Kingsbridge station ... Zebra 5 go to Kingsbridge ... tell Sergeant X and Garda Y to go to Kingsbridge ...' and so it went. I told my news editor about this flurry of activity and was told to get down there as quickly as possible.

I arrived at the station, out of breath and full of anticipation. I don't know what I expected to find there, but I knew in my bones I was on to something. Sure enough, the place was alive with gardaí and plenty of patrol cars and garda bicycles were strewn around the area. The gardaí were both inside and outside the station and walking up and down the platforms. But there didn't seem to be anything amiss. After walking around for a while, I saw an unmarked garda car with three detectives sitting inside. I strolled over confidently, the last of the brilliant investigative reporters, and asked nonchalantly what the story was.

Well, as everyone knows, policemen all over the world invariably answer a question with a question. These chaps were no different. 'Who told you we were here?' one of them asked.

Now this posed a problem. I couldn't very well say 'I've been listening to your radio, old boy.' Not only would that get me into trouble with these guys but it would also pose problems back in the office. The loss of the police radio would be a big blow to the workings of the newsroom in Middle Abbey Street. I was on a sticky wicket.

With what I can only describe as controlled panic, I came up with the brilliant lie: 'We got a tip-off,' I replied, straight faced.

Then followed the inquisition, the third degree...

'Who gave you the tip-off?'

'Sorry, I can't tell you that.'

'Why?'

'Because I don't know?'

'What do you mean you don't know?'

'It was an anonymous caller.'

'What did it sound like? Was it a man or a woman's voice? What did the voice say?'

The barrage continued. I couldn't back out now and played along with the charade, straight batting and lying through my teeth for all I was worth, trying to maintain credibility.

'The person must have given some information?'

'Can't tell you that.'

'Why?'

Then I had a brainwave. I decided to bargain with them: 'If you tell me what the story is, I'll tell you why I'm here and what my informant said on the phone.'

But they weren't going to give me any information and we kept on going around in circles for about ten minutes. In the end, I must confess, I cracked and blurted out: 'It was only a crank call. We get loads of them.'

I was just digging my own grave. They went on practising their interrogation techniques on me. I was fed up and totally frustrated by this time and said: 'Ah, he just said there was a bomb planted here.' I said that because I believed that that was what they were looking for as every hoax call we had got in the office related to bombs.

They laughed and said that wasn't the reason they were there. They convinced me that there wasn't a bomb in the station and I then believed the whole business was just another hoax. I went back to the office and told the news editor that there was no story. As it was late, I left and went home to bed. A night which had begun looking as though I was on to a really good story ended up a big disappointment. I quickly forgot about my frustrating experience.

The phone rang at 3 a.m. and woke me out of a very deep sleep. 'What in the name of Jaysus did you tell the cops down in Kingsbridge tonight?' roared Tony Myles, the assistant late night reporter.

Still half asleep and trying to gather my wits, I replied: 'Oh, I just told them we received a crank call that there was a bomb planted down there, but I assured them that it probably wasn't true, that it was probably a hoax call.'

'Well, all hell has broken lose,' said Tony, the old pro berating the stupid young reporter. 'They have called out the bomb disposal squad and have cordoned off the area.'

'Jes-us Chr-ist,' I moaned. 'Now I'm in the shit.'

I was a deeply worried young man, I can assure you. All sorts of fears rushed through my mind. But, amazingly, I didn't get into any trouble. The incident went by without any comment the next day from any of my superiors. So many other things were going on that yesterday's news – or non-news – was forgotten.

However, while I got off lightly in the office, I didn't escape quite as easily from the gardaí. At least twice a week for the next month a detective used to drop in looking for 'Mr Kilfeather in connection with an incident at Kingsbridge.' Every time the detective was seen entering the building I disappeared out the back door. Then, fortunately, the inquiry was dropped and things got back to normal again.

It was a narrow shave. It is important to have a sixth sense in journalism and to be able to extricate information from reluctant sources, but in this case, through inexperience and lack of judgement, I had made a bad mistake.

Afterwards, I found out that the gardaí were at the station to provide security for some train which was carrying a lot of money. If the gardaí had been straight and told me this simple fact there wouldn't have been any problem. But that was too simple. In those days the gardaí were reluctant to talk to reporters. They wouldn't even comment on the weather or on the most trivial of incidents. In fact, I think this order came down from on high. Anybody found talking to the press was in big trouble. Unless you had some contacts in the gardaí you were lost. I didn't have any contacts, nor had most of my colleagues.

Back in the 60s the only reporters who could get information out of the cops were the crime correspondents. We used to admire them for their tremendous inside knowledge. The two star crime reporters at the time were Jimmy Cantwell, of the *Herald*, and Sean Cryan, of the *Evening Press*. Both used to come under severe pressure from their news desks to provide lead stories. Both men were good friends and used to ring each other to check what they had so that neither would scoop the other and insure that neither got into any trouble with demanding, over-zealous news editors. Survival was the name of the game. They wouldn't or couldn't run an operation like that today.

It was a stupid policy by the gardaí to refuse to disclose even the smallest, most elementary piece of information because it caused all sorts of confusion. When the press was forced to speculate the gardaí complained about inaccurate reports, yet they were doing nothing to help the situation. The gardaí usually came off worst in these situations. Today, the gardaí have set up a press office which acts as an important link with journalists. This has made a big improvement, although there is still a long way to go before it can be considered perfect.

One particular case which springs to mind in the 60s which clearly showed the obduracy and arrogance of the guards, involved a riot which took place on O'Connell Bridge, Dublin. Some protesters – I think they were members of the Dublin Housing Action Committee – decided to make their case by sitting down on the bridge and disrupting the traffic. The gardaí, after making an unsuccessful attempt to negotiate their removal, eventually decided to use force. A few batons were brandished with gay abandon and some people were injured. One of the injured was a reporter from the *Irish Independent*. Naturally, when this chap got back to the office he wasn't going to write a eulogy about the gardaí. With his head still spinning from the blow of a baton he wrote a scathing report on Garda brutality.

The news editor felt the report was a bit emotional and one-sided (and who could blame the writer?), so I was asked to get the Garda response to give our coverage some balance. Do you think I could get any co-operation from the men in blue? Not a chance. I spoke to about three very senior officers, pointing out that we had a strong report coming out the next day highly critical of the gardaí and we would like to carry their side of the story. Not only did they not appreciate being given an opportunity to comment, they were downright abusive. 'We don't have to talk to anyone, we don't have to explain our actions to anyone, we don't care what you write.' That was the reply. One senior gentleman went so far as to tell me to 'fuck off.'

However, it was as a result of that O'Connell Street incident that the whole business of gardaí dealing with riot situations was examined at top level. Relations with the press were also carefully looked at around that time. Eventually the gardaí learned how to deal with protests and press queries. There is now a much better attitude and a more civil relationship exists between the gardaí and the press. Not that everything is all roses and light. Far from it; there are still instances where photographers and reporters are being hindered by misguided, over-zealous gardaí while trying to control protest marches or street incidents. These are isolated instances, but they do exist.

* * *

Another serious incident, which occurred in the mid-70s, also did not did nothing to increase my esteem for the gardaí. I had been sent to the Mansion House to cover a highly controversial Sinn Féin rally. I left the meeting before it ended and walked back towards *The Irish Times*. I had almost reached the bottom of Grafton Street when I noticed a man following me closely, step for step. Next thing he jumped in front of me and flashed a badge and shoved me into a doorway. I hadn't a chance to look closely at the badge, but presumed he was a detective. He immediately began quizzing me about the meeting. His attitude was not exactly friendly. He asked me my name and address, which I gave him. He then laughed derisively and said 'Tell me the truth.' He wouldn't accept that I lived in Co. Wicklow. Subversives don't live in rural areas. He kept insisting that I tell him my real address and I told him I knew quite well where I lived. I then told him I was a reporter. He thought this hilarious. He didn't believe me. This guy believed nothing. I was getting angry at this stage and I fumbled in my pocket and produced my press card. That produced a dramatic change in his demeanour. He became very conciliatory. 'Oh, yes, Frank. How are you, Frank? Sorry about that, Frank.' He was acting as though he had known me all his life. 'Could you tell me what went on at the meeting?' he asked, all courtesy. I wasn't in the mood for his sudden change of tack. Having been taken aback by his belligerent attitude and unreasonableness, I wasn't in the mood for co-operating with him. Having been roughly bundled into a doorway on one of the most public streets in Dublin with hundreds of people passing by wasn't the best way to win friends and influence people. I said he knew damn well what was going on inside at the meeting. It was a public meeting and was probably crawling with undercover detectives. They also probably had a few bugs placed in the hall. 'If you want to know what went on, ask your colleagues who are inside,' I told him. 'Failing that, read *The Irish Times* tomorrow.'

That was the end of that. I then went back to the office and did my report on the meeting. I was tempted to write a piece about the 'obstruction of a journalist in the line of his duty,' but I refrained from doing so. I was annoyed about the incident for a long time. It was no way for the gardaí to act. He had no right to lay a hand on me and push me into that doorway. He probably thought he was 'protecting the State', or some other high-falutin excuse, but he was going the wrong way about it. I'm part of this State and that was no way to treat a citizen.

* * *

During the visit of President Reagan in June 1984, I had another first hand encounter with the gardaí acting out of control. A policy decision was apparently made to ensure that Reagan would see no sign of any opposition to his visit to Ireland or disagreement with his foreign policy. The gardaí followed this directive with absolute dedication and enthusiasm. There was no sign of any protester along any of the presidential routes. Any marches that did take place were re-routed far away from American eyes.

At 8.06 p.m. on Sunday, 3 June, President Reagan's cavalcade passed the Bank of Ireland building at Ormond Quay, beside Capel Street Bridge, on its way to a banquet in Dublin Castle. As it did a tall young student with glasses and a wide-brimmed hat moved towards the crush barrier, waved an anti-Reagan poster and shouted 'Reagan out.' Instantly, a Special Branch detective appeared from nowhere, jumped on his back and flung him to the ground, cracking the back of his head on the pavement with a horrific thud. I was standing beside him and jumped out of the way. So did two fathers with young children on their shoulders. The student's friend tried to defend his injured colleague, who was now on the ground semi-conscious, but he was roughly bundled away. The motorcade sped by and the incident was over in seconds.

The young man lay stunned and shocked in Capel Street for about 10 minutes, lying on the pavement. He then picked himself up and walked with his friend to Middle Abbey Street. The Special Branch walked a short distance behind them. I followed them, accompanied by a colleague from the *Irish Press*, walking on the other side of the road. In Middle Abbey Street I asked the injured man a few questions. He said he was a student at Trinity College and was not in favour of Reagan's visit.

> 'All I did was put up a poster. I did not think that this could happen in a country like Ireland. I just held up the poster and the next thing I was smashed to the ground.'

As we were talking a patrol car swung around the corner and three gardaí jumped out and grabbed the students. I asked what they were doing. They asked me my name. When I informed them I was a reporter they looked for identification. I showed my press card and special Reagan Visit accreditation card and they warned me to 'clear off.' I inquired what were they charging the student with. They wouldn't answer, but when I persisted, they laughed and said 'The Offences Against the State Act' (a very powerful law whereby you can be detained for a period without any explanation or charge being made against you). It's a catch-all charge which is often used by the gardaí when they want to hold someone for questioning.

Later that night I rang the gardaí to see what had happened the young men. They explained they had been released without any charge being preferred against them. Exactly what I thought would happen.

I don't want to appear too anti-Garda – and things have improved over the years – but here was a case of a student holding up a poster, getting knocked to the ground, detained in a Garda station and then released, basically for doing nothing unlawful. It was a case of excessive zeal by the gardaí and if I hadn't been there to witness it I wouldn't have believed it. I wrote a detailed report of the incident in *The Irish Times*, but it went by without any public reaction. I found the whole thing quite disturbing.

Threats, Bribery and Intimidation

Most reporters at some time in their careers have been threatened, offered bribes or subjected to intimidation, verbal or physical. These usually do not amount to anything serious or dangerous, but they occur nevertheless and they can be unnerving and unpleasant at the time. On every paper I have worked on I have been subjected to some intimidation or veiled threats.

The first threat I ever received took place 35 years ago in a cemetery, quite an appropriate place to be given a warning. It wasn't serious or too malicious, but just enough to make you think more carefully about what you were doing.

The *Irish Independent* rang me in Wicklow and said they wanted a fairly comprehensive report on the funeral that afternoon of the King of the Gypsies in Rathnew cemetery, two miles outside the town.

'The King of the WHAT?' I asked, quite surprised. 'Yeah, apparently this guy was King of the Gypsies and he has died in Spain. His relations and friends are bringing him back and burying him in Rathnew, where he originally came from,' said the voice in Dublin.

I was given a few instructions as to what type of report they wanted. The *Independent* was very keen on this story. It's not every day there is a royal funeral in Ireland. In fact, if it happened today they would send down one of their own reporters and a photographer. However, in those days there was a lot of penny-pinching, so they had to rely on me, their Wicklow correspondent. When I eventually got into the 'big time' and got a job with the *Independent* in their Dublin office, I was cut five pence on a bus fare to Dun Laoghaire by an over-conscientious news editor who seemed to think he was dispensing his own money. I don't know what he was like when he was young and on the road, but he certainly had a very suspicious mind, which didn't do me any favours.

The funeral was supposed to be at 3 p.m. I was there 15 minutes early to ensure that I wasn't going to miss this 'scoop.' I also knew the *Independent* were prepared to pay well for this one and I wasn't going to screw up. Three o'clock came and went and there was no sign of any funeral. It was a lovely sunny day and as I sat on a tombstone in the tranquility of the cemetery, I began to think the *Independent* had been misled. It was not unusual for a newspaper to get a bum tip-off or even set up for a hoax.

I was just about to leave, and had made up my mind to send the *Independent* a hefty bill for my time, when a large very expensive looking hearse and about ten also very up-market black limos pulled up with a screech of brakes, a cloud of dust, and a babble of very loud voices. Within minutes the place was alive with a lot of very upper class gypsies. Many of them were dressed like company executives, beautiful suits and accessories. In fact you would have been convinced they were executives except some of them had ear rings. They had chartered two planes to bring the family and mourners to the funeral. It was all very impressive, quite befitting a royal funeral.

I immediately moved in among them, notebook in hand, asking a lot of questions, but not exactly getting many answers. At least not getting many straight answers. Gypsies are suspicious of outsiders and someone like me snooping around at a sensitive time like that wasn't going down too well. Still, I had a job to do, so I continued asking my questions. I was trying to find out the King's name, his age, how long he was King, who elected him, when did he leave Rathnew etc? All quite basic stuff, or so I thought. Suddenly, I felt about five of them close in on me. I began to feel a bit worried. Maybe outsiders were not allowed to attend this private occasion? They firmly and courteously shepherded me away to a quiet, leafy corner, where they began to ask a succession of questions. The tables were being reversed in no uncertain terms. Who was I, they wanted to know. What paper did I work for? Who told me about the funeral? What was I going to write? I told them the truth and said this was considered to be important news and the *Independent* was anxious to get a report on it.

'Yeah, it's important alright,' said one rather large gentleman in a three-piece suit with a very brown, weatherbeaten face. 'And you better do a good job on it,' he added menacingly.

'Of course,' I replied, 'What else would I do?'

'We don't want any disrespectful report appearing tomorrow,' my captor insisted.

'Why would I do that?' I asked, explaining that I was just there to get the basic details and send them to Dublin.

'Because we are used to newspapers twisting things about us and we don't want to see it happen again on this occasion,' said one of the mourners.

I assured them that they had nothing to fear and that I wasn't in the business of making up funny stories and that I wouldn't try to ridicule the occasion.

The big man, who appeared to be the leader (maybe the next King?) said I had better be right as they would be reading all the newspapers the next day. Then he added the words which will always remain in my mind: 'If you try to make a joke out of this, we'll find you ... it doesn't matter where you go on this planet, we'll find you.'

Well, as you can imagine, I sent the straightest, most accurate and reliable story I have ever written in my life to Dublin that day, warning the news editor not to change a word in it or it would have serious repercussions for me. Anyway, the gypsies must have liked it and I never heard anything further about it.

* * *

Around the same period in the early 60s I walked into a much more dangerous situation. There was a large fertiliser plant in Wicklow town at the time. It was the biggest factory in the area and a good employer of local men. Unfortunately, one day there was a major leak of a highly toxic chemical from the factory into the nearby harbour and bathing area. This posed a serious danger to swimmers and marine life. I sent the story to the *Evening Herald*. It turned out to be the lead, spread across five columns. It was an important story and I thought I had written it well; that I had done a good professional job.

My satisfaction was turned to fear three days later. A man who fancied himself as one of the civic leaders of the town met me as I was walking to my office. He caught me by the lapels and pushed me up against a wall. He then stuck his face into mine and snarled: 'Do you know the fucking damage you have caused this town by that sensational story about the fertiliser plant? You have ruined this town. No tourists will come and you have frightened the locals off swimming ....' He continued to abuse me for a few minutes, issuing all sorts of warnings about my future, and shaking me at the same time. He was a big chap and very strong. His fingers around my throat were so tight that I felt I was going to choke.

He withdrew his hands and I mumbled my excuses. I explained that other newspapers also had carried the story. It wasn't the sort of thing that could be suppressed. It was important that the public should know about such a danger. I don't remember much of the conversation now.

After getting a few more rough shoves off the wall and further abused, he moved on. I told nobody about the incident but it was a real eye-opener as to the reaction in a small town to a bad press. I would have been within my rights to report him for assault, but I decided to let it pass.

* * *

Another occupational hazard in journalism is bribery. There is always someone out there who feels he can get anything he wants by putting a few quid up front. Most attempts at bribery arise out of court cases and they are usually of a pathetic nature. I was only six months in the business when I was sent to cover Drogheda District Court.

A man was given a hefty fine for making poteen. It was an interesting case and there was some very good evidence in it. It was definitely a newsy story and highly readable. However, as I was leaving the court building afterwards the poteen-maker sidled up to me and whispered:

'That'll be alright, I presume,' pushing a handful of fivers into my pocket. Quite taken aback, I said it would not be alright and pushed the money back to him. That was an awful lot of money at the end of the 50s, as I was earning two pounds, ten shillings.

Then there are the cases of people being drunk or disorderly, or maybe up on an assault charge. They are highly embarrassed and nervously come to you afterwards begging you to keep the story out of the paper. They offer you money and ask you not to use the case. The usual excuses are 'because my mother is dangerously ill in hospital and if she reads it she will die', or 'if my boss reads this I'll lose my job.' Some of these cases can be quite harrowing, but you cannot start to make an exception for anyone, otherwise the floodgates will open. An old editor on one of the provincial papers I worked on remarked once: 'They should have thought of their mother or their job before they made a fool of themselves.' I suppose that is a bit harsh but it is true. We could not bend the rules for some and headline others. Thinking that they can buy their way out is pathetic. Some defendants seem to think that it is the done thing and arrogantly offer a bribe without any apology or embarrassment. I have never heard of a reporter taking money to keep a story out of print. It could have happened, but I certainly never heard of it.

A well-known Dublin journalist once jokingly remarked: 'There is no need to bribe journalists, just flatter them.' Now, there's some truth in that. There may not be much dishonesty in broadsheet journalism, but there are quite a few big egos, people who believe that what they write should be engraved in stone. Many are intoxicated with the opium of the by-line and feel they have a greater influence than in fact they actually have.

When it comes to subtle intimidation, politicians are masters. In the provinces they may know the managing director or the editor and if they are not getting their way with you or are unhappy with a story you wrote or didn't write, they will always come up with the veiled threat, 'Otherwise, I'll have to talk to so and so about this.' Politicians are generally quite demanding and most of them are quite paranoid. They are always looking for publicity and will go to any lengths to achieve it. When they do get publicity they sometimes feel that it wasn't properly presented in the media. They then start to pick on the reporter, accusing him of misquoting, misinterpreting or not giving the whole story. They always feel they are not getting enough space in the papers. They will come to you complaining that what they said had been cut so drastically that the report did not make sense and what they believed to be the most important part of their speech never saw the light of day – the report picked out one paragraph and sensationalised it etc., etc. It happens all the time. Politicians are very insecure and this builds up their paranoia. They are always under threat from somewhere, often from within their own party. They sometimes think that reporters are out to get them, or that their opposite number is more favoured by the press and therefore gets more publicity. They will point out all the work they are doing in their constituency, but stress that they are not getting credit for it, while their opposite number, whom they will allege does not work as hard, is constantly getting his picture in the paper. Daily bitching from politicians, no matter how high up they are on the political ladder, even at ministerial level, is an almost daily experience for reporters, but it is generally not malicious and it is often done with a rueful smile. On the other hand, there are the politicians who like to bully and say they will have you fired.

However, the greatest intimidation I have ever suffered was at the hands of the GAA while I worked as a junior reporter in the provinces. Thirty-five years ago, the GAA felt it could dictate the amount of publicity it should get. If it was getting three pages of the paper, it pressed for four; if it was four, it should be five. It could not tolerate any form of criticism. If you criticised any aspect of the GAA there had to be some ulterior motive behind it, some plot, trying to do it harm. It had the classic siege mentality and if you became embroiled you got badly burned.

In my early days in Wicklow, I attended a few football and hurling matches which put warfare into the halfpenny place. I naively thought my job was to report on the outbreaks of violence as well as the match itself. I always fully reported vicious incidents, on and off the pitch. Being a keen sportsman, I love all forms of sport, but I believe in fair play and I don't like to see a few thugs on the field or a similar breed in the crowd ruin the spectacle for everybody else. Some of the things I saw were quite shocking. Yet, while I may have thought they were shocking, some of the officials of the clubs concerned did not think such behaviour should be commented on in the media. Successive meetings of the County Board condemned me for giving the GAA a bad press. 'He mustn't have been at the match I attended,' was one of the favourite remarks, as the delegates made excuses for the behaviour of their teams on the field. 'He's harming the Association and bringing it into disrepute,' was another. They brought a new meaning to the word sensitivity. Reports had to be all one way – complimentary – or they set out to impede you, even at the highest level.

There was a prominent GAA official who had big political ambitions and numerous articles began to appear regularly in the national press about him. These articles weren't exactly complimentary and he became quite incensed and began to behave totally irrationally. He tried to put two and two together and came up with seven. He concluded that I was behind this 'campaign to vilify' him. Nothing could have been further from the truth. Admittedly, I did act as correspondent for the *Independent* and *Evening Herald*, but I never wrote any of the articles which offended this individual. He made it his business to cause as much trouble for me as possible. Every County Board meeting he and his supporters condemned me and my paper for being 'irresponsible.' Then he found out that I played rugby for Blackrock College on Saturdays and I was, therefore, in his narrow-minded opinion, 'not qualified' to report on our national games on Sunday. This all happened in the bad old days of the 'ban', when bigotry, with a capital B, reigned supreme. The atmosphere was really torrid. Looking back on it now, more than three decades later, it was unbelievably oppressive, vicious and insidious. I felt scared at times and was also worried that I would lose my job because I had heard that they had been in contact with head office about this 'trouble maker.' They began asking for a 'real reporter' to be sent out to cover our national games.

It was a chapter in the GAA's history that they need not feel too proud about. Even Jack Lynch, the former Taoiseach, was once banned from the GAA for attending a rugby match. He had just captained the Cork senior hurling team in a victorious All-Ireland final, one of the famous four in a row, in 1943. He was told that by attending the match he had suspended himself. 'What that meant,' said Lynch many years later, 'was that I was seen either going into, or coming from the final Irish Trial, and someone had reported me.' The hypocrisy was so bad in those days that the person who would report you would be there to see the rugby match himself.

It got to the stage in Wicklow where a motion was put down to have me banned from all GAA grounds in the county. They spent three hours debating it while I sat taking a shorthand note of all the abuse and trying to look as calm and unconcerned as it is possible for a 21-year-old to be in a very rough adult world. Luckily, I had a lot of friends in the GAA and they spoke in my favour, although I did not like the way some of them went both ways by qualifying their support with claims that I was young and inexperienced and did not know what I was doing. As it transpired, the motion to have me banished from all the GAA grounds in the county was defeated. It reached the point where I was half hoping that I would be banned from their grounds because I was fed up with their antics and constant harassment. It was something I could do without. After the vote I resumed covering the matches on Sundays in hail, rain and snow. There were still the odd rumblings, but no further action to stop me doing my job. The standard of football and hurling did not improve either and the Sabbath was the one day of the week that I never looked forward to. But it was one of the hazards of working on a provincial paper in those times. It was, in retrospect, great experience and taught me to grow up pretty fast. Today the infamous 'ban' is gone, as is most of the bigotry, and things have certainly changed for the better. However, covering GAA affairs in Wicklow 35 years ago has left a life-long scar on me.

The Beef Tribunal

In the early days of the old Soviet Union, innocent people had a fear of being sent to Siberia. There was a similar feeling in Dublin journalism in 1991. In this instance, it was the fear of being sent to report on the Beef Tribunal. Reporters ran for cover, made up excuses to get out of it, begged news editors not to send them, explaining that they had other urgent matters to attend to. I used to go up to Dublin Castle at the beginning of the tribunal to help out our team there.

However, in no time I was put on it full time and ended up leading the team – a claim to fame I could well do without. It was undoubtedly the worst perience of my life. None of us know how long we are going to live, but I'm ite sure the long-drawn out beef saga has shortened my time on this planet. ing incarcerated in the castle for two years has left deep scars. In fact, the emory of it is so bad that I put off the writing of this chapter for months. It was idoubtedly the most complex and onerous assignment I have ever had the isfortune to cover. It was very intense, with solicitors' letters flying all around the place; there were accusations, recriminations and threats; there were numerous rumours of people going to be sued or threatened with some legal action.

Due to the intricate nature of the evidence there was always a danger of making a mistake. Trying to explain to the public the complicated operations of government departments, the workings of the beef, finance and insurance industries, day after day, was mentally and physically exhausting. Trying to understand and unravel the huge morass yourself was difficult enough, but putting it into English for the ordinary man or woman on the street to understand was another matter. So much had to be checked and double-checked. There were times we sat in the press room and looked at each other and said: 'What in the name of Jaysus was that witness talking about?'

None of us realised it would last for so long. When it started on 21 June 1991, they were laying the foundation stone for a hotel in nearby Christchurch Place. When it finished the hotel was in full operation. When the tribunal commenced, *The Irish Times*' reporters were using typewriters; when it ended we were all using computers. The terms of reference were far too wide. A big chunk of my life went in that tribunal. It had its good side of course. The regular reporters condemned to cover it built up a good working relationship and a fine camaraderie developed. Only for that there would have been a few nervous breakdowns. I must say, in all modesty, we did a damn good job. It showed how newspapers could provide a really first class information service for their readers.

Yet, because it went on for so long, we became battle-weary and started asking ourselves 'Is anyone out there reading this any more?'

Then, to relieve the monotony, we set up a forecast 'book', with predictions as to when the nightmare would end. You paid a pound a guess and the winner took all. One day the chairman of the tribunal, Mr Justice Liam Hamilton, came into the press room and I asked him if he would like to 'buy a line.' He diplomatically declined and said: 'Would any of you hazard a guess as to how long it will take me to prepare my report?' There were no takers. As it transpired, he took a year.

Another day, when he dropped in for a chat, I rushed to stand in front of a poster we had erected on the wall, which I did not want him to read.

The poster said:

'Cows may come
And Cows may go,
But the BULL in this place goes on forever.'

He might not have appreciated the joke. Although, on the other hand, he probably would, because he showed throughout the tribunal that he had a good sense of humour. This is probably one of the reasons that kept him and the rest of us battling on. There were some bumpy and distinctly unsettling moments when major controversies erupted during the hearings. While he got some very good publicity and became a household name, which was unusual for a judge, he also came under a lot of fire. It wasn't an easy job to handle, but he proved he was the best person for it. As politics and law became entangled, issues sometimes built up to fever pitch. He made it perfectly clear that he was not going 'to allow this tribunal to become a political football.' He held his nerve admirably.

Yet he was not able to get the information that was vital to the tribunal. He could not get any evidence on Cabinet discussions. The matter came to a head when the State legal team, acting on the instructions of the Attorney General, Mr Harry Whelehan, intervened to prevent one of its own witnesses, the former Minister for Industry and Commerce, Mr Ray Burke, from answering questions about a crucial cabinet meeting in June 1988. Mr Justice Hamilton, exasperated, said he had been appointed to carry out this inquiry and there were certain questions that he had to ask. Mr Whelehan then referred the matter of cabinet confidentiality to the High Court, where Mr Justice O'Hanlon ruled against him. Mr Justice O'Hanlon pointed out that it had not been unknown in other countries for totally corrupt governments to come to power and for their members to enrich themselves at the expense of the State. Were such a situation ever to arise in Ireland, the effect of Mr Whelehan's submissions would be to prevent any tribunal of inquiry from obtaining the information it needed to establish guilt where guilt existed.

I thought this was a good judgment. The point was being made that if Cabinet confidentiality operated as the Attorney General thought it should, then not merely could no tribunal ever uncover corruption if it existed at government level, but the whole basis of Irish democracy would be fundamentally deficient. The rights of the Government would be more important than the interests of the people. This victory was short-lived. The ruling was appealed to the Supreme Court and overturned by a three to two decision. I don't think this was a good decision and it doesn't do much for democracy. Besides, in practice, it is a bit of a farce, as every reporter, backbencher and civil servant knows within minutes of a cabinet meeting ending of what transpired there. As they say, there is no such thing as a secret in Ireland once more than two people know about it. The new Government under John Bruton said it would amend the situation and make the running of government more transparent. Later, it said that the matter was a bit more complex than they had at first thought, and a referendum would be necessary.

The highlights of the tribunal were the appearances of the former and the then current Taoisigh, Charlie Haughey and Albert Reynolds. The inquiry had been going into long periods of boredom until Messrs Haughey and Reynolds arrived on the scene. This was what the public wanted. This was what news editors wanted. People could understand this. This was a change from listening to cautious accountants, meat plant workers and tedious civil servants. Attendance figures at the tribunal quadrupled. Politicians, party supporters, hangers-on and curious members of the public crammed the room, which was large, but not sufficient for such crowds. Some stood outside in the hall, others even tried to take over the press seats. We were under enough pressure without this. Tony O'Brien, of the *Irish Independent*, had to ask a woman and her two children to remove themselves from the press benches.

Haughey, who had originally set up the tribunal, was quite calm and controlled while giving evidence, although he got a bit tetchy at times when under heavy cross-examination. At the end of his evidence, one of the counsel for the State, Mr Henry Hickey SC, complained about the way in which Mr Haughey had been cross-examined by one of the tribunal's lawyers, Mr Eoin McGonigal SC. He said that no other witness had been subjected to the same intense, heavy questioning, which he felt had exceeded fair legal interrogation.

However, Mr Justice Hamilton, smiled, turned to Mr Haughey and said: 'I'm sure Mr Haughey has no complaints about the way he was treated during his visit?'

Mr Haughey replied he hadn't, but then, after a short pause, he changed his mind and made clear that he wasn't too pleased at the questioning he had been subjected to. He also took a swipe at Mr Justice Hamilton, whom, he said, had stated at the outset of the tribunal that he was going to deal with members of the press who had in the first week of the proceedings written inaccurate reports about him (Haughey). The press, he said, had treated the allegations made against him and the Government as fact, when in reality they were only allegations with nothing to back them up. This had very seriously reflected on him and his good name.

Mr Justice Hamilton said he had not done anything about this because he understood that Mr Haughey was raising the matter in 'another place'. Mr Haughey then left the witness box and walked slowly down the room, looking straight ahead, averting his gaze from the press bench as he went by, out the door and out of public life; his contribution to Irish politics over. He said he was now going home to his 'bucolic pursuits'. Albert Reynolds' performance in the witness box was considerably less articulate and his evidence rambled all over the place. Every time he was asked a question he answered with a speech. I understand it was the same in London when he took his libel action against the *Sunday Times*.

Reynolds loves to talk and once he gets going he can't stop. He is a natural affable, old style politician. Yet, he was highly impatient at the tribunal, and from the moment he entered the building, he let it be known that he was 'a busy man' and that he had 'a country to run'. He stressed that while he was there to help, they should expedite matters for him, as he had many important issues to deal with. He complained later to the chairman that the lawyers were repeatedly asking him the same questions. He said he couldn't be expected to keep on answering the same questions. He asked the chairman to point this out to the legal teams. Mr Reynolds maintained that all they were doing was 'going round and round the mulberry bush'.

He proudly told the tribunal that he ran the Government like he had operated his successful business ventures. He revealed his *modus operandi*: he was not a man to get bogged down in bureaucratic red tape. He boasted that he was a 'one-page man'. He always required a one-page synopsis of a situation. If he wanted any further information he knew where to go for it. He explained with obvious pride that he had been around a long time in business and that had stood him well in politics. He certainly provided the most explosive outburst of the whole two years of the tribunal when he accused the former Minister for Industry and Commerce, Mr Des O'Malley, of being 'reckless, irresponsible and dishonest' in the giving of his evidence. Counsel for Mr O'Malley asked him to withdraw the allegation, or modify it, to even substitute the word 'inaccurate' for dishonest. Mr Reynolds would not budge. This allegation resulted in plunging the country into a general election, during which Mr Reynolds use of strong words again came into question. He used the word 'crap' in a television interview and later had to apologise for it.

After his first day in the witness box he was upset when told that he was required to come back the next day. He repeated that he was a busy man and was prepared to stay there until midnight to finish his evidence. He said he usually worked long hours. For instance he had been awakened by a telephone call at 3 a.m. that morning to discuss the GATT Agreement. Mr Justice Hamilton said it would not be in the best interests of the tribunal to sit so late. While Mr Reynolds may be a man of limitless stamina, he himself was not. 'That is why you are Taoiseach and I am a humble President of the High Court,' he added jokingly.

Mr Michel Jacquot, Director of FEOGA, the EU's agricultural, guidance and guarantee fund, told the tribunal that all member states were watching the inquiry. He was sure that Ireland and the other states would benefit from the work being done. 'Ireland has given all the other states very good example.'

During cross-examination, Mr Jacquot was asked a heavy convoluted question, which he found hard to cope with. He then gave the unforgettable answer: 'That is like trying to determine the sex of angels'.

When his evidence was completed, the Mr Justice Hamilton asked: 'By the way, what sex do you think angels are?'

Confused for the second time, the unfortunate Frenchman replied: 'I don't know, but I'm named after the Archangel Michael ... and he was masculine.'

Half way through the tribunal hearing – after about a year – Mr Justice Hamilton said that if the questions relating to beef exports had been properly and fully answered when they were put during *Question Time* in the Dáil there would have been no need for the tribunal. So, there we had it in a nutshell. A year into the tribunal's proceedings, we got this gem of information, that this £30 million extravaganza would not have been necessary if the civil servants had drafted proper answers to be used in the Dáil. All we could do was laugh in the press room.

In fact, the evidence showed that the civil servants were delighted when one of their younger colleagues was able to give a reply to a deputy that was so minimal as to be meaningless. But it wasn't surprising really. Any reporter who has ever covered the Dáil knows only too well that this is par for the course. Deputies sometimes put down brilliant questions and the press wait with bated breath for the reply. Instead they get a convoluted load of meaningless verbiage in return. The Minister who reads out the answers has a file full of the detailed answers should the deputy get a chance of pursuing his question, which he never does really because there are so many other TDs pressing to get their questions dealt with. The Ceann Comhairle never allows Question Time to 'become a debate,' so many interesting, well constructed questions never get properly answered. A Minister can truthfully say afterwards that he never gave the full answer because he was not asked. It is sharp practice, but a trend that has been going on since parliament was invented. Ministers will only give the opposition the bare minimum amount of information on what they consider to be sensitive issues. If it is a TD from his own party he is likely to get a more comprehensive response. But a TD from his own party won't ask any difficult questions in public. Therefore, Mr Justice Hamilton's observation was quite correct. There would have been absolutely no need for the tribunal if the questions in the Dáil relating to beef had been answered properly.

In the second year of the proceedings, the public was well and truly fed up with the beef tribunal and most people certainly were not bothering to read the reports. It was all one big bore. It became the subject of satire and comedians joked about it on the Dublin stage. Yet, it was important that the papers gave it full coverage every day because of the amount of impropriety being revealed in so many sectors of our national life. But for us at the coalface, it was a thankless job. There is nothing worse than to have members of the public coming up to you and saying 'God, Frank, I gave up reading that months ago'. Because the tribunal was so difficult to report and to get to grips with, this attitude was annoying. Every journalist likes to think that his reports are being read somewhere out there. The public attitude was highly discouraging. The only bright spot in the depression was the attitude of the chairman, Mr Justice Hamilton. He conducted the proceedings in an impeccable manner, even though I suspect there were times when he was totally frustrated and exasperated by some of the long-drawn out legal submissions and technical arguments. Some of the stories being written outside the tribunal must also have caused him upset. But he stuck at it manfully. The tribunal was also run in a very civilised manner, with a coffee break at 11 a.m. each day. This was really a 'smoke break' for Liam Hamilton. He is one of the heaviest smokers I have seen in my life.

The big interest of the public was in the astronomical salaries of the barristers. The senior lawyers were knocking down about £2,000 a day, while the juniors were getting £1,300 a day.

Even on the days when the tribunal was not sitting they were getting paid. There were also quite a few lengthy adjournments. Nice work if you can get it. A total of £3.2 million was granted to Larry Goodman's lawyers and advisers by the Taxing Master, a figure that was quickly contested by the Government.

The public, as taxpayers, were right to be interested, but these figures seemed to dwarf the rest of the proceedings. The whole purpose for which the tribunal was set up was being hijacked by one issue. Yet, other outrageous issues being reported seemed to be ignored by the public, which could never get to grips with the intricacies of the inquiry. I suppose they just became weary of trying to understand the morass of words and technical expressions. I can just assure those people who suffered from lethargy that the press corps went to great lengths and did its best to try to make it as interesting as possible.

When the tribunal eventually spluttered to a halt in July 1993, the press corps held a wonderful party to celebrate the occasion. We drank toasts to the chairman, the barristers and the witnesses in their absence. Ballads, poems and monologues were composed and drunkenly sung or recited as the night went on. It was a night of hilarity and relief. We had shown that in this life, if you persevere long enough, all pain will end. With one bound we were free. One of the more sober members of the corps told me afterwards that he kept all the scribbled sheets of poems and ballads and that he was going to get copies made. Some of them were quite good, but I can assure you that, for legal reasons, they will never go on sale to the public. We then went back to our offices and tried to reacclimatise to the real world of journalism. We waited for a year for the report of the tribunal to be published.

The final kick in the teeth for those who had slaved in Dublin Castle for the duration of the marathon inquiry, was that the tribunal report, which was published in the middle of the summer of 1994, prompted no real response. The Dáil wasn't sitting at the time but was recalled a few weeks later to discuss it, but no Question Time was allowed. It was simply a 'set piece' debate, with each deputy making long-winded speeches. Most of the speakers obviously did not understand the issue and just took up a party stance on the matter to waste time. Nobody was following the debate, anyway. The reason being that the IRA announced its ceasefire at the start of the debate, effectively neutralising the proceedings in Leinster House. The report sank without trace.

Yet, the report contained important insights into how this state is governed and pointed out numerous irregularities. It was undoubtedly one of the most important and expensive overviews on the running of this State since its foundation and it was most unfortunate that it fizzled out the way it did. The indecent haste in which certain politicians rushed to brush it under the carpet was astonishing. The attitude was, 'It's all over now, forget about it, put it behind us; everyone is vindicated, no wrong-doing has been proved.' The Taoiseach announced that there would be no further long, drawn out, expensive tribunals in future.

An editorial in *The Irish Times* on 5 September 1994, described the three-day Dáil debate as a 'spectacular and brazen snow-job.' It said we had witnessed the not-inconsiderable failure of the democratic system as it operates in this state.

'Mr Reynolds and his party colleagues,' said the editorial,

'would certainly earn more respect for their positive achievements if there was the generosity and courage to acknowledge their past errors. It would be reassuring for those who recognise the damage which has been inflicted upon the democratic system in its failure to secure answers for parliament, for the judiciary and for the taxpayer on the way in which the State has conducted its business.

'We are still left with unanswered questions. And we are presented with members of a Fianna Fáil party in Government who declare, in effect, that if a similar set of circumstances presented themselves in the future, they would do the same all over again. It might. And they would.'

The tribunal report itself was disappointing and incomprehensible to the ordinary man or woman on the street. While it dealt with all the terms of reference, its conclusions were rambling and each finding was qualified, with the result all the main characters were able to say they had been fully vindicated and were able to welcome the report. Yet, if you dig deeply enough into the report things are not always quite that simple. There is plenty of strong information there, but only for the initiated. The former editor of the *Sunday Tribune*, Mr Vincent Browne, wrote that it was very difficult to make sense of the report.

> 'To understand it you really have to reconstruct it, as it is out of sequence, with documents repeated over and over again. Linkages between pieces of evidence seem to have been missed because of its presentation.'

Mr Browne said that compared with, for instance, the Glacken report on the Telecom affair, the beef report was a disappointing piece of analysis.

> 'It could be less than half its length with better organisation and editing. It also might well have been sharper, given the evidence before it and, indeed, the evidence that it has produced, albeit in such an amorphous form.'

The Irish Press Closure

The closure of the *Irish Press* group of newspapers in May 1995 did not come as a surprise. For the previous five years staff knew they were living on borrowed time. The group was losing money at an alarming rate and it did not seem to know how to stem the haemorrhage. The company was not able to come to terms with modern trends and the workers were demoralised at the lack of leadership. The staff were working for less money than their colleagues in other newspapers because they were not being given national pay agreement increases. They were being told to tighten their belts and were given a number of assurances that management would turn the company around. They waited, but it was all to no avail.

Management embarked on a series of disastrous initiatives, each losing massive amounts of money. The group was spiralling out of control. The journalists and outside observers knew the *Press* was doomed. I had many good friends in Burgh Quay. We worked side by side out in the 'field' covering all the news of the day. The group had some excellent, dedicated journalists. It was a tragedy to see them thrown out on the street. In the five to eight years before the closure they constantly spoke of their insecurity. There was always an air of gloom and they lived in constant fear. Their demise was hastened by Independent Newspapers Ltd which head-hunted some of their top writers.

While the collapse was expected, when it actually occurred there was shock, mainly because of the way it happened. Major recriminations followed. The boil had been lanced. The closure of a newspaper – a living, throbbing, vibrant thing – is a sad occasion. The *Press* newspapers were an Irish institution, part of what we are. Their disappearance is a massive loss to Irish journalism, and to Irish life generally.

Some people felt that I and my colleagues in *The Irish Times* should be glad of the demise of the 'opposition', but that wasn't the case. All Dublin journalists had the greatest of respect for the *Press* and its staff. As I have said, some of the best journalists in the country worked there. It had produced many fine reporters and writers over the years. In fact, my own father worked there as a political reporter and assistant news editor back in the late 40s and early 50s. I tried to get a job there 30 years ago, but luckily (as it has transpired) they could not take me on as there were no vacancies. Even in the good old days, the *Press* never had a lot of money and those on the staff always had to work harder and be more productive than the reporters on the other newspapers, but they certainly turned out a good product. It had an enviable record for producing all of the hard news, rarely missed a story, and what you read was tightly and factually written. It was the complete newspaper, with emphasis on the news, no waffle or pretentious pontificating. If you wanted the news you bought the *Press*. They covered the country like a hoover. It was a great paper to train on. You had to have all of the facts and your copy had to be accurately written. There were never any loose ends. It was a real newsman's paper.

For decades the *Press* had a tough news editor called Bill Redmond who was an extremely hard taskmaster. A strict disciplinarian, he also had very strong views on how reporters should dress. He had an old-fashioned idea that they should all come in in dark suits. Even though he had mellowed by the 60s, he asked Sean Lynch, a young reporter (one of the more flamboyant members of the staff) to go home and change into a suit. A surprised and upset Sean told me the story afterwards He had come in to work in a sports jacket and pink shirt and nice tie. 'I thought I looked very well,' said Sean, 'but he lost his head and demanded that I change into something more conservative'.

Because it was such a tough place to work, many journalists when they became experienced moved on to other papers or into radio. The *Press* was certainly a great training ground – the best – and anybody coming out of it could be relied on to do any story competently. By the early 60s, the three *Press* titles were easily, and deservedly, the most successful in their respective categories. They had just enough political radicalism to make them lively without being subversive, just enough sophistication to make them cultured without appearing elitist. Of course, there was the dreadful political bogey. It always followed the Fianna Fáil line. That was why it was set up by Eamon de Valera in September 1931. Dev described it as 'this great enterprise.' He wanted to 'break down the conspiracy of silence in the daily press'.

This meant the 'conspiracy' against him, or so he thought. Originally, he wanted to buy the *Freeman's Journal*, then in financial difficulties. The industrialist William Martin Murphy put an end to that when he acquired the paper and merged it with the *Irish Independent*. Dev said the paper wasn't owned or controlled by the party. The articles of association of the *Irish Press* said there would be a controlling director who would have:

> 'sole and absolute control of the public and political policy of the company and of the editorial management thereof. He may appoint at his discretion remove or suspend all editors, sub-editors, reporters, writers, contributors of news and information, and all such other persons as may be employed in or connected with the editorial department ....'

On the fiftieth anniversary of the *Irish Press*, Paddy Clare, the paper's late night reporter for many years, wrote about the hectic days leading up to the official opening. Paddy was one of the most unflappable and likeable characters you could ever find. He was the night watchman, the man who stays at his post until 4 a.m. and deals with all the late breaking stories. It had to be a very good story indeed to worry Paddy and it had to be really extraordinary to get him out of the office to cover it. On the fiftieth anniversary, he wrote:

> 'People were ringing up at all hours to find out when the paper would be out, if ever. Up to the last minute some people had doubts about it.
>
> In the meantime there was much coming and going. A lot of Americans had contributed to the founding of the paper and Yanks and Southerners were continually calling in, all bringing good wishes. Some I remember well.
>
> There was one who called himself Brian Boru O'Dunne, and another called Rory O'Moore Sarsfield .... All sorts of things were being said; they (the Free Staters) wouldn't let it come out .... It wouldn't last a month .... One politician said it would suit Mr de Valera better to rebuild the tenement houses in Cumberland Street than starting this nonsense.'

It was disengenuous of Dev to say the paper wasn't owned and controlled by Fianna Fáil. He ran it and his son ran it after him and another de Valera was running it when it closed. So for 50 years it was de Valera controlled. And Dev *was* Fianna Fáil. The party, right up to the day it closed, believed, quite correctly, that it would always get full support during a general election. The party may not have owned or controlled it, but to all intents and purposes it was their paper. As a political reporter in the old, barn-storming days of the *Press*, my father was close to Dev. He used tell me stories about Dev phoning the newsroom every night to know what was coming out in the paper the next day. He often had no hesitation in changing copy, in changing a whole front page. My father covered many of Dev's election campaigns. After giving a speech, Dev would come over to Dad and ask him to read back certain passages. If he was not satisfied he would amend it. He would even change the grammar. He was a stickler for detail. He also had a very strong feeling for history and for his part in it. He was always ensuring that posterity saw him in a good light, as a strong, articulate leader. He knew the power of words. To him the pen was mightier than the sword. Like him or hate him, de Valera did genuinely embody the self-image and aspirations of at least a large section of the Irish people.

However, despite the obvious political bias – and what paper hasn't a bias on something or other – the *Press* was an excellent paper. The life of the nation is much the poorer and Irish publishing is greatly diminished by its demise. *The Irish Times*, in an editorial on the closure, was generous in its praise:

> '*The Irish Press* group has a long and distinguished record in the life of this nation. In the manner of its founding father, Eamon de Valera, it had an instinctive rapport with the daily life, the interests and the concerns of Irish people. Traditionally, Burgh Quay stood for vigorous, high-quality journalism.'

The manner in which it eventually closed was truly high farce. The management tried to put the blame on Mr Colm Rapple, the group's business editor, a highly regarded finance writer. He had written an article in *The Irish Times* about the future of Irish newspapers for which he was immediately sacked. In this article he enlarged on several themes he had already addressed at a Ministerial Forum on the Newspaper Industry some weeks earlier. He referred to Dr Eamon de Valera's role as proprietor and shareholder of the Press group, and to the relationship between the operating company which runs the newspapers and its holding company, Irish Press plc. To dismiss him was disproportionate to his supposed offence. Indeed, the Press company had earlier been offered space in the same series to put its own point of view and had declined the offer. Other contributors to the debate in series came from the *Irish Independent* and *The Sunday Business Post*, as well as a former editor of the *Irish Press*.

Mr Rapple was later re-instated by the Employment Appeals Tribunal. The National Union of Journalists said this justified its stance in his defence and showed that the company was making him a scapegoat for the closure. The day Rapple's sacking was announced the NUJ stopped work to hold a mandatory union meeting to discuss the dismissal. The management then locked them out. However, a large number of militant NUJ members decided to occupy the building. But the real reason for the closure of the newspapers was the decision of the Supreme Court to set aside awards of almost £9 million which the High Court had granted to the company in a legal battle with its former partner Ingersoll Irish Publications. That increased the company's debt to the extent that its immediate future was in doubt.

It was such a sad sight to see the journalists occupying the building, holding out for a miracle. The sight of Jack Charlton, the Irish soccer manager, visiting the protestors, still lingers in the memory. 'I have always had good relations with the *Irish Press*, and when people are in trouble it is the right thing to do,' he said. The journalists worked hard to publicise the closure, seeking support from the public and urging well-known figures in public life to give them backing.

I was on night duty in *The Irish Times* when the sit-in was taking place. I kept in touch with the *Press* during the night to see if there were any developments. In the small hours of the morning, when I was going home, I would walk over to Burgh Quay and drop in a few copies of *The Irish Times*. The sight of Con Houlihan, the *Evening Press* columnist, standing on O'Connell Bridge with a can in his hand collecting money for the workers' fund was heart-breaking. The journalists left in the building published what they described as the 'lockout edition' of the *Evening XPress*. In this two-page paper they gave their views on the dispute and handed it out around the city to raise funds for the staff.

Eventually, the occupation ended. It had not been a success. They did not get their demands. The workers had shown solidarity, but in a way it was always destined to failure. There was a flurry of technical court actions. A few prospective buyers appeared, but this came to nothing.

Then, silence. Passing the building every day on my way to work, it was sad to see the premises falling into disrepair. Winos began sleeping in the loading bay areas at night and this space eventually filled up with old clothes, empty bottles and all types of rubbish. A fine newspaper was truly dead. All that was left were memories. Nearby, Mulligan's pub, the meeting place of *Press* journalists in the good old days, did not seem the same any more. You don't hear any laughter or newspaper gossip there any more. It's many the good news story was minutely dissected there over the years. And if you believed half of what was being said you were mad. Many of the scoops talked about were like the fisherman's tale of the one that got away.

Some commentators maintain that the problems of the *Press* went back to the early 80s. As emigration picked up and people started to move towards the cities, and as rural Ireland became urbanised, the *Irish Press's* older, rural readership was quite literally dying, and circulation fell.

As my colleague in *The Irish Times*, Fintan O'Toole, wrote after the closure:

> 'Its closeness to the heart of a very powerful vision of Ireland made the *Irish Press*, and in time its sister Sunday and evening titles, hugely successful. So long as Irish people remained largely rural, nationalistic and egalitarian, so long as the broader Fianna Fáil ethos which the papers reflected and sustained represented the core of Irish society, the Press group was the Irish media mainstream.'

Between 1980 and 1984, the group lost £5.3 million. Throughout the mid-1980s, cutbacks allowed small profits to be made, but, according to many working in the group, this was at the expense of the newspapers which were starved of resources.

On top of that, bad industrial relations hindered an orderly and necessary move to new technology, carried out by other newspapers in the late 1980s and early 1990s. The decision to turn the *Irish Press* into a tabloid proved a costly mistake, alienating its traditional readers without being strong enough to compete with newer tabloids like the Daily Star. A major mistake was the relaunch of the *Evening Press* as a two-section newspaper in 1991, prompted by the disastrous marriage with the Ingersoll Group. The link up with Ingersoll – because of the then desperate financial state of the company – was the last nail in the coffin. There then followed numerous internal rows and expensive court cases.

Over 640 people lost their jobs when the Press group closed. Some had over 30 years service with the company. The majority were members of SIPTU, working in the machine room, advertising, sales, and administration. There were also printers and other craft union members. Over 200 were journalists.

A year after the closure, there were no accurate records of how many former employees have found work. At this time, SIPTU sources suggested less than one per cent. Less than ten of the former journalists were in full time employment. Possibly up to 40 had regular freelance work, though for many that may mean one column a week. The rest had no work at all. Eighty-five members of the Irish Print Union lost their jobs. Ten found work in the print industry generally. Some left the industry and 30 went on desktop publishing courses. Most got no work. All newspapers benefited from the closure. The biggest beneficiary was Independent Newspapers Ltd, where sales of all their titles experienced phenomenal increases.

It is heart-rending to read the closing lines in Michael O'Toole's book *More Kicks Than Pence*. O'Toole was a long serving member of the *Evening Press* staff and wrote the popular Dubliner's Diary column after Terry O'Sullivan's death. He wrote:

> 'As I write (in the late spring of 1992) the Irish Press and its sister papers are preparing finally to leave Burgh Quay for a modern high-tech building in Parnell Square. The ghosts of 60 years will be left behind and with them, it is hoped, the ill-will that has dogged labour relations in the company for so long. For Eamon de Valera's 'great enterprise' it will be a new beginning – one that will lay the foundations for the next 60 years.'

It was not to be. All that remains are the memories.

Charlie Haughey

When Charles J. Haughey was acquitted in the High Court in 1970 for allegedly conspiring to import arms, he was understandably delighted. I had watched him sit through the trial, always neatly dressed in blue mohair suits, pale, quiet and impassive. The trial and his sacking from the Cabinet by the Taoiseach, Jack Lynch, had been a traumatic experience for him. He had earlier been ill in hospital after falling off a horse in the grounds of his home at Kinsealy. The relief when the verdict was announced was written all over his face. His supporters began to sing rebel songs at the back of the court and some ran to shake the hands of the jurors. It was a very dramatic and emotional scene.

He immediately called a press conference in a nearby hotel. A colleague asked him: 'Mr Haughey, how does it feel to be a free man again?' Haughey beamed and said: 'Great, great.' He was a happy man. The world was taking on a new perspective for him. For months he had been a worried, depressed and disillusioned, now this huge weight had been lifted from his shoulders.

I ventured the second question. 'Will you consider retiring from politics, Mr Haughey?' I asked. That was 27 years ago – more than a quarter of a century – but I still remember the withering look he gave me. I could see then why so many people are afraid of his temper.

He growled: 'Of course I'll continue on.'

How naive I was then. I was thinking like an ordinary member of the public, not like a politician. But I didn't understand the disease of politics sufficiently at the time. Haughey picked himself up, dusted himself down and started all over again. It was a long, slow, painful process. He knuckled down to it and climbed back to the top of the heap.

I got my first Dáil press gallery ticket in 1965, so I have seen Haughey in action for 32 years. When he eventually resigned as Taoiseach in January 1992, the most commonly used word to describe him was 'enigmatic'. That is a reasonably accurate assessment. It is not possible to pigeonhole him or to put labels on him. He is a complex person – a kind of Jekyll and Hyde. He can be charming in public or show great dignity and statesmanship, but at other times he can be quite offensive.

Politicians and civil servants used run for cover when he was annoyed about something. Even as a youngster his temper was well in evidence. The GAA suspended him for a year for striking a linesman. Then there was the infamous occasion when he threw a file at the secretary of the Department of Justice, Mr Peter Berry.

In the 60s, Haughey had very good relations with the press. He was probably the most popular minister in the Government with the press corps. He was invariably in good humour, always had some witty remark to make and was loved by photographers. He was accomplished at presenting himself for a good picture. He knew instinctively what the photographers wanted. However, from 1970 onwards – after the Arms Trial – he became totally paranoid about the press. He believed they were out to get him.

He even suspected that the British Secret Service was behind a lot of the bad publicity he got. He never felt any of the perceived bad publicity was his own fault. He maintained that he was doing a good job and was not being appreciated. All he was getting were brickbats. For a man like Haughey who revelled in being looked up to as a leader, a father figure, the wise one, this was hard to take.

There were, of course, some journalists who intensely disliked him and didn't care to hide their prejudices. There were journalists who did not trust him and suspected even his best initiatives. They resented what they perceived to be his Little Napoleon image, his efforts at playing the country squire in his mansion in Kinsealy, his island off Kerry, his yacht, the horses, the wine cellar and the political 'strokes'. The fact that two journalists' phones were bugged during his GUBU administration did not endear him to a lot of people in the media. It was something that was never forgotten. Yet there were many others in the media who gave him a fair shake, but when he lashed out at the press, he tarred them all with the same brush.

Many were suspicious of his wealth. This was quite an achievement on a Minister's or Taoiseach's salary, which, by any economic criteria, is not great. It was a modern day miracle of the loaves and the fishes. He would never talk about his wealth or how he got it. He maintained that it was nobody's business except his own. But that is not strictly correct. It is alright for a member of the public to say his wealth is nobody's business, but a politician, particularly a leading politician, is in a different category. The State – you and I – are paying his salary and you like to know, and are entitled to know, what you are getting. It was one of the taboo subjects which reporters were not allowed to ask him about in interviews. If you did the answer was a curt: 'Ask my bank manager'.

The other matter you had to avoid like the plague was the Arms Trial. He totally blocked it out of his mind and in 27 years has never spoken publicly about it. The real story of the Arms Trial will never be fully known, as the main characters in that drama, Haughey and Lynch, have never put anything down on paper for historians. The vacuum is filled with speculation. There is, of course, the transcript of the trial, but the judge made it clear that someone had committed perjury, leaving the matter hanging. What is more, both Haughey and

Lynch made it clear that they had no intention of ever writing or elaborating on those dramatic days. The matter has been conveniently buried. It may be many more years before historians dig up the real story. Judging from the secrecy so far, they will have a a tough job on their hands. Many of the main players are now dead and the trail is very cold.

Haughey was also very prickly about little, insignificant things. For instance he didn't like the media calling him 'Haughey.' He felt this was disrespectful. They should call him 'Mister Haughey' or 'Taoiseach'. This showed too much sensitivity and for a man in his position it was a bit pathetic. Other politicians, O'Malley, Reynolds, Bruton, Spring – all politicians, in fact, are generally called by their surnames. Haughey maintained otherwise and said that other prominent politicians were not called by their surname, instancing the media always calling Garret FitzGerald 'Garret'. This may only appear to be a small thing to the rest of us, but to Haughey it was of great importance.

The editor of the *Irish Independent*, Vinney Doyle, described in the excellent book *Talking to Ourselves* by Ivor Kenny, a conversation he had with Haughey:

> 'Once, when Charlie was in opposition, we had barely sat down to lunch when the hooded eyes looked across the table and he said, "I can't for the life of me understand why, when you are writing headlines, I'm always Haughey and FitzGerald is always Garret." Our style of layout is a three-column headline. I said: "Deputy Haughey, you try putting FitzGerald in there – count the letters. It won't go, but Haughey goes perfectly. That's the only reason.' He said, 'I don't believe you, but that takes the biscuit".'

Doyle added:

> 'He was capable of being slightly vindictive. We once ran a picture of Kinsealy taken from an aircraft. It's a spectacular mansion. He was extremely upset and protested to Tony O'Reilly that we were setting him up for potential IRA or UVF hits – to which I could only reply the IRA were hardly dependent on us for information about Kinsealy.'

Nevertheless, Haughey had lots of charisma and charm. He was brilliant during elections, especially when out canvassing. He would always come up with the right quotes for reporters. Once he forgot the chip on his shoulder he could be superb. A Fine Gael TD came up to me one time when Haughey was canvassing in an inner Dublin city constituency and said:

'Look at that ... he has the people in the palm of his hand. No other politician can do it as well. God, if only Garret could do that.' And that was coming from one of FitzGerald's own deputies. Privately, I have heard Fine Gael TDs express concern about FitzGerald's aloofness and wished he could mingle among the people like Haughey could do so effortlessly. The so-called common touch is such a vital ingredient in politics.

Of course, Haughey wanted people to look up to him. His image was all-important. Image is important to everyone, but to a politician it is crucial. You were either with him or against him. There did not seem to be a middle ground. Michael Noonan, the Limerick Fine Gael TD, in an interview on the Brendan Balfe RTE radio show, said: 'He wasn't the worst. His biggest fault was that he always wanted to be loved.' There is a lot of truth in that.

However, according to Machiavelli, wanting to be loved is a major weakness in politics. Margaret Thatcher, when she was prime minister, did not give a damn what people thought of her; she was single minded, determined, and quite ruthless in getting her way. This attitude was probably one of her greatest strengths, as well as being a disadvantage in other ways. Haughey deeply resented criticism. Yet, even when it was unfair or bordering on the libellous, he never took any legal against the media. He once said that if he was to take an action every time something libellous appeared about him, he would spend all his life in the courts.

While this is not strictly correct (there was plenty of constructive, deserved criticism of him during his reign) there was some that went too far and if he had sued he might have succeeded. I believe in strong criticism of politicians, but it must be fair and not pass into maliciousness and vilification.

His successor, Albert Reynolds, on the other hand, during his short period as Taoiseach, had no inhibitions about redressing what he considered libellous. He is reputed to have got over £150,000 in claims against newspapers, all settled out of court. A tidy sum, which did not endear him to newspaper executives or journalists. The outcome of his action against *The Sunday Times*, where he was awarded a derisory penny by the judge, after the jury awarded him zero damages, was met with great delight by most journalists. Reynolds is seen as being far too sensitive about his reputation. To then blame British justice for the decision was pathetic. Politicians should be able to take hard criticism and if they find it too hot in the kitchen they should get out. Reynolds never suffered the constant heavy, sometimes vicious criticism that Haughey was subjected to. Haughey could dish it out but he could also take it on the chin.

In his book *One Spin on the Merry-Go-Round*, Sean Duignan, who was press secretary to Reynolds, wrote about advising him not to sue newspapers, but he would not listen. Duignan wrote:

> 'Irrespective of the cost, he was not prepared to abide by Haughey's acceptance of the conventional wisdom that it would be counter productive for him (Haughey) to take legal proceedings against those who smeared and vilified him. "But, Taoiseach ..." Reynolds was adamant: "I don't care, Diggy. I'm not going to take that kind of thing lying down. Charlie felt there was nothing he could do about it, but if they tell lies about me, I will sue them, and to hell with the consequences".'

Of course, everyone would have the deepest of sympathy for Reynolds if there was a definite deliberate malicious allegation made about him in print. That should not be perpetrated against anyone. Every person has the right to their good name. Reynolds would have a right to damages in such a case. But in situations where a genuine mistake was made, or something slipped into the paper, an apology and correction, plus a contribution to a charity of his choice, should be enough. Reynolds does not see things that way and that was why he kept on with his anti-press campaign, ending in that terrible ordeal for him in London. This was something he brought on himself and it was hard for any journalist to feel sympathy for him. He says he is going to appeal. Maybe he will have better luck next time, but please, spare us the attack on British justice.

Haughey was very good to those who were loyal to him, who admired or praised him. He put them into cabinet, made them junior ministers or gave them some other prominent positions or perks. This meant that a lot of very talented people who could not be bothered playing up to his ego were left to rot on the back benches. This damaged him in the long term and left big weaknesses in every one of his governments. He was advised time and again to drop certain weak links, but he just couldn't do it.

For someone who could be quite ruthless, he could on other occasions show himself to be over-sentimental and a real softie. He was hard to read. Sometimes as hard as stone, other times as soft as jelly.

He was also a very generous person. The stories of his generosity are legion. He never hesitated to help people in trouble. I know a few of these cases and I saw the relief and happiness he brought to people. He also spared no effort to cut red tape when he saw bureaucracy stifling some worthwhile project. PJ Mara, who was press officer during Haughey's periods in government, maintains that he was the outstanding politician of his generation. In Tim Ryan's book *Mara PJ*, he says that Haughey will probably go down in Irish history among the three most influential figures of the last half century – the other two being Eamon de Valera and Sean Lemass. 'Some of his major achievements, when they are examined by historians,' said Mara,

> 'will be the periods he spent as Minister for Justice and Minister for Finance. He will be remembered as a particularly caring politician for the position of the elderly in our society. They, in turn, had great regard for him, as was evident in the affection shown to him by the elderly on his many trips around the country.'

Maybe that is going a bit too far – and it is, after all, coming from a close, naturally biased friend – but, nevertheless, it does contain a lot of truth. Haughey was revered by many and did do a lot of good. His supporters were fanatical; they looked on him as God, one of the greatest politicians that ever lived, a miracle worker. No matter how big the crisis 'Charlie will work it out.' I have seen close up the adulation of the people for him. They would not listen to any criticism of him. They accused the media of trying to harm him. It is not the function of the media to be for or against him. The function of the media is to objectively give the facts and not be influenced by personality. It has to be said that, while he was an exceptionally good politician, with a lot of good qualities, but it must also be pointed out that he did a lot of harm and was a major divisive figure in his own party during his last 25 years.

I felt he should have resigned as Taoiseach at the end of Ireland's Presidency of the European Union, especially as we had carried out our presidential duties with great success and aplomb. But he did not want to relinquish the reins of power. He simply loved power and all its trappings. He thrived on it and could not even begin to think of retirement. He stayed on until the issue of the bugging of two journalists' phones (Geraldine Kennedy and Bruce Arnold) was resurrected in January 1992. It was reported that he had known about the bugging, even though years earlier, in his previous government, he had denied all knowledge. He was brought down by his former Minister for Justice, Mr Sean Doherty, who claimed on a television show that Haughey did in fact know of the bugging. In a statement given to a press conference on 21 January, he said:

'I am confirming tonight that the Taoiseach, Mr Haughey, was fully aware in 1982 that two journalists' phones were being tapped, and that he at no stage expressed reservation about this action.'

He went on to say:

'I did not seek nor did I get any instruction from any member of the Cabinet in this regard, nor did I tell the Cabinet that this action had been taken. Telephone tapping was never discussed in the Cabinet.

However, as soon as the transcripts from the tapes became available, I took them personally to Mr Haughey in his office and left them in his possession.'

That was the end of Haughey's political career. Yet, looking back on his controversial reign, I still thought he would get out of it. Reporters had come to the conclusion that he was unsinkable. Haughey gave a lengthy and detailed rebuttal to the allegations, but it was no use: he was finished. There was not going to be any Houdini act this time. He resigned as Taoiseach, and a few days later as leader of Fianna Fáil.

If he hadn't been so wildly ambitious and power crazy, he could have seen that the end of the Irish Presidency of the EU would have been an ideal time for him to bow out. He could have gone out in a blaze of glory instead of under a dark cloud. Many political observers and those who had an interest in succeeding him believed that he was going to retire after the EU presidency. However, when asked about retirement in a radio interview, he said he felt in good health and pointed out that Chinese politicians and some other world leaders stayed on into their 80s. That set the alarm bells ringing for a few members of his party who believed that he was going to stay until he was 'carried out,' or, as one Fianna Fáil deputy put it 'until someone puts a stake through his heart'.

I cannot emphasise the point sufficiently in this book: to be a politician requires incredible qualities – self-confidence and determination, not to mention, of course, an extremely hard neck, which the ordinary mortal totally lacks. Politicians are a strange breed and Haughey was a superb politician. There is no doubt that he had lost his sure touch in his last years.

Watching him in action from the press gallery in the Dáil or at press conferences, it was obvious his political footwork was not as good and the magic was not there any more. He was not impressive in the Dáil. His performances generally were very poor. His thought process seemed to have slowed down. He couldn't think fast on his feet any more. He treated the Dáil with contempt and would only give the most minimal replies to opposition questions.

Supplementary questions received monosyllabic answers or silence. He was irritable and impatient. Some political observers maintain that this was because he was worn out with all the party heaves against him over the years. They claimed that he had never been in full command and that he always had to be looking over his shoulder; he could never be his own man. Certainly, as far as I could see, he was a very feeble man in his last year or two. Some observers believed that his health was letting him down and as a result he wasn't as confident as he used to be.

Looking back over the years, he had been an incredible fighter and a survivor. No Irish leader weathered as many heavy political storms. He overcame four attempts to unseat him as leader of Fianna Fáil and cheated death three times – once in a car crash, once when his boat sank and a third time when a light plane he was travelling in crashed in Kerry. Most of us in three lifetimes would not experience such trauma.

A little thing about him that always fascinated me was that he never wore a watch. Most of us would not be able to get through a day without looking at our watch. He never wore one and said he did not need it; he maintained that there were plenty of clocks around to look at or people to tell him what time it was. He was probably the only leader of state in the world who could be seen without a watch on his wrist.

Love him or hate him, and like de Valera, there is no middle ground, we will never see his likes again. Politics are boring without him. He has left an indelible mark on Irish political history, both for good and for ill.

He then set off to enjoy his retirement. Each morning he rode his horse along Portmarnock strand. A Land Rover and horse box brought his favourite steed to the beach and Charlie went along afterwards in his chauffeur-driven Mercedes. He concentrated on his estate at Kinsealy and when the weather was suitable sailed away on his yacht. He spent his holidays on his island off Co. Kerry. He vowed not to make any political comments and generally kept out of the limelight. He said shortly before his retirement that he would find it very difficult to relinquish the reins of public life: that he was not the kind of person to spend the rest of his live tending to his garden. Yet, when the time came, he showed that he really could happily take to retirement. He also retained his keen interest in the arts. It was an idyllic existence.

However, this bliss was shattered by reports that he had received £1.3 million from Ben Dunne. Haughey quickly denied this. Nevertheless, Ben Dunne and other witnesses at the Payments to Politicians Tribunal – initially set up to look into the financial affairs of the former Minister, Michael Lowry – said he had in fact taken the money. They said that at the end of the 80s Haughey had run into financial difficulties and needed money badly. Ben Dunne's sister, Mrs Margaret Heffernan, told the tribunal that she had heard rumours that the money had been handed over. When she went to ask for it back Haughey maintained that he had never received the money and claimed that Ben was 'unstable'.

Later, as the tribunal investigation intensified, Haughey changed his story and his lawyers admitted he had been given the money. The admission caused shock and outrage to the public. The opposition in the Dáil demanded that another inquiry be held to ascertain if any other prominent wealthy people or companies had contributed to assist Mr Haughey continue his lavish lifestyle which had earned him the nickname The Squire of Kinsealy.

Many of the more sceptical members of the press and public were not shocked by the revelations. For years newspapers had been trying to find out how he could live in such luxury on the relatively low salary of a senior politician. Most investigative reporters came up against a blank wall when they delved into the matter. His financial affairs were too well buried for anyone to get at. All that remained was innuendo and gossip. Because that's all it was, Haughey had to be given the benefit of the doubt.

We had to assume that he had some other means of financing Kinsealy and his other expensive, finance-draining projects. The strict libel laws did not help. Even when Cliff Taylor, of *The Irish Times*, reported that Dunne had handed over the £1.3 million, the paper could not use Haughey's name. It had to say 'a former well known politician' got the money. Yet, every dog in the street knew this person was Haughey.

In the end it was only by sheer accident that Haughey got caught. The whole matter had started off as an inquiry into former Government Minister Michael Lowry. It was in the course of that affair that the investigation tumbled upon Haughey.

On 10 July 1997, the day after Haughey's lawyers made the sensational disclosure that he had in fact been given the money, *The Irish Times* editorial said:

'A ghastly vista has opened up for Irish politics as a consequence of Mr Charles Haughey's acknowledgement that he received more than £1.3 million from Mr

Ben Dunne between 1987 and 1991, at a time when he was leader of Fianna Fail and the Taoiseach of this country.'

The editorial also stated:

'Through his actions, Mr Haughey has brought shame on the country, on himself, on his family and on Fianna Fáil. As Taoiseach and party leader, he placed himself under a financial obligation to one of the country's wealthiest businessmen. And while both Mr Haughey and Mr Dunne are insistent that no favours were asked and none given, the very fact that such an eventuality could have arisen is indefensible. Mr Haughey embraced the role of a kept man, rather than face life without the trappings of grandeur inherent in his Gandon mansion, his island, his yacht, his art collection and his horses.'

I was in the Dáil on the day of the disclosure and politicians of all parties were stunned. They believed the whole body politic had been sullied and degraded by the news. Politicians I spoke to at the time were extremely angry. One politician said:

'People are always saying politicians are on the make, trying to line their pockets .... That is completely untrue, but what will the public think after this. We'll be crucified.'

When he appeared before the tribunal in Dublin Castle on 15 July 1997 his evidence was that from 1960 onwards his financial affairs had been handled by his accountant, the late Mr Des Traynor. He said he had no knowledge of where the money to support his lifestyle was coming from. 'In hindsight, it is clear that I should have involved myself to a greater degree in this regard,' he said. This performance was strongly attacked by the media which maintained he was passing the buck to a dead man.

Mr Denis McCullough SC, for the tribunal, in his summing up, contended that Haughey had lied three times before owning up to his guilt. He said Haughey lied in his letter to the tribunal of 7 March when he denied receipt of the money. He also lied in a statement of 3 June when he accepted 'as a matter of probability' he had received the money but didn't know about it. He also lied in his 7 July statement about the details of a conversation he had with Des Traynor about Margaret Heffernan's approach to Haughey to find out whether he received the £1.3 million.

The findings of the tribunal were published on 25 August 1997 and they were scathing of Haughey. Mr Justice Brian McCracken, in his excellent report, said the tribunal could not accept or believe much of Haughey's evidence. It stressed that it was unacceptable for a Taoiseach's lifestyle to be supported by gifts. It said Haughey shrouded his gifts in secret off-shore accounts to hide them from the Revenue Commissioners. It said that his attitude towards the tribunal might be in breach of the law and the papers should be sent to the Director of Public Prosecutions.

In just over four pages dealing with Haughey's evidence, Mr Justice McCracken used the phrases: 'Unacceptable and untrue ... quite unbelievable ... equally unbelievable ... not believable ... most unlikely ... incomprehensible ... the tribunal does not believe ... factually incorrect ... quite incredible.'

For the 73-year-old Haughey, who loved to put on the appearance of a cultured gentleman solving the country's problems and promoting the arts, it was all a disaster. His life had fallen down around him. It wasn't just the money and the major problems that this posed for him. No, it must have been the humiliation of having seen his high place in Irish society crumble so publicly that hurt most. His pride must have been hurt. That was the biggest blow, especially coming in the twilight of his life. It was an ignominious end to a turbulent, controversial career. He was no longer the Great Survivor.

And Finally ...

It was September 1958 when I got on the train at Connolly Station and set off to start work on the *Drogheda Argus*. I can still remember standing on the station platform, full of excitement, tinged with a certain trepidation, wondering what the future held. My life was beginning. I can still vividly see the little Dublin porter on the gate checking the tickets and get the smell of the thick fumes from the engine. It does seem like only yesterday. Unfortunately, it's nearly 40 years ago and the mileage on the clock is now fairly high. Writing this book about so many incidents and people in the distant, misty past has been quite traumatic. It was a bit like lying on the psychiatrist's couch. It brought back a mixture of all types of emotions. It's been a long, winding road, with a lot of highs and lows, but overall there has been much enjoyment and fulfillment. Nowadays, I seem to be taking on the role of the grand old man of letters. Colleagues come up and ask me questions like 'Who was Charlie Haughey's barrister at the Arms Trial?' or 'When did the Dublin bombings take place?' They are constantly looking for advice or contacts.

Anxious parents ask me to advise them on how little John or Mary can get into journalism. They stress that the child is 'very good at English' and has his or her heart set on becoming a journalist. I genuinely find it difficult to be of assistance. Life in the newspaper world has changed so much that I'm reluctant to give an opinion. There are now a number of colleges of journalism which produce a certain quota of graduates every year. After graduation, it is a combination of ability and luck. The latter is probably the more important factor. I firmly believe that if I was starting off again next week, I would not have a chance of getting into the business. Today they are looking for highly qualified people with plenty of confidence. I had neither qualifications nor a lot of confidence, but I did have a love for the business and plenty of enthusiasm.

There was no such thing as colleges of journalism back in the 50s and it was simply a case of learning by your mistakes. This made it quite a precarious existence. And, take my word for it, mistakes were made on a grand scale. On the other hand, not many youngsters were interested in journalism then. It wasn't exactly looked on as a very respectable occupation. I remember a woman saying to my mother that if she couldn't get her sons into the bank or medical college, she could always throw them into journalism. Not very flattering. But now the wheel has come full circle. Journalism has become one of the glamour professions. I'm quite bemused at my new celebrity status. It takes a bit of getting used to. Looking back, it is amazing to see the dramatic changes that have taken place in the newspaper industry. This particularly applies to the last 15 years. Once change began, it escalated rapidly.

The business has been transformed out of all recognition. There is now a completely new working environment. New technology has had a major impact. Computers have made things so much easier. The days of dealing with dirty black carbon paper and typewriters with broken keys are long gone. You now type the story onto a computer, press a button and it flashes down the telephone line into the newsroom. In the old days, we were one step away from the era of the carrier pigeon. Messenger boys used to arrive every hour to the Dáil or the courts to collect our copy and take it back to the office. It was a slow and cumbersome process. There were a lot of problems. One day a drunken messenger boy was cycling back to the office with some important Dáil copy. Without him noticing, the copy fell on to the road. Luckily, an hour later, Ned Murphy, of the *Irish Independent*, who worked on the Dáil press gallery, was on his way home and found the stuff and personally delivered it to the office. When I worked in the provinces in various district offices, I used to have to walk to the station (which was usually outside the town) and place my brown envelope full of copy on the train. If the train was delayed, the copy might not get into the paper. Yes, communications were very slow indeed. Even trying to use a public telephone could pose major problems.

On many occasions I had to queue up in the rain waiting to send a story while teenagers hogged the phone, laughing and talking with their boyfriends. Other times you became frustrated going from one telephone kiosk to the next trying to find one that wasn't vandalised. Back in the 60s if someone told you that one day there would be such a thing as a mobile phone, you would look at him in amazement and tell him to give up the drink. Yet, as they say in biblical parlance, it has all come to pass. Every second person seems to have a mobile phone now. Recently, I was coming home from work on the DART when the driver announced that there was engine trouble and we could not go any further. Immediately, a forest of mobile phones appeared and the commuters were bellowing out instructions to their wives not to put on the dinner but to collect them at Blackrock station. It was a clear sign of the times.

Another great invention was the fax machine. There was time when you could spend hours on the phone taking down lengthy press statements from various people. For instance, after a Budget every vested interest in the Stat would want to comment on how they were going to be affected by the chang Now you just ask them to fax it through and you have it within seconds.

As newspapers are always battling against deadlines, time is of the esse All these innovations have made journalism a lot easier. While it is nice sentimental and look back on the good old days, I would not like to se back. Sentimentalists like me will naturally look back with nostalgia to t of the hot metal process – the smells, the heat and the noise of the paper going to press. It provided an atmosphere of urgency and excitement.

Today, they are replaced by the silent computers and a cleaner and healthier working environment. The old buzz is no longer there, but it is a lot more efficient. Sentiment can be fine in its own way, but the technological transformation in recent years has been a big boost to the industry. It has improved our conditions immeasurably. The speed at which it all happened surprised everybody. It seemed to take place overnight. One day all the old machinery was there and next it was a thing of the past. The days of the linotype operators and the hot metal people are now only a distant memory. A special museum to that printing era was recently opened in Beggars Bush, Dublin, where a lot of fine old machinery and equipment is on display. It is nice to see it being preserved and it is well worth a visit. Communications have improved considerably in recent times, but there is still a long way to go. We have a relatively more open and transparent society. People are more inclined to talk to the press. In the old days they were afraid of reporters. Now everyone is prepared to talk and some are quite capable of using the media for their own ends. It's a lot easier being a reporter today than it used to be.

There are press officers and public relations people to provide information or introduce you to someone who will fill you in on the situation. In the old days nobody wanted to make a statement about even the most trivial matter. How often have I heard the remark, 'It's more than my job's worth'. There was a real fear there, and getting information out of some individuals or organisations was like pulling teeth. One thing I've always enjoyed about journalism is that you learn something new every day. That's what makes it so interesting. Every day brings different stories, new people to meet, new situations. Its unpredictability is fascinating. Every day presents you with a challenge and you don't know whether you are going to be lucky and get the story or just resign yourself to ~feat and hope things will improve tomorrow. Luck is a vital element in every

~. Luck means ringing someone for a comment and catching him seconds
~he goes out the door. The *Irish Independent* rings five minutes later and
~ and there is no way of contacting him. You have the story and the
Independent reporter loses out. The following day the roles may be
one profession where you should never think you know it all.
~nks that is in for a rude awakening. When you enter the
~d be given something about which you know nothing. You
~ch and you can spend hours trying to get to grips with the
~e you can never get complacent. You never chuckle at
~f a story. You could be next.

* * *

163

Whilst it is great to see journalism changing for the better, there are a few regrets. Unfortunately, the industry doesn't produce characters anymore. It used to be a business full of characters and eccentrics. But there is no room for that breed in today's more serious world. The old characters wouldn't last a week on a modern paper. There is no patience, understanding or sympathy for such people. I can't imagine the drunk and frustrated reporter in the *Irish Independent* who flung his typewriter out the window 35 years ago being kept in his job today or the man who flung the reporters' engagements book into the Liffey being too easily forgiven.

The weak now get knocked out of the way. All the new breed are career journalists, highly ambitious who take themselves very seriously. When my generation started, we were just glad to have a job. We just provided a service and never let ourselves or our views seep into our stories. The young reporters today believe they are changing the world. Maybe they are right, maybe they are. I don't know. In our day we believed we should learn to walk before we ran. In those days by-lines were very scarce.

The chief sub-editor decided when a story was good enough to warrant a by-line. Nowadays, young reporters put their by-lines on everything they write, whether it is good, bad or indifferent. The one good thing about the old system was that when the chief sub-editor decided you were worth a by-line you could be sure it was a damn fine story. I remember a group of us in the *Irish Independent* 30 years ago bringing out a reporter and buying him several pints because he had got a by-line. Young reporters today are brighter, better educated and a lot more determined than we were. They are not as easily put off as we were. But we are all prisoners of our own era and every child eventually becomes wiser than its parents. Papers in the old days were timid and reporters, even the young ones, weren't encouraged to rock the boat. There were no brownie points for being too pushy. The public now is also younger and brighter and expects a lot more from newspapers than it used to. People aren't just buying a paper to read the death notices or to see the television programmes. They are more critical, they want to be fully informed and entertained. They won't accept lazy reports. They will ring to ask why certain details were left out. They are fully entitled to do this: they pay their money and they should get full value.

A lot of fun has gone out of journalism. Competition is now quite intense between the Irish papers. The English papers are now over here in big numbers and they are increasing the pressure. Each paper is going to greater lengths to scoop their rivals. There isn't the same friendships and camaraderie between reporters of different papers as there used to be. There is more suspicion and mistrust. There is also a lot of sniping between papers by columnists. Sometimes this borders on the childish and is petty and unedifying. We have even reached the stage where columnists of the same paper will take each other on in public, which must be the height of stupidity.

There is also a sourness creeping in and it's not nice to see. Strong rivalry can be healthy and good for the business, but some of the ankle-tapping in the circulation war is quite pathetic. It is important not to take yourself too seriously in this business. Just write your reports straight and fair and to the best of your ability. Keep your prejudices to yourself. If you do that you will be doing a good job. Some reporters develop an inflated opinion of themselves. They think the public is hanging on to their every golden word and that they are influencing people in a big way. That is a mistaken belief because the public will always make up its own mind regardless of what anybody is writing in a newspaper.

One of my favourite authors is John Steinbeck. He was a journalist in his early days. He once wrote to a friend:

> 'What can I say about journalism? It has the greatest virtue and the greatest evil. It is the first thing the dictator controls. It is the mother of literature and the perpetrator of crap. In many cases it is the only history we have and yet it is the tool of the worst men. But over a long period of time and because it is the product of so many men, it is perhaps the purest thing we have. Honesty has a way of creeping in even when it was not intended.'

London: Verso, 1996